The Complete Guide to
Selling Your Own Home in California

By Kathy Gottberg

The Complete Guide to
SELLING YOUR OWN HOME
in California

By Kathy Gottberg

Printed in the United States of America

Published by:

Zyrus Press Inc.
PO Box 17810, Irvine, CA 92623
Tel: (888) 622-7823 / Fax: (800) 215-9694

www.zyruspress.com
ISBN 978-1-933990-16-3

Acknowledgements

This book is dedicated to my mother, Alice Pfeif, (1933—2007). She inspired me to love to read and never told me I couldn't write.

I also gratefully acknowledge my husband, Thom, who reminds me that I get to make it up, and who helps to make what I create worthwhile.

Table of Contents

PART ONE

CHAPTER ONE

1. When to sell
2. Other timing considerations
3. Property condition—both physical and legal
4. Trends in the real estate community

CHAPTER TWO

1. Knowledge of the California real estate market
2. Legal forms and disclosures
3. Time and effort
4. Personal comfort level dealing with people/strangers
5. Negotiation skills
6. Overcoming common misconceptions

CHAPTER THREE

1. How the listing process works
    a. Questions to ask during your broker/agent interview
2. How is the commission handled?
3. What is agency?
4. Arguments agents use against becoming a FSBO
5. Timing on listing a property through a broker
6. Who is a Realtor and who is not?

CHAPTER FOUR

1. Discount brokers
2. Internet FSBO services
3. Paying a buyer's broker
4. Lease option or rent-to-own
5. It's up to you

PART TWO

CHAPTER FIVE

1. Gathering data

CHAPTER TEN

1. Purchase offers from buyers without a broker
2. Don't be afraid of the truth
3. Filling out the purchase offer
4. What about the good-faith deposit?
5. Purchase offers from a buyer with a broker
6. Do you have to pay a commission?
7. Handling the commission in a new way
8. What differs when a real estate agent is involved?
9. Comfortably anticipating your first offer

CHAPTER ELEVEN

1. Counteroffers
2. Closing costs
3. Taking backup offers
4. Other contingency safeguards
5. Contingency problems
6. Your right to include contingencies
7. Possession
8. Canceling escrow
9. Home warranties
10. Homeowners' associations, CIDs, or condominiums
11. Personal property
12. What's included?
13. Final walk-through inspection

CHAPTER TWELVE

1. How financing is affected by the current market and vice versa
2. How mortgage loans work in California
3. Loan assumptions
4. New purchase-assist loans
5. Types of common loans available
    a. Fixed rate amortized
    b. Adjustable loans
    c. Government loans
6. Other loan types and terms to know
    a. Conforming loans
    b. Nonconforming loans
    c. Jumbo loans
    d. Balloon payments

PART THREE

CHAPTER THIRTEEN

CHAPTER FOURTEEN

Table of Forms

Forms in book and on CD

Forms on CD

Forms referenced

INTRODUCTION

To be or not to be . . . a FSBO
(For Sale By Owner)?

Is it possible to sell your home yourself and save a large amount of money? Absolutely! Is it easy and simple? Not always. Fortunately, with the comprehensive information in *The Complete Guide to Selling Your Own Home in California* and the accompanying CD containing all the necessary legal forms and worksheets required to sell residential property in the state of California, you now have everything you need to successfully accomplish the goal of selling your home yourself.

However, if you decide instead to sell your California-based property using a real estate broker, this book will also help you save lots of time and money. When sales volume and prices drop, both the real estate brokerage business and the real estate marketplace are thrown into a state of flux. Because of that, you can no longer sit back and expect an agent to have your best interests in mind at all times, regardless of how big a fee is to be paid.

Now, with the aid of this book, you will know what to expect and what to ask for, every step of the way. Once informed, even if you do sell using a broker, you can be sure you are getting your money's worth, and you should still save a significant amount of money without having to do all the work!

Nearly 25 years ago I became a real estate broker, not to become an agent for others, but to learn the business from the inside out and to save money buying and selling my own properties. Do I think you need to spend 20 to 25 years learning the same things? No! Things have changed considerably since then.

Now, thanks to the Internet and other current technologies, the extensive California real estate inventory previously held secret from the public is widely accessible. Plus, contained within this book are all the forms, explanations, disclosures, and real estate savvy you'll need to sell your home, with or without a broker.

As a matter of fact, selling your home today is not an all or nothing experience. You can do some of the work yourself and at the same time take advantage of the resources of the brokerage community when useful, and still save money. Sometimes, just one detail can make all the difference between your home selling quickly or sitting on the market for months at a time. One question, asked at the right moment during negotiations, could save you $5,000, $10,000, $20,000, or more. Yet, if you don't know what to ask, when or who to ask, or are unaware of the necessary steps to take, you are at the mercy of others and subject to the whims of the market.

To keep the process simple, this book is organized into three parts. In Part One I address the choices you now face and reveal some of the mysteries of the For Sale By Owner (FSBO) experience. Part Two is filled with the elements every seller needs to know before, during, and after the successful completion of a sale. Part Three is for trouble-shooting or to use as a reference when a task is at hand or if you find yourself facing a roadblock. This final part also includes some simple marketing techniques that all sellers should at least be aware of before beginning the sales process.

In addition, the accompanying CD from *first tuesday* contains all the legal forms a homeseller needs for any phase of a transaction. For 30 years, *first tuesday* has been a leader in the California real estate brokerage education and forms market. Until now, finding forms to legally transfer real estate in California has been one of the greatest challenges facing those in the FSBO market. Feel free at any time to jump around in the book or to browse the CD to find anything that directly tackles your current concerns or questions.

Can you do it? Again, maybe yes, maybe no. The goal of this book is to *realistically* prepare you for the job of selling your own home should you make the decision to do so. Your preparation requires a commitment of time and energy to learn the necessary steps. You also need to develop a willingness to talk to people, make appointments, and negotiate. Most of all, you need the resolve to stick it out, even if circumstances become challenging.

Ultimately, if you are the kind of person who likes to turn your problems over to an expert and are willing to pay $10,000 to $20,000 or more for the convenience, you might want to call a real estate broker today. On the other hand, if you resent paying a real estate broker anywhere from 4% to 6% of your home's sales price knowing you could keep all or some of that money by doing it yourself, then becoming a FSBO might be your best decision.

In the end, the wisest choice would be to read this book completely before making up your mind. Only then will you know if you have what it takes to join the growing group of people who confidently saved thousands of dollars by selling their home themselves.

Kathy Gottberg

Timeline

Buyer	Seller
	Seller begins to think about selling.
Buyer begins to think about buying	
	Seller begins gathering information about pricing and market conditions.
	Seller decides to become a FSBO or list with Broker.
Buyer talks to lender and pre-qualifies for a loan	
	Seller hires Home Inspector.
	Seller fills out all necessary disclosure forms (included on CD accompanying book).
	Seller orders termite report and preliminary title report.
	Seller "stages" home so it shows advantageously.
	Seller arranges with Internet real estate marketing service and uses available photos and brochures to market property on the Internet.
Buyer starts researching homes and prices on the Internet and does so for 3-6 months before proceeding.	Seller takes photos, gathers school and local facilities information, and then makes up a color brochure/flyer about the property.
Buyer looks at 16 houses physically or 8 houses after researching the Internet before making an offer.	Seller puts out "For Sale" sign with brochures and begins showing property.
Buyer views subject property for the first time.	Seller shows home to Buyer for first time.
Buyer comes back for second look or calls with questions.	Seller shows house again, answers Buyer's questions, and gives Buyer blank purchase agreement from accompanying CD. Seller also gives Buyer all disclosures at this time.
	Seller verifies that Buyer has been pre-qualified with a lender.
Buyer fills out purchase offer, signs it, and hands it to Seller with deposit.	
	Seller reviews the offer and either accepts it or fills out a counteroffer (on CD).
Buyer receives Seller's acceptance or counteroffers until agreement is reached.	
	Seller contacts Escrow Company and makes an appointment to open escrow.
	Seller takes signed purchase agreement and deposit to Escrow (or Title Company).
	Seller reviews instructions prior to them being mailed to Buyer for signatures.
Escrow prepares escrow instructions and documents, and mails them to Seller and Buyer.	Escrow prepares escrow instructions and documents, and mails them to Seller and Buyer.
Buyer returns signed escrow instructions and documents to Escrow.	Seller returns signed escrow instructions and documents to Escrow.
	Seller obtains copies of all reports not already given to Buyer (preliminary title, pest control, natural hazard, lead paint, etc.), and hands them to Buyer.
Buyer contacts Lender and provides them with copy of purchase agreement and escrow instructions.	
	Seller provides Escrow with current loan pay-off information and any information about HOA for home and assessment bonds.
Lender provides Buyer with RESPA disclosures regarding costs of loan and closing.	

Timeline cont.

Buyer	Seller
Buyer's lender orders appraisal.	
	Preliminary title report ordered out by Escrow for Seller approval.
Buyer finds and makes appointment with Home Inspector.	
	Seller makes home available to Buyer's Home Inspector and Appraiser.
Buyer completes all forms required to obtain new loan on property.	
Escrow prepares all closing documents and mails them to Buyer and Seller.	Escrow prepares all closing documents and mails them to Buyer and Seller.
Buyer receives final approval on loan.	
Buyer removes all contingencies.	
	Escrow obtains payoff information for existing loan on property and prepares loan pay-off documents.
Buyer selects Property Insurance Carrier, makes arrangements for coverage, and then notifies Lender and Escrow.	
	Seller arranges for movers and picks date to vacate property as per contract agreement.
Escrow receives new loan packet with all loan documents for Buyer to sign.	
	Seller arranges to have all utilities and mail taken out of his name and puts in Buyer's name.
Buyer has final walk-through inspection at property.	Seller allows Buyer final walk-through inspection.
Escrow calls for Lender's funds.	
Buyer deposits down payment and closing funds into escrow.	
	Seller contacts his Home Insurance Carrier and arranges cancellation for day after move.
Buyer arranges utilities in his name.	
Escrow sends grant deed to Title Insurer and loan documents to Lender.	
Deed recorded.	Deed recorded.
	Seller picks up sales proceeds at Escrow.
	Seller vacates property as agreed.
Buyer moves into property.	
	Seller calculates how much money he saved by selling property himself!
Buyer receives supplemental tax bill and pays it separate from regular property tax bill.	

PART ONE

If your home is already for sale,
you might want to skip this section
and go directly to the "How To's"
of handling a sales transaction in
Part Two.

CHAPTER ONE
The decision to sell

The decision to sell your home is always momentous. In most cases, it is the highest valued asset you own. Therefore, it is completely natural that you would be a bit nervous about making the right decision, as well as desire to make a choice that would ultimately put the most amount of money in your pocket.

Your decision to sell is unquestionably affected by a variety of considerations. Before you decide, it is wise to reflect on each of the following issues carefully.

When to sell

Timing has a profound effect. If you have to sell your home immediately because of a job transfer, family health considerations, or any one of many possible personal and financial emergencies, then your options shrink. The faster you must sell your property, and the shorter your deadline for moving, the more vulnerable you are to the whims of the current real estate market.

What are market whims? When there are more properties for sale in any given area than there are buyers, then that market is called a Buyer's Market. In a Buyer's Market, the buyers have the upper hand since they have many properties to choose from in the marketplace. They can negotiate prices downward and be more selective as to the condition and qualities they want in a property. If you are a seller in a Buyer's Market, and you need to sell quickly, it might take longer than you would like and you probably won't get the best price for your home.

On the other hand, a Seller's Market is when there are lots of buyers and few homes available for them to purchase. When this happens, sellers have the advantage since they can demand higher prices and are under less pressure to negotiate. In a Seller's Market, the length of time a property will be on the market before it sells is usually much shorter than during a Buyer's Market. For example, during the Seller's Market in 2004, the average time a property remained on the market was less than 30 days. In contrast, during a Buyer's Market, an average market time of 120 to 150 days is not unusual.

Clearly, either type of market will affect the sale of your property. If you need to sell right away, be aware that market conditions will affect your net proceeds from the sale, regardless of whether you decide to sell it yourself or list with a broker. If you do not need to sell right away, you can use that to your advantage. For example, if your desire to sell is fueled by a decision to move into a smaller home, then it might be wise to check to see if it is a Seller's or Buyer's Market before making the leap.

Keep in mind, however, that even if a Seller's Market allows you to come out on top when you sell your home, you will lose that advantage when you become a buyer under the same market conditions. The ideal scenario would have you selling locally in a Seller's Market and then relocating to a new community where homes are less expensive and in a Buyer's Market.

Other timing considerations

Something else to consider when deciding to sell your home is your income tax position. We will cover income taxes in more detail later, but be aware that the new Internal Revenue Service (IRS) rules on paying taxes on the equity profit in your home favor those who have owned their home for over two years. If you have lived in your home for less time and know that it has appreciated substantially, yet do not need to sell quickly, you can save a sizeable amount of money by waiting for the two years to pass before selling.

The time of year is also something you should consider. Historically, one of the slowest times to sell your property is during the traditional holiday period between Thanksgiving and Christmas. However, those in the real estate business know that when a property is for sale during this time, sellers are highly motivated. The same is true during the late summer months when many sellers, buyers and agents are on vacation.

One of the best and most active times of the year to sell is during spring and early summer. Anyone with children knows that it is easier, and less of a hassle, for a family to move when the children are nearing the end of their school year. Also, if people are relocating, this is the best time for them to look at homes in a new location.

Regardless of the time of year, selling your home means that you must be available to field phone calls and schedule showings. If you have a choice as to when you will be putting your home on the market to sell, you may want to avoid any period of time when you personally feel that you will be unable to give it your full attention.

Property condition—both physical and legal

The condition of the property definitely affects the price you will receive. If you do not have to sell immediately, you may want to take the time to complete all repairs, maintenance, and upgrades before you begin marketing. Buying a home is an emotional experience for most buyers. Even if you promise to do repairs or alterations in the near future, prospective buyers looking to find their dream home will likely be unable to envision those improvements. Making repairs and doing maintenance in advance allows you to present your home in the best possible light and reap the most favorable price.

What about remodeling before you sell? It is probably not the best move. According to *Remodeling Magazine* in their "Remodeling Cost vs. Value Report 2006," the average cost of an improvement is seldom recaptured on sale. For example, the report states that even though fixing up an average bathroom is ranked at the top of the more profitable remodels, it only recaptures about 84.9% of the cost.[1] Plus, the expense does not take into account the time, trouble, or headache of performing such a job. Based on this information, remodeling your bathroom in a neighborhood where all the homes are in similar condition will rarely be beneficial in terms of a financial return.

However, if your home has a bathroom or other feature in a shabby or dilapidated state, you should probably make repairs or modifications as necessary. These improvements become more critical if your home is surrounded by houses that contain similar features which are updated and in good condition. Bringing your home up to the neighborhood standard could help you receive a comparable sales price, as well as experience a much shorter time on the market. Of course, if you want to remodel so you can enjoy the upgrade while living in the home yourself, then go right ahead. Just don't expect to make extra profit because of it when you go to sell your home. Remodeling before a home sale should always be done with an eye on the bottom-line benefits, rather than your emotional desires.

Of course, the condition of a property actually extends beyond the mere physical aspects. If you are in the process of a divorce, have lost a family member, or other circumstances exist that alter your ownership of the property, these conditions will affect your sale. You may need to resolve these legal issues before you attempt to sell since each has the potential to hinder your best efforts.

Trends in the real estate community—now is a great time to be a FSBO!

Good news! The best time in history to sell your home yourself is right now. The changing state of the real estate market and the benefits of current technology have recently come together to give homesellers access to both prospective buyers and increased information. Best-selling nonfiction books like, *Freakonomics* point to some of the shifts at hand in the real estate brokerage community. Other publications like the *Wall Street Journal*, *Money Magazine*, and the *New York Times* jointly emphasize the changes that are now occurring for buyers and sellers due to the ever-increasing access to real estate inventory on the Internet.

A large part of the change is due to disintermediation. Disintermediation is the label used by economists to describe the transformation that happens to a market due to the technology of the Internet. It generally occurs when consumers eliminate the middleman and have direct access to previously protected and guarded information. Disintermediation happens when discount sellers of any type flood the marketplace with alternative products, services, and lower prices. The most well-known examples of this changeover are visible in the travel, bookselling, and stock market industries.

Until recently, the real estate industry has resisted similar evolutionary changes due largely to the leadership of the National Association of Realtors (NAR) and their huge lobbying efforts. Although founded in 1908 as a consumer advocate group, NAR has evolved into the second largest political donor in our country today.[2] It is no surprise then that NAR works hard to protect its $60 billion-a-year industry.[3] And, although real estate commission fees have dropped slightly from the historically traditional 6% to 5.1% within the last several years, they still have not fallen in proportion to the dramatic increase in current property values and the direct access to information and services now available over the Internet.[4]

But things are changing. The Department of Justice (DOJ) is currently looking into issues of price fixing and restraint of trade within the real estate industry. At the same time, access to Internet real estate inventory and information is growing. Added to that is increasing consumer dissatisfaction with paying high real estate fees. As each day passes, the options available to the home selling and buying public are multiplying.

There is no going back. According to the California Association of Realtors (CAR), over 70% of all California homebuyers credit the Internet as an integral part of the home-buying process. With increases like this, it won't be long until the entire home-buying public will be able to access for-sale properties through the Internet instead of being forced to use real estate brokers. This access to inventory and alternative services will force the real estate community to change. The public, and especially FSBOs, will continue to reap the benefits of these current changes far into the future.

CHAPTER TWO
What does it take to be a For Sale By Owner (FSBO)?

If you are convinced that now is the best time for you to sell, then your next step is to decide whether you want to do it by yourself or to use all, or some, of the services of a real estate agent. It is not my intent to sway you one way or the other, but merely to present you with enough information to make an informed decision. Before deciding to either do it yourself or use a professional, consider the plight of the travel industry. Until recently, nearly everyone used a travel agent to book airline flights, hotels, and vacations.

Now, due to the Internet, the average person has access to information that was previously very difficult to obtain. Today, it is possible to book flights, cruises, vacations, and hotels without ever having to speak to a live person! In some ways, the For Sale By Owner (FSBO) market shares with the travel industry the progress brought about by the information now available on the Internet.

But make no mistake, selling your own home requires more sophistication and effort than it takes to plan a holiday. In many cases, there is a valid reason why real estate brokers charge the percentages they do. As you will learn, selling a home requires the coordination and knowledge of a number of activities that are not commonly known or, until recently, easily available to the general public. However, by buying this book, you have already taken a huge step toward acquiring the knowledge and resources necessary to market your property, locate a buyer, and complete a transaction. You will discover that there is not only a great deal to learn, but a number of actions you must take as well. So, what exactly does it take to successfully sell your home yourself?

Knowledge of the California real estate market

Unless you are a real estate agent, or you have sold four or five of your own homes in California in the last couple of years, you are undoubtedly unfamiliar with the practice of selling a home. In fact, the process can seem overwhelmingly complicated for an outsider at first glance. That is why it is essential that you educate yourself before you tackle the job.

This book is a simple guide to learning what you need, and, unlike the majority of other resources available, it is written specifically for the California real estate market. While the California distinction might not seem important, a significant difference in the sales process exists between every state in our country. Each state operates under different laws, regulations, and guidelines regarding the sale and transfer of property. Most FSBO books and websites tend to generalize the information they offer so they can market their materials nationally. However, this book exclusively targets the California real estate market and its rules, regulations, and unique practices.

Yet, even though this book contains the knowledge and advice necessary to successfully sell your California-based home yourself and save thousands of dollars, you are the one who must evaluate whether you have the time and desire to learn what it will take. If you don't have the time or desire, you may be best served by going with the more traditional route of hiring an agent to sell your home.

Still, even if you do decide to employ an agent, this book will teach you what you should know about the process so you will ultimately make or save money. In today's ever-changing real estate market, and with your potential profit on the line, all of us need to know as much, or more, than our advisors when faced with the decision of when and how to sell a home.

Legal forms and disclosures

Congratulations! You have, with the purchase of this book and the enclosed CD, all the legal forms and disclosures you need to sell your home yourself in California—with or without an agent. A huge obstacle in the past to selling your own property was the monopoly that the real estate brokerage community had on access to appropriate forms. There are still some California brokers today who want you to believe that you can only use their real estate forms if you want to complete a "legal transaction." Don't believe them!

The forms on the enclosed CD are time-honored and proven to work with all aspects of real estate sales and escrow transactions. All of the disclosure forms required by law as of the date of this book's printing are included on the CD. Not only are these forms easier to understand than those commonly used by the real estate broker industry, they are also much easier to fill out. All you have to do is follow the directions provided in this book and on the CD when faced with individual tasks.

Time and effort

It is very important to be honest with yourself about how much time and effort you will need, or would be willing to devote, to sell your own home. To successfully sell your home yourself, and to reap all the financial advantages that such an activity provides, it takes a strong commitment on the part of at least one member of the family. Ideally, the entire family should make the commitment since, as I will discuss later, everyone in the house will be affected.

Most real estate agents know that, in spite of the fact that many people are attracted to the idea of saving a real estate commission and consider going the FSBO route, many homeowners who begin the process will quit within the first month. That is why a number of agents will contact you the moment you advertise or put a "For Sale By Owner" sign out in your front yard. Statistically, most FSBOs get frustrated and give up within a few weeks. By staying in touch with you, agents believe you will eventually list with them. They are often right—especially if you lack the right information or are filled with unrealistic expectations concerning the time and effort it will take to successfully sell your home.

In fact, as the old real estate saying goes, "The quality of the sign in the FSBO's yard indicates how long it takes for them to list with an agent." That is because the quality of your "For Sale" sign demonstrates the level of your commitment. A simple, plastic "For Sale" sign stapled to a picket stake shows that you haven't invested much thought in the idea of selling your home yourself. A custom metal sign with a plastic carrier holding color brochures says that you intend to make a go of it. Don't believe me? Watch your neighborhood. Chances are very good that when you see a shoddy FSBO "For Sale" sign in someone's yard, you will very shortly see a broker's sign instead.

Of course, being a FSBO offers some unanticipated benefits to certain homesellers. Some people enjoy the experience of getting to know the many people you will encounter during the marketing and sale. Others absorb the information as a valuable educational experience and appreciate the advantages of learning about the real estate market from the inside out.

Most importantly, few tasks will reward you as well financially as that of selling your own home. The important thing is to be sure you have marshaled your resources and recognize the amount of work and time it will take beforehand. Being mentally prepared will help to insure that you stay with the process, even if it takes longer than you expected or requires more dedication than you anticipated.

Personal comfort level dealing with people/strangers

One thing a good real estate agent does well is converse with people, and most agents love to talk! That ability to communicate is very important when selling your house. Most buyers will not only want to see the house a few times before making an offer, they will also ask dozens of questions. In response, they expect you to have the information they inquire about and will likely ask questions that seem highly personal or even silly. When selling your home as a FSBO, you will have to deal with these prospective buyers directly and by yourself.

Friendly and open-minded communication is a key factor in selling your home. As a FSBO, you must make yourself available to just about anyone who seems interested and wants to arrange a time to see your house. I recommend making appointments, but there are people who will still knock on your door and ask about your home, so be prepared both emotionally and with a tidy and well kept home.

Not only must you deal with prospective buyers who may not be financially qualified to purchase your home—after all, how will you know their qualifications until after you've met them—there are also a number of others who will be involved in your sales transaction. A few of these others include an escrow officer, a title officer, home inspectors, and appraisers. Plus, some buyers will show up with a real estate agent without prearranging whether you, or anyone, will pay the agent anything at all. If you are an introvert who finds it difficult to talk to people, to say no when you need to, or to pick up the phone when necessary, then you might want to select a family member who will take on the communication responsibility and help you with this important aspect of a home sale.

Of course, if you sell your home yourself, you have one great advantage; you and your family know more about your house and your neighborhood than any real estate broker ever could. If you have the nature to deal with people and won't take offense if they don't fall in love with your property, then chances are good that you can do a better job of selling your home than any person you could hire.

The personal safety of the seller, his family, and his property are another concern of every homeseller. Naturally, a certain amount of care and precaution are always necessary in any activity when dealing with strangers. But, as long as a FSBO practices normal patterns of safety for himself and his family when advertising, taking calls, and inviting prospective buyers into his home, then there is no more risk as a FSBO than there is when marketing a property with an agent.

Negotiation skills

Another recommendation for a successful FSBO is what I call negotiation skills. Negotiations are different than communication or people skills as previously mentioned. Negotiation skills include the ability to listen to other people's opinion of your house and not take their views personally. Further, it is the ability to accept what another person says or does and then turn it around to make it work for both of you.

Arriving at an agreement with a prospective buyer to purchase your house is more than just arriving at a price you will accept and they will pay. A number of important resolutions must be reached as the transaction unfolds, and the process is helped or hindered by your ability to communicate and reach a consensus.

Just as a doctor is not allowed to operate on family members, so too is it often recommended that you have an outside, impartial person negotiate some of the more sensitive issues in a transaction. A sensitive issue for one family might be a buyer's criticism and removal of the decor or furniture. Some sellers might be touchy about comments related to the actions of their children. Other sellers might take offense to derogatory remarks about the neighborhood or the asking price. Each of these issues can create roadblocks to successful negotiation. Most likely, a homeseller who routinely encounters negotiations in his normal line of work will have the best success.

Overcoming common misconceptions

As in any industry, misconceptions about the marketing and sales process are often circulated and used against your potential success as a FSBO. We have already addressed the most obvious misconception—that selling your home yourself is an easy thing to do. However, the flip side of that misconception is equally flawed—that it is so difficult that you can't hope to succeed and will eventually give up and list with a broker.

In the final analysis, the biggest factor affecting the sale of your house will probably be the *timing*—your personal time frame for closing a sale and the timing of your current local real estate marketplace—when you decide to sell. However, in spite of the timing, with concentrated efforts on your part, attention to detail, and the application of the information in this book, you can succeed at achieving your goal.

Another misconception is that by selling your home yourself you will *always* save a great deal of money. Certainly, I believe that you can save a considerable sum by following the recommendations in this book, but it is not always assured. For example, homesellers who fail to research the local real estate market (as advised in this book), may initially price their property below market. Beyond that, there are also those who do little to locate buyers until it is too late to aggressively market their property. Then, because their individual circumstances demand immediate action, they must sell at a deep discount.

A similar misconception comes from buyers who believe that since you are a FSBO and are not marketing your property with a real estate agent, they are the ones who will save money when they buy from you. Some buyers even believe that the amount of commission you are saving should automatically come off of the purchase price. Although it is completely your choice whether you decide to share some of the savings with your buyer, it is helpful to anticipate some of their motivations.

It is also occasionally believed that you need a lawyer to sell your home. In reality, although you may choose to have a lawyer review your documents to make sure that you are doing everything necessary, it is not required in the state of California. In contrast, some other states like New York and Georgia require the use of a lawyer to close every transaction. Historically, the process of buying and selling homes in California has been standardized and regulated to the extent that only in extraordinary situations are the services of attorneys needed.

The more of the aforementioned qualities you embody as a seller, the easier it will be for you to successfully sell your own home. Other information you will find useful is how the average real estate broker or agent markets and sells property. Even if you represent yourself as a FSBO in the sale of your home, it is absolutely beneficial for you to know how real estate brokers function because real estate agents represent the majority of available buyers. In the next chapter, I will discuss how the real estate industry works and how you can use it to your advantage.

CHAPTER THREE
Do you need a broker?

This book is not intended to convince you to either sell your home yourself or to list with a real estate broker. Instead, I will share some of what I have discovered about real estate during the last 20 years to help you make a much better and more informed decision, no matter how you eventually market your property.

Knowing how the real estate brokerage business works and being aware of both its strengths and its shortcomings, can greatly benefit anyone who decides to sell their property.

How the listing process works

The majority of homesellers list and sell their homes through a real estate broker. When you sell a home through a real estate broker, the charge for that service, called a commission, is almost always a percentage of the purchase price. Although commissions are by law negotiable in order to encourage competition among brokers in the marketplace, they are usually set based upon what a broker believes sellers will pay. According to a report by the U.S. Government Accountability Office, average commission rates in 2003 were an estimated 5.1%.[1] I personally know of a few brokers that charge less than this amount, but most agents where I live still charge something closer to 6%, which is historically the standardized rate charged by most large brokerage firms.

The good news is that you will find brokers who routinely list for lesser amounts. The bad news is that paying a higher commission does not guarantee that you will receive better service or be represented by a more knowledgeable broker.

Who gets paid what amount in a standard commission breakdown? Say you decide to list your home with a nice agent named Sally who is the mother of your daughter's friend. If you do, you must agree to pay a commission based upon what Sally's broker requires her to accept. Even if asked, Sally will likely say that she is unable to discount her fee. She's right. Sally is not really your agent; she is merely an agent of her broker, who is legally your agent. It's the broker who controls how much commission is charged, plus how his agents will conduct themselves and carryout the practice of marketing and selling your property.

So, although Sally is probably the only person you will see from her office, technically you have listed your home with her broker, not Sally. Should you want to negotiate a commission beyond the range of what her broker typically allows, Sally's broker must become involved and approve of any modifications you want to make. Unfortunately, with this type of system, every agent in any particular broker's office charges what his broker demands, regardless of the agent's competency, quality, or years in the business. Of course, every broker is supposed to train, guide, and oversee all of his agents, but that doesn't always happen to any significant degree.

Now, Sally may be a wonderful person, but you have no guarantee that she will do what you want her to do, that is, to locate a buyer for your home quickly and for the highest price possible, and to do it with a high degree of competency. One part of the problem is that the California real estate industry has a relatively simple and easy entry system. That means that Sally could have become a real estate agent last week after taking and passing one real estate related college course, and then getting 70% or better on a three-hour multiple choice test. Sometimes a new agent's enthusiasm and energy more than makes up for their lack of experience—other times not.

According to the California Department of Real Estate (DRE), the number of new sales agents in the field soared to 62,983 during the year preceding June 2006.[2] Based upon previous numbers, this represents a 16% increase in the number of real estate sales agents in the state during 2006. In other words, one out of every six agents was licensed and new that year. DRE figures also show that turnover is very high.

Other statistics show that during the last three years in the state of California, up to 46% of all active agents were new! These reports demonstrate that when you go looking for an agent and want to list your home, you have close to a 20% chance that they will be inexperienced and potentially untrained. Yet, the amount of commission charged is usually the same as a well-seasoned professional.

Alternatively, just because your agent has been in the business for 20 years doesn't mean that they know everything there is to know and can do the best job. A large number of agents work only part time or have their licenses placed on hold in an inactive status. A popular saying is: "Instead of 20 years experience, some people have one year's experience 20 times." Remember, unless you ask a series of questions, you have no guarantee that the person you are trusting to sell your house has much more experience than you do.

So what sort of an agent should you hire? First, I recommend that you ask your circle of acquaintances for their best referral. Then, interview several agents before deciding. Just as you would interview a prospective employee for a business, I believe it is wise to ask a number of questions. The questions I suggest you ask are as follows and can be found on the Seller's Pre-Listing Interview of an Agent, form 339.

1. What is their experience selling real estate?

Don't just take their word for it. Ask to see references, and then call and check with at least one or two of them. Although it might seem to involve a lot of work to check up on your agent, remember that they are similar to an employee you will be hiring to handle the sale of a large amount of your assets in the near future. Don't you think you ought to know how well they work?

Also consider the fact that they will have access to your home and will be showing it to others while you are not at home. If you are using an agent that has been referred to you, be sure and ask the person who did the referring why they liked their agent and how they worked.

Do you need to like your real estate agent? Not necessarily, but you do need to trust them. Upon introduction, some agents may appear aggressive or abrupt, but that may mean that they are very busy and focused. However, if they are too busy to help you or to submit to an interview before you list your property, chances are good that they will be too busy to take your calls once you have listed. Most importantly, don't let any agent intimidate you into doing anything you are not comfortable doing, and always follow your gut when in doubt.

I also recommend that you think very carefully before listing your property with friends or relatives. If you do list with a friend or relative who has a real estate license, make sure that you ask them all

SELLER'S PRE-LISTING INTERVIEW OF AN AGENT

This worksheet is used as a source of questions asked by a seller of real estate during an interview of an agent to determine the agent's credentials and the marketing activities the agent or his broker will perform to locate a buyer and close a sales escrow.

Agent or broker interviewed: _____.

Company: _____. Date of interview: _____, 20_____.

Interview conducted by: _____.

Documents agent brought to the interview: _____.

The Local Real Estate Market:

1. What trend is taking place in the local real estate market? _____
   1.1   Are we in a a buyer's market, or a seller's market? _____
   1.2   How will the current trend affect your marketing and sale of my home? _____
   _____

The Agent's Real Estate Experience:

2. What is your experience as a agent listing and selling real estate? _____
   _____
   2.1   What is the average price range of homes you've sold? _____
   _____
   2.2   Can I get a list of your recent sales? _____
   _____

3. What professional designations do you hold? _____
   _____

4. Is your practice primarily listing with sellers or is it representing prospective buyers? _____
   _____
   4.1   Do you work mainly with homesellers or homebuyers? _____
   _____
   4.2   How does your working mainly with homesellers or homebuyers benefit me if I list my property with you?
   _____

5. What is the source of the majority of your business? _____
   _____
   5.1   Do you have a marketing farm as a source of listings? _____
         a.   Where is it located? _____
   5.2   How will your farm benefit me and assist you in the sale of my home? _____
   _____

6. How many homes have you listed during the past six months? _____
   The addresses of these homes? _____
   _____
   _____
   6.1   In what price range were your listings? _____
   6.2   What percentage of these listings taken during the past six months have sold? _____%
         a.   Did you or did some other agent locate the buyers who bought your listings? _____
   6.3   What is the current average number of months for properties listed in the local MLS to be on the market before they sell? _____
   6.4   What percentage of the listing price was the sales price of the MLS listings which sold? _____%
         a.   On homes you sold, what was the percentage of the sales price to the listing price? _____%
               Why? _____

7. Why are you the best person to list my home for sale? _____

_____

_____

   7.1   Can you get a higher price for my home than other agents? Why so? _____

         Why not? _____

   7.2   Did you obtain a property profile on my home from a title company? _____

        a. What does the profile disclose? _____

   7.3   Do you have a list of comparable properties which have recently sold? _____

        a. Have you prepared a comparable marketing analysis and set the market value of my home? _____

        b. What is your opinion of the fair market value of my home? _____

        c. Will my home sell for that price? _____. How long will it take?_____

   7.4   What listing price would you recommend for my home? _____

        a. What would cause you to recommend a price reduction if you had the listing? _____

                    _____

        b. How much time will pass before you recommend a price reduction? _____

8. Are you working with any prospective buyers who would be interested in a home like mine?_____

_____

   8.1   [If so] Can we set up an appointment with you to show the home to the prospective buyer?_____

_____

Marketing the Property:

9. What type and to what extent will you market and advertise my property for sale? _____

_____

   9.1   Is your marketing and advertising policy in writing so I can get a copy? _____

        a. Do you have a flyer distribution system? _____ What is it? _____

        b. Do you place a container in the front yard and keep it supplied with color brochures? _____

   9.2   Who pays for the marketing program on our property? _____

   9.3   If you do not perform marketing as agreed, can I cancel the listing? _____

10. Do you or your company maintain a website? _____

   10.1 What is the nature of your company's internet presence? _____

   10.2 Can you show me how our property will be presented to prospective buyers online? _____

        a. How many photos will you place online? _____

        b. Will a virtual tour of my home be available online? _____

        c. When will my property listing be placed on the website for the local MLS? _____

11. Will you keep me updated each week with a written report on your marketing activity? _____

      By email?_____By fax? _____

   11.1 Can your weekly report include what activity took place during the prior seven days and what activity is anticipated for the next seven days? _____

   11.2 Will you advise us weekly on feedback from agents and prospective buyers as to what we can do to help better market the property? _____

   11.3 Will you advise us on the net sales proceeds we can expect? _____

        a. What information do you need from us? _____

12. Do you work with an assistant or as part of a team? _____

   12.1 Who will I be talking with on a day-to-day basis if I list with you? _____

   12.2 Who on your team will be handling marketing? _____

        a. Property showings? _____

        b. Disclosures? _____

        c. Escrow instructions? _____

   12.3 Do you use a marketing or transaction coordinator? _____ Who is it? _____

13. How do you handle the showing of the home to other agents and prospective buyers? _____
_____

    13.1 How do you arrange the appointments? _____

    13.2 Do you arrange a caravan or open house? _____

    13.3 What security problems do lock boxes present? _____

    13.4 What advance notice will we get before showings? _____

            Do you call first? _____

    13.5 What is done to pre-qualify the buyer financially and determine whether the home is suitable for them before it is shown? _____

    13.6 What privacy issues should we be concerned about? _____

            Pets? _____ Valuables? _____

    13.7 What do we need to do to prepare for a showing? _____
_____

Seller disclosures to prospective buyers:

14. What forms do I have to prepare and sign to tell prospective buyers about the home? _____
_____ Why? _____

    14.1 When do I fill out the property disclosure forms? _____

    14.2 What must I disclose? _____

    14.3 How do you use these disclosures? _____

    14.4 Are they part of your marketing package? _____

    14.5 When is the prospective buyer told about the property's condition?

          a. Before I accept his offer? _____

          b. After we enter into an agreement? _____

15. What third-party inspectors or appraisers would be involved in a sale of my property? _____
_____

    15.1 Home inspectors? _____ Pest control operators? _____

           Hazard advisors?_____Lead-based paint analysis? _____

           Environmental inspectors? _____ Occupancy inspectors? _____

           Ordinance compliance inspectors? _____

    15.2 Who pays for these inspections and reports? _____

Management of escrow instructions:

16. What steps do you take to assist and coordinate the opening and closing of a sales escrow? _____
_____

    16.1 Once you have opened escrow, do you remain available to answer questions and get escrow closed?
_____

    16.2 What can be done to avoid contingencies which allow the buyer to cancel escrow? _____
_____

          a. How do you handle a loan contingency? _____
_____

Fee arrangements:

17. To sell a home in my price range, what does your real estate office charge? _____

    17.1 Is your fee the same as most other agents? _____ Why? _____

           Why not? _____

18. If you bring me an offer for a price less than the listed price for the property and you recommend that I accept it, do you renegotiate the fee? _____

    [If not,] Why not? _____

19. If my home sells and I decide to buy another home using your services, do you discount your fees on both these sales? _____ By how much? _____

20. What happens if I decide to cancel the listing because I become unhappy with your services? _____
_____

20.1 Do I owe you a fee if that happens? _____
        How much? _____

21. What other services do you or your company offer that I should know about before I decide to list my home?
_____

22. _____
_____
_____

23. _____
_____
_____

FORM 338   03-07   ©2007 **first tuesday**, P.O. BOX 20069, RIVERSIDE, CA 92516 (800) 794-0494

of the same questions that you would ask any potential listing agent, and qualify and compare them to all the other agents you have interviewed to take the listing. Remember, unless you feel obligated to hand over some money to a friend or relative, they are taking on a very important task and you deserve to have a qualified agent representing your best interests. In some cases you might be better off selling the home yourself and just writing them a check.

Also, avoid bringing in your licensed friend or family member at the last minute so they can get part of the commission. If you do decide to list your home with an agent, treat your relationship during the listing period with as much respect as any business partnership.

2. Ask potential agents for their area of specialty.

Some agents specialize in listings. What this means is that they have a very strong focus and campaign to attract people who want to list their homes. They advertise extensively with this in mind.

However, once your property is listed with them, they continue to look for more new listings believing that someone else within the brokerage community who works with buyers will sell your house once they place it in a Multiple Listing Service (MLS). An MLS is where local properties are showcased for all local brokers and agents. This might be more than enough to sell your home, but it is beneficial to know how your potential agent will work in the future.

3. Always question the "buyer-in-the-pocket" routine if an agent uses this when attempting to obtain a listing from you.

If any real estate agent says that they have an eager buyer looking for a home in the area and would love to list and show your home, then suggest they show your house tomorrow and assure them that you will pay them a commission if it sells. This pitch by a listing agent is a common come-on. It is unlikely that they have a "ready, willing and able buyer" and are just trying to get you to list with them. Even if you do decide to list with this particular agent, tell them you want to know the name of the buyer and when exactly your home will be shown to them.

4. Ask how your house will be advertised—then get it in writing.

Some agents may brag about how their office is part of a large national chain and talk about all the money for advertising and promotion it spends. Unfortunately, once you have listed your home, you might never see your particular property featured. Such agents usually respond by saying that when they get buyers to call their office, they will then direct buyers to your property. That's fine. But why not insure that they also promise to advertise your property in particular, in specific ways?

For example, if you want newspaper ads, say so. If they advertise on television, be sure your house will be included. If there is a flyer distribution system, ask for it. Be adamant that your front yard has a container with an ample supply of color brochures available for those who drive by. Don't leave the marketing of your property to chance. Ask your agent to put it in writing.

5. What kind of Internet presence does the listing real estate office have?

In this day and age, it is extremely important that when your property is listed that it is put on the Internet immediately with lots of photos, as well as a virtual tour. Not only are these visual enhancements available through the broker's personal website, they are also readily available through the MLS for all local real estate agents to view.

It is essential that your property have wide exposure in this area because, according to a survey done by the California Association of Realtors (CAR), homebuyers who used the Internet as an integral part of the home-buying process increased to nearly 70% in 2005.[3] The report went on to emphasize that the Internet is becoming a major source of information for buyers in California and should be used in conjunction with the aid of a real estate agent.

Thus, the Internet is an indispensable tool for every serious homeseller. Another report by the National Association of Realtors (NAR) implied that the percentage might be closer to 77%. But just because this information is well known doesn't mean that the agent who wants to list your home will actually do what it takes as quickly as possible. You must insist that they commit in writing exactly what they will do to market the property widely and effectively on the Internet.

6. Where's their "farm"?

Did you know that most real estate agents normally focus on certain areas, types of properties, or types of clients, which is called their farm? It is important before you list with anyone that you know where he or she will be focusing. If your potential listing agent works with first-time homebuyers and you have a large-family home or a retirement-type home, it won't get the attention you probably expect. If your home is in a great school district and you believe that is one of its greatest assets, then you might want to find an agent that deals with families or relocations, or whose farm is located within the district. Find out how your agent works and use that to your advantage.

7. How often will your agent contact you?

A classic homeseller complaint is that once they have listed their property for sale their agent stops calling. Don't be that type of seller! Ask when you can expect marketing reports from your agent before you list, and then hold them to it and cancel the listing if they don't perform. A short email or phone call once a week is not asking for too much from someone you have employed to sell your home. You deserve to know if there has been any action on your listing and what other agents and their clients say after they look at your home.

8. Does your agent have an assistant?

It is better to find out right upfront who you will be dealing with on a regular basis. Often when dealing with many of the most successful agents, you will be passed to their assistant much of the time. Because you may end up dealing with them as much or more than the actual agent on a day-to-day basis, you have every right to know about it before you sign a listing agreement.

9. What are their selling percentages?

During the listing interview, most sales agents routinely provide you with a Comparative Market Analysis (CMA), form 318, that outlines comparable properties in your neighborhood that were listed and sold. Most of these statistics will be from homes sold through the local MLS and its reporting system. The agents will then suggest what they feel is a marketable asking price for your home.

At this point, ask them how closely the sales price of the homes they listed in the past six months was to the asking price that they recommended. Request exact figures and percentages. What you want to know is how good they are at coming up with asking prices. In other words, did they recommend a price of $500,000, and then actually sell the property for $450,000? If they did, that means that the home sold for 9% less than what they recommended to that seller.

What is the average price reduction across all the agent's listings? Is that average similar for all the homes listed in your local area—or just from that agent? If the average price reduction for that agent's listings on a sale are close to 10% less than what they list at, the listing price the agent suggests to you is probably 10% higher than market value as well. Sometimes certain cities or locations follow that same general percentage price reduction across all listings.

Unfortunately, at other times, some agents will tell you what you want to hear by implying that they think they can get you more money than other agents, hence a higher asking price, just so you will list with them. Later, when your home has sat on the market for a few weeks or months, they will attempt to convince you to lower the price claiming changes in the market or other excuses. Such an agent would never admit they had baited you to list with them by suggesting a too-high asking price!

Remember, even though there is a slim chance that you might make a little more if you list your property higher than the market, you can also turn off or miss potential buyers because they resent that your property is overpriced and would rather not view it or make an offer. Don't let an agent manipulate you by listing your property for far more than it is worth.

10. How does your agent handle showings?

This is much more important than it sounds. If you want your home to sell as quickly as possible, it is best to make your home as neat, clean, and presentable as possible—and make it easily available for showing. However, it is common courtesy for an agent to give you a little warning before showing up on your doorstep. A 24-hour advance telephonic request is considered reasonable.

Will your listing agent be present during all showings or will he or she give out your phone number to all local agents and tell them to call first? Unless you have unusual circumstances, it is generally not necessary for a listing agent to be present at a showing. Far more important is for you to request that they pre-qualify prospective buyers before dragging them through your home. Even if you list with a broker, you'll discover that every showing takes your time and effort. So make sure your prospective buyers are pre-approved by a lender and suited to your home and neighborhood before any agent shows your house.

Also, if your teenage children are home alone in the afternoon or you have pets that might get out of your home or yard, you need to express your desires about managing showings before you actually list the house. Your agent might not bring it up because the agent usually prefers no limitations on access. Just remember, you are the employer, they are your agent, and your wishes should be followed.

11. How does your agent coordinate your sales closing process with escrow and others?

Once you do find a buyer and an offer is made and accepted, how does your potential agent proceed? Even though a large portion of the work has been accomplished, you should still expect to be guided through the escrow process to closing. Many agents will want to turn you over to the escrow officer and move on to the next deal. Make sure that they don't dump you in this manner.

Unless closing details are handled correctly and in a timely manner, your sale might fall through and you will be back where you started. While there are some things only you can do, there are also a number of things that your agent can and should be doing as well. Your agent needs to stay on top of everything until the final day and be available to respond to your questions and needs throughout the closing process.

12. Question the agent about the fee they expect and whether it is negotiable.

Remember that the brokerage fee is **always** negotiable.

13. Ask why they are the best person for the job.

Should they be unable or unwilling to answer, you will learn something very important.

How is the brokerage fee handled?

It is a good idea to understand the chain of command in any listing process regarding the brokerage fee. As I said above, when you are listing with an agent, you are actually listing with the agent's employing broker. If you list your property for a 6% fee, then your listing agent will receive only a percentage of that fee.

For example, if Sally lists your $400,000 home at 6%, and another agent comes along with a buyer to purchase the property, the other real estate office will usually receive half of the commission you agreed to pay. In this example, it would be 50% of $24,000. Then Sally receives a pre-agreed percentage she contractually gets from her employing broker, which is somewhere between 40% to 80% of the commission received by her office. If her office gets 50% of $24,000, and her percentage is 50%, Sally will make $6,000 on the transaction. As a chunk, it appears to be a large amount of money. However, if that is the only sale Sally has made in several months, and she has been working full time on sales, then her pay scale is relatively low.

A major benefit to the current commission structure is that a homeseller does not owe a fee unless a buyer located by the agent closes escrow and the property sells. The major detriment to this type of structure is that most real estate offices charge close to the same commission even though the level of competency, quality of care, and protection given clients varies greatly. Regrettably, it remains up to each individual homeseller to determine which brokerage office will actually provide the best overall results.

What is agency—and how does it affect the sale of property?

Another important aspect of listing your property is called agency. If you decide to list your property, the conduct of your real estate agent is guided by what is called agency law. Agency law comes into play whenever someone is hired to represent another person in dealings with others—like when a seller hires an agent to represent him when dealing with buyers in real estate transactions. In that situation, an agent owes you a duty which requires them to follow agency rules and regulations, like:

1. They must represent the principal (you) with an utmost degree of care, integrity, honesty, and loyalty.

2. They must be obedient to your directions.

3. They must account for all money they collect.

4. They must disclose all adverse material facts about the property.

Because the duties owed clients by their agents are not well known by the public, laws were enacted to correct the situation. Real estate law in California now requires that you as the homeseller read and sign an Agency Disclosure Addendum, Form 305, that outlines the above listed agency duties when you sign a listing agreement with a broker, and again before you accept an offer involving a real estate agent.

Further, an additional agency disclosure provision in the purchase agreement confirms the type of agency each agent involved has undertaken. This may indicate that the real estate agent who brings you an offer from a buyer is not acting as your agent, even when you are the person who will pay them. Sound confusing? It can be, but the mandatory written disclosure does help to clarify who is working for whom.

It has been common practice for many decades for the seller of a home to pay the real estate commission. On the flip side, it is customary that the buyer seldom directly pays any commission, even when they think the agent they have been closely involved with has their best interests in mind. To resolve the issue, California concluded that the agent working with the seller is the seller's agent, and if a separate agent is working with the buyer, that is the buyer's agent—even though both are paid by the seller.

What does paying the commission mean to you as a seller? It means that if you list with an agent (the employing broker), you are owed the very highest agency duties—nothing less. Agency laws make your real estate agent more than a mere employee, they must affirmatively care for and protect you in the marketing of your property and the handling of your sale. You should have no hesitation asking for and demanding a high quality of attention and advice every step of the way.

Further, if you decide to sell the property yourself and an agent comes to you with an offer and wants you to pay them, the purchase agreement needs to confirm who the agent represents. Chances are good that even if they want you to pay for their service, they will be the buyer's agent and have the best interests of the buyer in mind, not yours. Just remember, if you are paying a commission, any amount or method of payment they ask for is entirely negotiable. Even if the agent says the commission is a "set amount", nothing is set until the employing broker and you agree to a fee. Always remember that commissions are negotiable!

In the end, agency law does not allow anyone, the seller, the buyer, or the agents to withhold any facts about the real estate that might have an adverse effect on the property value or the decision of the parties. I will discuss other disclosures in more detail in a later chapter, but for the time being, remember that if you do decide to use an agent when you sell your property, you deserve to have the highest quality of care and skill possible. Don't settle for less.

Timing on listing a property through a broker

The time line for listing your property with a broker is essentially the same as for when you sell your property yourself. The major difference is that the agent should be doing all of the sales related marketing, packaging, and coordination for you—after all, that's why you are paying them. Should you decide to list your property, use the time line on page xv to ask your agent how they will handle certain details. Ask them to tell you specifically what you will be required to do—and if they say the forms and disclaimers are up to you—don't be afraid to ask for their help every step of the way.

For example, once you have received an offer from a buyer and escrow is opened, the escrow or title company sends you a stack of papers to be filled out. Don't hesitate to call your agent and ask them to come over and help you go through the forms. At the very least, they should be available by phone to answer your every question.

Even the busiest agents have assistants who are available to help you with your inquiries.

Another area that you should insist on help with is the escrow process. As mentioned above, some agents act like their job is finished once the purchase agreement is signed by your new buyer and you. However, all agents know better. Be adamant that your agent (the listing agent) works with you and escrow to make sure all the details and paperwork between you and the buyer are handled correctly. It is not the duty of the buyer's agent to keep you informed of the progress. Remember, the buyer's agent owes his loyalty to the buyer. It is more than reasonable to expect your agent to keep you informed as each of the essential elements of the escrow process are completed and fulfilled.

For example, ask your agent to let you know when the buyer has submitted his loan application, again when he receives loan approval, and then when the loan will be funded so escrow can close. Ask them to keep in touch with the buyer's agent so you will know in advance if there is the slightest problem with the buyer's prompt performance. If you requested a weekly report from your agent from the time you listed, insist that your agent keep up the weekly reports throughout the escrow process.

Arguments agents use against becoming a FSBO

Whenever you meet with a potential listing agent or broker, you will probably hear a number of common arguments they will make to convince you to list with them. Naturally, they will list all of the reasons that they are better than other agents, as well as what they will do for you throughout the process that others may not. That is good. However, if you mention you are considering selling the property yourself, you will likely hear the following arguments:

Argument 1.

The number one argument you will hear is that according to a 2005 survey done by NAR, "the median price of a home sold with the assistance of an agent was $230,000 compared to $198,000 for FSBO sales."[4] Clearly this data sounds impressive. Unfortunately, it ignores the fact that the more expensive the property, the more the seller does not need or want to do the work himself. You will hardly ever see a home in the $1 million range where the owner wants to sell it himself.

Also, consider the fact that the survey done by NAR was done throughout the country. There are very few areas in California where the price is only $200,000 to begin with. Obviously, the statistics are badly skewed by averaging the data on very high home prices and very low home prices spread across the country.

This argument is easily countered by one used against the health insurance field. For example, when a person has health insurance that covers every little thing, they are much more likely to go to the doctor for a cold than those with no insurance or a high deductible. Statistics of these two categories of people might look as though those who had insurance were more likely to get sick than those without. In other words, an argument could be made against buying insurance since you would be healthier. Statistics can obviously be used to support whatever side you are trying to promote.

It is possible that an unsophisticated seller might accidentally price their property too low without the benefit of a real estate agent. However, most of the people who succeed as For Sale By Owners (FSBOs) are not unsophisticated. As a matter of fact, it is likely that a FSBO knows more about the process (especially after reading this book) than the average homeseller ever will. Arriving at an appropriate price to sell your property is very important, but it can be done in several ways—some of which we will talk about later in this book.

Argument 2.

The second argument is that most FSBOs will have problems in the area of understanding and completing the paperwork necessary to sell your home. For those who don't buy this book, this can be true. Without the forms that accompany this book, FSBOs have a difficult time getting usable real estate disclosures and purchase agreements, and a harder time trying to fill them out. This lack of readily available forms and the information to fill them out is obviously self-serving to the real estate industry.

Now that you have purchased this book, you will have all the necessary forms, to both market and sell your property. Additionally, escrow officers are also available to help you with forms if they feel that you will be opening an escrow at their office.

Argument 3.

The third big argument that real estate agents will use is that they can be invaluable in helping you stage and present your property. The point they make is important. It is often difficult for a homeseller to see their property objectively, and an objective observer can be beneficial. But listing your home is not the only way to make sure that your property shows to its highest advantage. That is why I offer several other alternatives later in this book.

Argument 4.

Another argument is that the training and available resources of the agent are so invaluable that you as a FSBO would be at a tremendous disadvantage without them. Again, some of this is true.

However, after over 20 years in the business, I can promise you that some agents know little more than you do about selling homes. This will be especially true after you finish reading this book, with forms in hand. Remember, in 2006, nearly 1/6 of all real estate agents have been in the business for less than one year, and 46% for less than three years. There are some excellent professionals out there, but you have to hunt and interview to find them.

Argument 5.

A real estate professional is critical in the negotiation of your sale. This common argument suggests that a FSBO might not get as high a price. Negotiations can become tricky, and certainly some people are better at it than others. However, the high rate of agent turnover establishes that only a small portion of agents are actually more skilled in this area than the general public. If you as a seller do not feel competent in the negotiation arena, then there are brokers, agents, and even lawyers who can be hired for just the single function of negotiating with a buyer you have located—and at a lot lower fee than 5-6% of your sales price.

Argument 6.

The last argument I heard was how much safer it is to list your property than to do it yourself. This argument promotes fear and suggests that an agent will somehow protect you. Nonsense! I believe that even if you do list your home with a real estate agent, you must exercise a degree of caution whenever strangers plan to enter your home—and that includes unknown agents as well! This caution extends to your home whether you are present or away. By following the guidelines I offer in this book, you should be as well protected as you would be through any listing.

Who is a realtor and who is not?

Finally, I thought it might be useful to clarify the title of "Realtor." Although it is commonly believed that all real estate agents are realtors—they aren't, even though it is occasionally used in error. Technically, in order to call yourself a Realtor, you must be a member of NAR. A large national trade group of real estate licensees, NAR offers guidelines and suggests business practices. NAR promotes many good things within the real estate brokerage community, but as with any trade union, they are extremely protective of their name and promote the necessity of their members as an essential element in any home sale. With that in mind, I have attempted in this book to use the term professional, or real estate agent or broker, rather than the word Realtor.

The very best real estate brokers earn a great deal of money and are worth it when you cannot do it yourself. They not only professionally market and sell your property, they also keep you informed every step of the way. Unfortunately, not all agents are equal and many have not been prepared for the task. If you do decide that you want to have a real estate broker handle your property, make sure that you get the very best available. After all, there isn't much difference in how much they will charge you, but there is a world of difference in the quality of service they bring to the transaction, the attention they will provide, and how long it will take to sell your home.

CHAPTER FOUR
Other FSBO options

Now that you have a clearer picture of what a normal brokerage listing process looks like and some of the background as to whether or not you have what it takes to be a For Sale By Owner (FSBO), there are other options to consider. Because the real estate market is so dynamic, everyone has more choices, but they are not as well known.

Before you make your final decision to sell your property yourself or to enlist the help of an agent, you need to know a few of the new alternatives you now have to both save money and get maximum exposure for your property.

Discount brokers

Driving around your neighborhood, you may have noticed a new type of sign that implies that you can save money when you list a property. The companies behind these signs are called discount brokers. Help-U-Sell and Assist-2-Sell are two of the largest franchisers of these discount brokers in the country, and both are extensively available in California. Others exist under a variety of names, and if one seems predominant in your area, you might want to consider them in your search when contemplating using a broker.

Keep in mind, even if you don't use the services of a particular real estate agent or discount broker, every licensee you talk to can provide you with information about the market and your home—so don't be afraid to speak up and ask questions.

Discount brokers customarily work in what is now being called an "a la carte" way. What that means is that you can usually pick and choose the type of work that you want them to perform for you, and then pay only for the services you receive. Each company is a little different and has a different fee structure, so you will need to check around.

Most discount brokers offer to do certain aspects of traditional brokerage for a set flat fee. Usually, the more you want done for you, the higher the fee. For example, Assist-2-Sell offers three main packages:

1. **MLS for less:** As mentioned before, every real estate community has a local industry-established database containing all the properties presently for sale that are handled by agents. This database is called a Multiple Listing Service (MLS). An MLS is usually exclusive to real estate brokers and their agents and is their primary resource when it comes to locating properties to sell.

   Because most properties sold in California are sold to buyers who use real estate agents, it is extremely beneficial for your home to be listed in an MLS. However, the only way you can get listed in an MLS is to come to some arrangement with a real estate broker.

   An MLS listing normally provides for photos and many facts and figures about each property. In addition, it also offers a specific commission amount that will be paid to the broker who brings a buyer who purchases the property at the full listed price. When an agent working with a buyer sees a property listed in an MLS, they immediately know how much the seller is offering to pay them if they produce the buyer for that property.

   Normally, when you sign a listing, your broker routinely inputs your property in an MLS offering a buyer's broker half of what you have agreed to pay as the commission. Discount brokers must arrange the fee differently. They typically charge a set flat fee (usually less than $500) for the services they will provide to the seller under a listing.

   However, if you want MLS exposure, the discount broker needs to state an additional amount offered to the buyer's broker. This is usually half of whatever is the customary fee charged by brokers in your particular location (generally half of 6% or a total of 3%). This percentage amount offered to the buyer's broker is only payable if any MLS agent brings you a buyer who purchases your home, and as with all commission fees, it is always negotiable. However, if you find the buyer yourself, you will only pay the flat fee charged by the discount broker.

This option is called "MLS for less" because, instead of paying a full commission, you are usually only paying slightly more than half. While providing maximum exposure, this option will save you almost half the standard fee.

2. **Direct-to-buyers:** This is an option a homeseller can choose where the discount broker will advertise the property throughout their company system, but will not place it on the MLS. This service is usually much less effective, but definitely costs less. In this category, you save any amount that would be offered to a buyer's agent (usually somewhere around 3%). In most cases, you will probably find that this option offers you little more than what you can do yourself.

3. **Paperwork only:** This option is for those FSBOs who are intimidated by the prospect of filling out the forms by themselves, but feel they can handle the marketing on their own. This option does not require a listing, but will provide you with all of the necessary forms, along with someone else to fill them out. This alternative might also include overseeing the process of closing escrow.

Even though some discount brokers like Help-U-Sell and Assist-2-Sell are national companies and offer that network, the local offices are all individually owned and operated. Local franchises offer a benefit with brokers and agents who are familiar with the local market and can meet with you face-to-face. However, a detriment is that each broker and his agents must be interviewed extensively to find out how well they will provide the services being offered.

Discount brokers also tend to attract a large number of agents that are either new to the field or do not have the character traits to make it in a more traditional brokerage office. It is unlikely that an agent who is highly active and successful will be working for a discount broker, so you must consider the quality and experience level of those who will be helping you.

Let's face it, if you are expecting all of the help and services that a highly successful and professional broker can provide, then you will have to go with a traditional broker. However, if you are willing to do much of the work yourself and don't need the handholding done by a conventional broker, then discount brokers can fill an important need.

Internet FSBO services

Another option that you have as a FSBO is to take advantage of some of the Internet websites that cater to FSBOs. Some of these sites are owned and managed by real estate brokers around the country. Others hold themselves out as real estate advertising companies. Either way, they offer today's FSBO more choices.

Just like discount brokers, many Internet FSBO sites offer a menu of a la carte items that anyone can purchase. The more help you want, the more it costs. For example, FSBO.com offers sellers a number of different packages. The least expensive choice provides sellers with a listing on their website, including eight photos. The next choice throws in a yard sign. The most expensive package sellers can purchase is a flat-fee listing in your local MLS. In that case, the amount sellers would pay would be similar to that mentioned in the subsection above.

This option can definitely save you money and help you get the buyer exposure that you need to succeed. The downside is that there are dozens of Internet FSBO sites, and the challenge is picking one or more that has the widest coverage. Another example is ForSaleByOwner.com which advertises that it receives more hits than any other FSBO site. User reviews, available through Internet traffic rankings on Alexa.com, are mixed. Before selecting any service, I would recommend that you ask for references of satisfied clients and research your options carefully.

Another option available through Internet website brokers is to pay a small percentage of the sales price to the online broker if, or when, the property sells. Usually, the percentage is less than what you would pay through a traditional broker — and obviously, the service you receive would be less. I believe that if you want the best exposure through the MLS, at the lowest price, you are better served by going through a local discount broker or a flat-fee Internet broker rather than those brokers who want a percentage of the asking price for their services.

As I mentioned above, the services you receive from these types of brokers or companies will be limited and subject to the personality and knowledge of the individual you happen to find. If you contract with them with the expectation that they will do the same job as a traditional broker, you will most likely be unhappy. Most of the time, you will get exactly what you are paying for. Hopefully, after reading this book and knowing what to expect, you will not be disappointed. For those who understand the benefits, and use them to their advantage, discount and Internet brokers can be beneficial.

Paying a buyer's broker

Another option you might use is relatively easy, but again, not as well known. To begin with, if you decide to become a FSBO, you must prepare yourself for the large number of real estate agents and brokers who will contact you to try to get you to list your property with them. There is no way around this situation unless you list with a traditional or discount broker. Then you are considered off-limits.

When real estate agents contact you, they will try and convince you that they are your best option to help sell your home. It is also likely that they will tell you that they have a buyer just waiting to look at your house and buy it. Instead of getting anxious that you might lose the perfect buyer for your home, you need to assure them that even if you don't enter into a listing agreement with them, you will pay them a buyer's broker fee if they bring you a buyer who purchases your property. This is assuming you are willing to pay a reduced fee (half of a normal full commission) for a ready, willing, and able buyer today!

I personally sold two homes I owned using this method. It is an excellent way to reach many buyers because the vast majority of them work with real estate agents since it costs the buyer nothing. What do you have to pay them? It is likely that they will want to handle their commission in one of two ways. If they ask you to commit to writing that you will pay them a fee before they show the property to their buyers, you can list the property for one person only, called a single-party listing. Be very certain that anything they have you sign has the names of the specific buyer, a time frame for presenting the offer, and the specific amount you are willing to pay as a flat fee or percentage of the price. Chances are good that you should be able to negotiate a commission somewhere between 1.5-3% in this type of situation.

Another way that a broker might handle your FSBO situation would be for him to show the home to his buyers, and if they are interested, present you with an offer to purchase. On the real estate purchase agreement routinely used in California, a section on the form allows the broker to write in a fee amount. This is located on the form near the end of the contract where he must confirm his agency relationship with the person he is actually representing in the transaction. (See Form 150 §14)

Remember, even if you are paying the commission, he will probably confirm he is working exclusively for the buyer. If he has already filled out the form, he will probably have filled in the commission amount with a higher percentage than you will want to pay. Assuming everything else in the contract is acceptable, you can counter the amount with one you will agree to pay.

So how much commission is reasonable? This question is entirely negotiable. Just remember, a bird in the hand is worth two in the bush. I have seen dozens of homeowners get very attached to their home and begin asking for an extra thousand here or there just because they have a ready buyer. We will cover this in more detail when we talk about negotiations, but remember that a buyer who likes your home and is willing to pay a decent price is what you have worked so hard to obtain. If the buyer comes with a broker attached, then finding a way to come to an agreement is a good thing since you have achieved a large part of your end goal.

If you have listed your property through the MLS, then whatever amount you offered to pay is usually the percentage the buyer's broker will expect to be paid, even if they offer a lower than listed price. If you have done all the marketing yourself without the MLS database, and are happy with the price offered, then agreeing to an amount of 2-3% is quite reasonable.

You also have the right to raise the price of your property to help cover the commission. Just keep in mind that if you priced your property right in the first place, an increase might knock prospective buyers out of the game should you decide to get greedy. Always keep the objective of selling your home in mind, and go from there.

You do not have to list your property with anyone to benefit from the real estate professional community. Even if you don't interview them in advance, they will come knocking. By offering to pay an acceptable commission to an agent that brings you a buyer rather than through a typical listing agent, you can use them to your advantage and still save a large amount of money.

Lease option or rent-to-own

Another option you have as a homeseller is to offer it as a rental with an option to purchase. If the property you own is already a rental, you likely have buyers (your tenants) who are interested in the home right now. Otherwise, you can advertise your property for sale to others who don't have the savings for the down payment, but would still like to own their own home.

This option works best if you don't need any cash out of your equity to buy another house or pay bills. If you rent your property and give the tenants an option to buy it later, you avoid any real estate commission and may have established a monthly cash flow until they exercise their purchase option. Both are nice benefits and are often used when the real estate market is very slow and interest rates are high or the mortgage market is tight.

How to go about correctly structuring a lease option involves co-ordination, which we will cover in more detail in a later chapter. Most importantly, you want to make sure to get everything in writing. Also, the forms you need to write up this type of transaction are included on the Forms CD accompanying this book. Just know that this is another option you have at your disposal when it comes to selling your property yourself. (See Form 163)

It's up to you

These marketing methods are the main alternatives you have when becoming a FSBO or listing your property with a broker. The common denominator in all of it is you—and the time and effort you are willing to put into locating a buyer. There are definitely choices to be made and more to learn, but chances are good that if you have read this far you are sufficiently motivated to become a FSBO. With the help of this book, the forms CD, and that motivation, I believe that you can successfully sell your home for a respectable price and save yourself a great deal of money on the commission—so keep reading!

PART TWO

The nuts and bolts
of every real estate transaction.

CHAPTER FIVE
The art of pricing

Setting a proper asking price is one of the more challenging aspects of being a For Sale By Owner (FSBO), but it doesn't have to be. It is actually a very simple procedure. Once you know how agents go about pricing properties, and you will after reading this chapter, there is no reason why you as an owner cannot come up with the perfect asking price for your home.

Setting an appropriate price is important because it can either reward you for your efforts or frustrate you with inaction. So before you jump to conclusions about pricing, there are a number of things to do before arriving at a final number—including letting go of any of your preconceptions about the value of your home. What you paid for your property, what you imagine your property is worth, or how much cash you are in need of has no actual bearing on the price you will receive in today's market. Naturally, you want the highest obtainable price, but never at the risk of antagonizing and alienating prospective buyers.

Actually, selecting a suitable asking price for your property is an art. Two important characteristics of this art are a sensitivity to the marketplace and the ability to be objective about your own home. I have seen intelligent and capable people become overly sentimental about their house by believing it to be far more valuable than comparable properties and pricing it out of the market. I have also witnessed people who, after originally paying too much for their property or finding themselves in a financial crunch, setting a price based on the profit they hope to make or the net proceeds they need from the sale of their house, regardless of its actual present-day value. In the end, the real estate market functions independent of our emotions or personal needs.

The art of pricing is sifting through and analyzing the available data before arriving at a fair and realistic market value for your property. What is fair market value? Fair market value is defined as the amount you would willingly sell your home for in a normal marketplace and what a willing and able buyer would pay. It's that simple. Unfortunately, too many of us read the newspaper, listen to the nightly news, and talk to our neighbors with the assumption that that information is all we need to set a reasonable price. Wrong. Again, the price we are looking for is what you can realistically sell your house for and what someone else will realistically pay in today's market.

How do you arrive at that amount? Below are a number of avenues you can use.

Using the local real estate community

The most important thing to do when pricing your home is to find out how much comparable homes have sold for recently. That data alone is the best indicator of your home's fair market value. In the past, just about the only way you could get this information was to talk to a real estate agent. Every local real estate board tracks and monitors the properties that each of its members lists and sells. Local title companies also track recent sales through deeds recorded with the county and this is available to local agents. When a potential homeseller contacts a local agent, that agent routinely provides the homeowner with a Comparative Market Analysis (CMA) using the information obtained through a Multiple Listing Service (MLS) and one of the local title companies. (See Form 318)

There are now other options, but this is still one of your best—even as a FSBO. You can call a number of local real estate agents and tell them that you are thinking about selling your home. You might even tell them that you will probably be doing that as a FSBO. Who knows? You might actually meet an agent that is so impressive that you do decide to list your home with them immediately. If not, it is still beneficial for you to have an agent look at your property and give you their opinion of the value. Not only will this help you arrive at an estimated asking price for your property, you will also have given your property some exposure to an agent that might eventually bring a buyer to your doorstep.

Keep in mind that the real estate community is very competitive and it is in their best interests to help homeowners. (I say that as a real estate licensee myself.) Most of them realize that even if you don't use them to sell your home, you might want to use them to buy your next one. Unless an agent is extremely busy or has a bad attitude, most will be willing to help you and work with you in a variety of ways. If you find one that is too pushy or difficult to work with, just open the phone book and call another one. Better yet, look around your neighborhood and call one that has another home for sale in your area. They will already have much of the information you need and are usually eager to work with neighbors. Just be prepared for their on-going desire to list your property. Know that, and have an answer to give them when they begin to inquire about the listing.

If you are comfortable with the idea of using the real estate community to obtain a CMA, I would recommend that you talk to at least three different real estate agents and compare the information that they give you. Again, select agents that seem to be doing a lot of business in your neighborhood. Watch the newspaper and notice who runs ads for homes in your area. Once you have received their CMAs, you will probably find that all of them differ somewhat in the price they suggest and the comparable houses that they give you. That's okay—what you want to do is analyze their data and compile it in a way that seems most reasonable. If you receive a CMA from three or more real estate agents, you will have a pretty good idea of what you can set as an asking price.

One last thing, make sure that the information they give you is current. Because the real estate market changes measurably about every six months, you want comparables within that length of time. Pricing is a reflection of what is happening in the marketplace—and the marketplace is always changing. By gathering current comparables, you will have a glimpse of what to expect in regards to your own property.

Getting an appraisal

Another way to arrive at a value is to hire a licensed appraiser. Whenever you get a new loan on a property, the bank requires that you pay for an appraiser to tell the bank what the property is worth. How does an appraiser arrive at a price? Basically, they use the same information that the local real estate agents use when giving you a CMA. The only difference is that the person who appraises for a bank has a contract with the lender and has taken additional courses, beyond those that typical real estate agents have taken, to refine their evaluations. However, the facts and figures they use are usually the same.

If you are uncomfortable asking real estate agents for a CMA, you can always contact a professional appraiser and pay them to tell you what they think your house is worth. The price for this service is typically $250 to $450. One advantage to having your home priced by an appraiser is that you can then tell any prospective buyers that a licensed California real estate appraiser established the price. This might help you succeed in obtaining an advantageous price. However, keep in mind that if you hire an appraiser, there is a likelihood that the price they arrive at for the property may be lower than what you expected or hoped to receive.

When it comes down to it, an appraisal amount, just like a CMA from a real estate agent, is really just one person's opinion of value. And what anyone considers to be valuable is somewhat subjective. So, even though everyone is using a reasonably consistent method to set the price, each person giving his opinion of value is deciding what property features will be given weight and which will be ignored.

The process goes something like this. An appraiser will conduct a routine inspection of your home. He will then gather data on other properties that have sold in the area. He'll then compare the features of each of the properties, such as the square footage, the location, the amenities, the age, and the condition of each property, to your home. Finally, he will add or deduct dollar amounts for the differences in qualities between the other properties and yours, and arrive at a price range.

Again, even though the process and the data is the same in most cases for both appraisals and CMAs, the properties that are selected and the weight given to each feature of a property which adds value, is subjective. For that reason, just like with the CMA, most appraisals will come in at slightly different prices. Sometimes the prices are dramatically different.

A drastically different value would most often occur when a property is very unusual. If your home is unique and very different from any property that could be used as a comparable, the process of weighing the value of the uniqueness is even more subjective. It is always easiest to arrive at a price for a home in a subdivision where a number of other homes have sold that are very similar to your home. If your property has a number of features that are not easily priced, then you will likely come up with a wide variety of opinions of value.

Using Internet sites to set prices

A new option that has only recently become available through the Internet is Automated Valuation Models (AVMs). These sites use computerized crunching tools and pull data from a variety of other websites, including public records, tax assessments, deeds, and other property characteristics. By using an address and a zip code, an AVM uses mathematical models to compare properties. However, because each site uses different criterion, the results can vary widely and are generally considered to be unreliable.

One site, Zillow.com, offers what it calls a "Zestimate" for no charge. By typing in your address and zip code, it gives you a Zestimate along with an aerial map of comparable properties. But remember, by Zillow's definition, a Zestimate is a cross between an estimate and a guess. Use such information with that in mind.

Older online valuation programs like HouseValues.com, HomeGain.com, and Domania.com also provide the same type of information. However, because they serve as lead generators for local real estate agents, they require your name and address, and then the information is passed on to local agents who pay a fee to receive your contact information. If you use these sites, be prepared to provide your name, address, and a phone number as well. An agent will contact you later.

My opinion is that the information that these sites provide do not give you what you should consider a definitive price for your property. Using my current home as an example, Zillow.com said it was worth $657,000, while RealEstateABC.com said it was only worth $587,000. Certainly, I might hope that the higher value was correct, but the different valuation is too wide to provide a dependable asking price for a property. Still, the information obtained can be added to other data you use to price your property. Just don't consider them to be an authority on value.

Using a title company

Title companies are a vital part of every real estate transaction in the state of California. Their primary business is to provide title insurance, which is an insurance policy saying that the title you are transferring to your buyer is marketable and free of all encumbrances except those they list. Like other insurance policies, you don't need them until you need them. However, when your ownership is attacked, they can be highly beneficial.

Because title insurance is an essential part of every real estate transaction, title companies work hard to help the real estate community. They are also competitive. Some of the largest title companies in California are Chicago Title, First American Title, Fidelity National Title, LandAmerica, and Old Republic Title. There are many more, which makes the job of selecting one even more challenging. The key of course is to use one with both a great reputation and a solid financial background.

One of the things they will do for you as a seller when asked is to provide you with a list of comparable properties. They will search the recent sales that have been recorded by the county clerk and recorder and give you a list of them. Just go to the phone book and look up a title company. Call one, or perhaps two of them, and tell them that you are a FSBO and that you would like recent comparables for your home. Usually within a week, they will have them available for you to come by their office and pick up.

Because they want to work with you when you eventually sell, they will probably not charge you for this service. Not only should they give you a current list of homes sold in the area, but you will also get a chance to see how accommodating their office is with regards to you as a FSBO. They often have other information for FSBOs, so be sure to ask. This is one good way to "interview" a local title company for use when you sell your property. You should also ask for their list of fees regarding the services they provide for title and escrow to help you make the choice of which company to use in the future.

The comparables provided by the title company will not contain an estimated price for your property. Nor will they necessarily be the comparables most closely related to your home. The real estate community has more of a familiarity with the differences and similarities of a particular subdivision or area, whereas the title company's data relies mainly on location and square footage. The list that they give you will be based on general information; however, consider it more data to use to arrive at your own conclusion for a price.

Doing your own CMA

Armed with information from all of the above sources, you are well on your way to selecting a price. Another necessary step is to "drive" the neighborhood. In the weeks leading up to setting a "For Sale" sign in your own yard, begin canvassing your neighbors and attending every Open House held nearby. When attending these events, try to remain as objective as possible when you are comparing that property to your own home. See as a buyer would see. Judge as a real estate agent would judge. Notice what you like and what you don't like, and then objectively compare the differences to your home.

Besides attending every local Open House, spend several weeks looking at the local classified ads. See what homes are selling for in your surrounding area. Get on the Internet and see what homes are for sale in your area. Just about all homes that are listed can be accessed through Realtor.com for no cost or obligation. Sometimes you have to do a little bit of detective work, but it is now possible, because of the Internet, to gather most of the information about homes that are listed on the market just by searching.

In addition to looking at properties on the Internet, collect flyers from neighborhood houses that are for sale. Look at the photos and compare the amenities. Again, attempt to remain as objective as possible in regards to your own home. You do not have to defend your home, and you will likely be unable to persuade a buyer to pay you more than it is worth, so save yourself some later grief by spending some time doing an honest comparison.

Play it like a game. When you see a new "For Sale" sign go up in the neighborhood, attempt to guess what the asking price will be. The more you do it, the better you will get. This is an extremely important step that has to do with thousands of dollars of potential income, so don't rush it.

Lastly, always remember that the asking price is not always the sales price. When you view other homes for sale in your neighborhood, keep in mind that the actual value will be determined only when a sale of the property has closed escrow. Be sure and attach a great deal more weight to the comparable properties which have sold, and the actual price they sold for, than to the asking price of homes which are still seeking buyers when doing your own CMA. (See Form 318)

Putting your personal time-frame into the equation

One other item has an affect on the value of your home and should be considered. Remember, the fair market value of your home is what a willing seller will sell for in a normal market and what a willing and able buyer will pay. Well, the market is seldom normal and neither are the circumstances of either the buyer or the seller. In

Pricing Elements to Compare
(Use the Comparative Market Analysis, Form 318)

1. **Square footage**: If the square footage in your home and/or the rooms in your home are much larger or smaller than others in your neighborhood that have sold, it will definitely affect pricing. Add or deduct appropriate dollar amounts to the chosen comparison properties.

2. **Location**: Every city has areas that are considered more or less desirable than others. What do others say about your neighborhood? If it's positive, that will add to your valuation; if it's negative, then you will receive less for your home than if it were in a more desirable area.

   Not only must you objectively evaluate your neighborhood, but the exact location within the neighborhood also has a bearing. Are you on a busy street or near a freeway? Does your backyard face a commercial strip or back up to train tracks? Are your neighbors the messiest in the area?

3. **Floor plans**: Most subdivisions have similar floor plans. Usually there are floor plans that are more desirable than others. Find out what yours is and adjust accordingly.

4. **Garages**: Does your home have a one-, two-, or three-car garage? How does that compare to the properties that have sold in your neighborhood?

5. **Age and condition of property**: If your home is older than all the others in the neighborhood, no matter how great the condition, that factor will affect value. If the condition is perfectly maintained, that will benefit the price. Adjust accordingly.

6. **Size of the lot**: Is your lot size comparable to all of your neighbors' or do you have an especially large or small lot? This variation in size affects price.

7. **Amenities**: Do you have a fireplace, pool, spa, patio, porch, or anything else that is a unique and desirable quality? Or is your home bare-bones while all of your neighbors have upgrades and amenities? Add or deduct as needed.

8. **Special outdoor features**: Do you have a unique and special view? Are you next to the ocean or a park? These desirable qualities can also affect the price.

9. **Average marketing time or days-on-market**: The length of this period affects the price since time on the market enables you to determine if the property sold was on the market for a longer than normal time. If it sold faster than most comparable homes, the price might have been a bit low. If the period was longer, the price might have been a bit too high.

10. **Asking price vs. sales price percentage**: By noting the percentage difference between the asking price of comparable properties and the price they eventually sold for, you know what to expect. This percentage difference also helps you price your property correctly.

    For example, if a large number of homes in your area were listed for $450,000, but routinely sold in the area of $405,000, then the sales percentage is close to 90% of the asking price. If comparables show that your home is worth $450,000 in today's market, with a 10% spread between the asking price and selling price, you would list your property at $500,000, knowing that in the end you will probably get something near to $450,000.

    On the other hand, if the pricing spread in your neighborhood is 2%, you would list your property near $460,000 and still come out the same. The sales percentage spread changes with different locales and different markets. This information will help you arrive at a correct asking price that will entice prospective buyers to make an offer.

What about the good things? Are you conveniently located? Does your neighborhood rate higher than others? Are you in the best school district in the region? All of these elements affect the value of your home.

COMPARABLE MARKET ANALYSIS FOR SETTING VALUES

This Comparable Market Analysis (CMA) worksheet is prepared by the seller of a property, or his agent, to provide an estimate of the value of the seller's property based on the sales price of other similar properties sold within the past few months, each adjusted in price to reflect the dollar valuation of their distinctions from the seller's property. On locating recent sales through the County Records and completing a visual inspection of the comparable sales, note in the column for each comparable property, at any itemized features which is distinguishable from the seller's property, the dollar amount of the adjustment to the comparable property's price by, 1) deducting the dollar value of the feature the comparable property has which the seller's property does not, or, 2) adding the dollar value of the feature the comparable property does not have which the seller's property has.

Date prepared _____, 20_____, by _____. Application/order # _____.

Features:	Subject property	Comparable No. 1		Comparable No. 2		Comparable No. 3	
Address:							
Proximity to Subject							
Sale Price	$		$		$		$
Sale Price/Gross Living Area	$ per sq. ft	$ per sq. ft		$ per sq. ft		$ per sq. ft	
Data Source							
Verification Source							
1. Sales Information:							
1.1 Date of sale							
1.2 Concessions (sales/financing)							
1.3 Fee simple/ leasehold							
1.4 Age of improvements							
1.5 Special HOA assessments							
1.6 Bonded assessments							
2. VALUE ADJUSTMENT:	DESCRIPTION	DESCRIPTION	+(-)$	DESCRIPTION	+(-)$	DESCRIPTION	+(-)$
2.1 Zoning Compliance (nonconforming/ illegal)							
2.2 Easement/ encroachment							
2.3 Use restrictions (CC&Rs)							
2.4 Retrofitting/water conservation							
3. Location/area:							
3.1 Neighborhood trend:							
3.2 Street amenities							
3.3 Lot size/shape							
3.4 Vehicle access							
3.5 Schools/churches /institutions							
3.7 Inside/corner lot							
3.8 Utilities available							
3.9 Environmental hazards/ nuisances							

VALUE ADJUSTMENT	DESCRIPTION	DESCRIPTION	+(-)$	DESCRIPTION	+(-)$	DESCRIPTION	+(-)$
4. Landscaping:							
4.1 Quality							
4.2 Maintenance							
4.3 Soil condition/ drainage							
4.4 Topography							
5. Improvements:							
5.1 Age of improvement							
5.2 Construction type							
5.3 Highest and best use							
5.4 Design/style							
5.5 Energy efficiency							
5.6 Maintenance/ obsolescence							
5.7 Exterior conditions							
5.8 Interior conditions							
5.9 Garage/carpet							
5.10 Central AC/heating							
5.11 Gutters and downspouts							
5.12 Windows/ screens							
6. Livable Space:							
6.1 Gross livable sq. ft.							
6.2 No. of bedrooms							
6.3 No. of baths							
6.4 Kitchen/ appliances							
6.5 Living room							
6.6 Dining room							
6.7 Family room							
6.8 Basement/ storage							
6.9 Attic/access							
7. Amenities:							
7.1 Fireplace/ woodstove							
7.2 Pool							
7.3 Fences							
7.4 Patio/porch/deck							
8. TOTAL Price Adjustment:		☐ + ☐ -	$	☐ + ☐ -	$	☐ + ☐ -	$
9. Adjusted Price of Each Comparable:			% $		% $		% $
10 Value of Subject Property:	$						

either of those cases, the price can be lower than market, and in other cases, higher than market, depending upon the special needs of either you, as the seller, or any particular buyer.

For example, if you have been transferred out of state and need to move immediately, your motivation to sell your home will cause you to consider accepting offers at lower prices than you would if you didn't have to move for another year. Likewise, if a buyer needs to get settled in a new location immediately, chances are good that they will pay a slightly higher price for your house if they can move in right away. Similarly, if the market is very repressed and you have grown weary of marketing, you might just take the first reasonable offer you receive since you may not have seen an offer for a very long time.

If you believe you need or want to move right away, you will want to price your home very close to fair market value right upfront. If you are just shopping the market, you might want to put your home 5-10% above that amount. If you needed to move yesterday, then you will want to price your property so competitively that every prospective buyer that has an interest in your neighborhood will want to see your home. The best way to do that is to price your home just under what everyone else is asking.

Another aspect of timing has to do with what is going on in the marketplace. For example, in early 2004, my husband and I noticed that the market was literally jumping with buyers! Because we routinely read the newspaper ads and watch the "For Sale" signs in our neighborhood, we clearly saw the inventory rapidly diminishing. On the other hand, when a property came on the market, it was several thousand dollars more than a comparable one had been just weeks before. Because we had previously toyed with the idea of selling, we made the decision to sell our house for $50,000 more than we would have been able to get only three or four months prior. We sold the home 35 days later.

In other words, if you see the real estate marketing exploding and you've considered the idea of selling in the near future, don't wait; now is a good time to sell. However, if you see homes sitting for sale for months at a time, with price reductions everywhere you look, you might want to think about your timing or the price you are asking for. In the end, if you have a choice as to when to sell your property, it is best to match your sale with a rise in the local real estate sales cycle.

What it comes down to is this—there is no one perfect price for your home. Again, the fair market value is what a willing and able buyer will pay and the price that a willing (but not desperate) seller will accept. You will find that any home, no matter what the condition or where its location, will sell if it is priced right for the current phase of the market. If you find your home is not selling and it has been on the market for longer than comparable properties in your neighborhood, then chances are good that you have priced your property too high. If you don't need to sell, then take it off the market and wait for the inventory of properties to decline. Have to sell and sell now? Then lower the asking price.

What real estate agents may tell you about pricing

Because I recommend that you use local real estate agents and their CMAs to help you arrive at your pricing, you might want to be prepared for some of their sales pitches in advance. One point they will likely stress is that according to a survey done by the National Association of Realtors (NAR), FSBO owners received approximately 14% less than comparable homes that were listed and sold using a Realtor.[1] Real estate agents would like for all sellers to believe that you will lose money if you try to sell your home yourself. Of course, they have a lot at stake—basically a 5-6% commission in most cases—so it is in their best interest to promote this data as fact.

What might this data really reveal? The sales amounts used are on the lower end of the national average for real estate purchases, basically $230,000 for those sold by brokers and $198,200 for sellers without agents. Clearly, these amounts are on the lower end of the scale, so they point to the fact that most of these homes are not in the state of California. Also, it is highly likely that most homes sold by FSBOs are in a lower price range. These are the people, like you and me, who are willing to do the work for the savings to be had. Sellers in the high-end market, or one that is rapidly appreciating, don't have nearly the same desire or need to become a FSBO. These types of sellers list and sell their properties so the resulting blended averages of their sales prices show a significantly higher average.

Actually, The Los Angeles Times reported in early 2006 that, "The median price of a home in California was $548,430 in December, compared with the national median of $209,300 in the same month."[2] When you consider these prices and their disparity, it highlights how difficult it is to compare a national percentage to California's market. In addition, it is widely known that many in the FSBO community sell to family members at a significant discount without the use of a broker. That could clearly account for the huge discrepancy.

Regardless of NAR's national survey, you as a FSBO should take note that pricing is indeed one of the critical factors when selling your home. Your greatest risk with pricing is to hurry through the process and not gather all the available data as suggested. However, armed with the recommended information, you are as protected as those sellers working with an agent when it comes to arriving at an excellent asking price.

Actually, listing with an agent does not guarantee that you will sell at the best price either. When selling a home recently, we asked two highly respected agents to give us a CMA. One came in at a range that was over 15% less than the other broker. Because we had been watching the local market ourselves, we went with the second agent's price — and got it as a FSBO—two months later. In the final analysis, you know your neighborhood and your home better than anyone. Keep your eyes open, pay attention, and you will arrive at a fitting asking price.

One final suggestion

Don't forget your friends. Once you have gathered all of your research, invite one or two of your trusted friends over to review the data and to offer their opinion based upon your data. Be sure to promise them that you won't mind their being completely honest, but that you may or may not decide to use the price they suggest. Of course, most of the time, your friends will err on the generous side, although they may occasionally come in lower than expected. Friends can often help you to see your home and price more objectively and prepare you for the arguments of future buyers.

Remember, everyone sees value in a different way. Just because the opinions of other people differ from yours doesn't make them wrong or right. Your goal is merely to price your property in a way that attracts and grabs the largest number of prospective buyers at the highest price possible. All your homework will help in this area.

Coming up with an exact price

When finally selecting your asking price, pay attention to what the amount sounds like and looks like on paper. What do I mean by that? Well, which sounds more expensive: $1 million or $995,000? Obviously, these numbers are extremely close in value, but they sound different. Retailers are especially wise in these matters. That is why you continually see retail goods priced at $9.99 instead of $10. Real estate professionals know the same thing. They know that lower numbers sound better and look better to potential buyers. Why not use that perception to your advantage as well? When it comes to placing a price on your flyers and what you tell others, be sure to select an amount that sounds as though it's a bargain.

Learn the art of pricing

All appraisers and real estate agents who provide CMAs use the above information to arrive at the market value for a home. As described above, most go about it in a similar way. But once they have gathered the information, they basically use what I call "art". The opinions of the best appraisers and agents reflect a sensitivity to the marketplace that sifts through and analyzes the data to arrive at the current market value of a property.

However, while some people excel at setting value, there are other agents and appraisers who are less than perfect. That is why I believe that if you take the time and relish the process described in this chapter, you as a FSBO are just as capable of coming up with a great asking price for your property as anyone.

Remember, avoid wishful thinking. If you want to be successful at selling your house yourself, it is best to not think of yourself as a mere home seller, but as a person who knows how to sell homes. Select a price that reflects the market and your circumstances, and you will be well on your way to a successful sale.

CHAPTER SIX
Getting comfortable with contracts and paperwork

Most owners who sell their own home report difficulty when filling out and understanding the paperwork required during the sales process. In this chapter, I tackle those concerns. In case you haven't yet looked it over, the enclosed CD is key to your feeling comfortable with the purchase agreement and the necessary disclosures you will need to sell your property. (See Form 157)

Be aware that you may jump ahead at any time and check out the forms whenever needed. In the meantime, I will start at the beginning and explain the legal background and requirements for selling property. If you already know how to use the forms, or don't now care to know, just skip ahead. Disclosures will be covered in the next few chapters.

How real estate is transferred

Real estate is normally transferred in the state of California by means of a grant deed. Just where exactly is the grant deed to your home? If you are like most homeowners, it's in a file stuck somewhere in the back of your closet with all your important papers. You should have received a file when you closed escrow on your home, and then afterwards, when other information arrived in the mail, you added to the file. Chances are, if you have owned your home for longer than a year, you probably haven't seen or looked at this file since then.

It's time to dig it out. That file will likely contain the grant deed that was used to convey the property from the previous owner to you. On the deed, there will be what is called the "legal description" and usually the common street address. It will have the previous owner's name as well as your own. The deed should also contain some official looking markings that verify that it was recorded by the county recorder. You actually don't even need to find the deed because it now exists as part of the county records and you, and anyone else, can get a copy by contacting a title company and asking for their help.

Other than obtaining the legal description for future contracts you will be writing, you will also want to notice who is named (technically called "vested") as the present owner of the property. Vesting is the manner in which you hold title and ownership to property. If you are the sole owner, the vesting will be in your name. If you purchased the property when married, the vesting will name both you and your spouse. The reason vesting is important is because it determines how the new deed must be filled out and who is to sign in order to transfer the property to the new buyer.

The longer you have owned your home, the more likely the chance that there are names on the ownership or vesting that you may have forgotten. In other words, when you purchased your home, you may have bought it with an ex-spouse or a co-signer on the deed. It is always a good idea to check to make sure that you and whomever else is on the deed is in agreement about selling at this time. Should there be a name you've forgotten about, you'll want to immediately find them and come to an agreement to obtain their consent to sell before you begin marketing. Once everyone who is a vested owner is in agreement, you are on your way.

Your mortgage papers

What about your loan? Before you sell, it is good to know how much you currently owe on the property so you can calculate the amount of your net sales proceeds. The best way to do that is to look on your monthly payment coupons for any loans you have. Actually, located in the file where you found the grant deed to your property, there will likely be the original loan papers for your property. The two most important loan documents will be the note and the deed of trust. These documents will only be copies, because the note and trust deed are your promise to pay your mortgage holder, and they hold the originals.

Either through the loan documents or your monthly payment statements, you may be able to arrive at a current balance for your loan. If you have more than one loan on your property, you will want to calculate that balance as well. If the balances of the loans are not listed, you can call your lender and ask for current loan balances. With that information, you will be able to deduct the loans from your asking price to determine the gross amount of equity in your property.

In addition to the balances of all loans on the property, you need to gather together the names, phone numbers, and fax numbers of all the lenders involved so you can turn them over to an escrow officer when you sell the property. Escrow, as closing coordinator, will arrange for the paperwork on a loan assumption or a payoff of all existing loans. Escrow must first obtain official statements of your loan balances. Then escrow will be required to figure exact payoff amounts and make prorations as necessary. Having all addresses and information will save time in the long run.

Title insurance

Within the property file that you received when you bought your house, there should also be a copy of your title insurance policy. This would have come in the mail a month or two after you closed escrow on the property. The policy is a bulky document that very few people actually read, but it was purchased to protect you in case there was a problem with your deed or title that was unknown when you bought your home. Thankfully, it is hardly ever used, but like most insurance, it is important when needed.

In most counties in California, it is customary for the seller to pay the premium to the title company for this policy to protect the buyer, so chances are good that it did not cost you anything when you bought your house. However, when you go to sell your house, the buyer will expect you to purchase a policy in their name to protect their title.

You may have actually purchased a title policy yourself more recently. If you refinanced your home or took out a second loan, your lender required you to purchase a policy to protect their lien rights in your property under a trust deed. The reason I mention this is because, if you purchased a policy within the last five years, you may be entitled to a discount from that title insurance company when you go to buy a policy for your buyers. This discount is a called a "short-term rate." Be sure and ask about it if you think it might apply. You would be required to use the same title company that issued that loan policy, but the savings should make it worthwhile. Likewise, if you bought your property within the last couple of years, ask the original title company if they offer a short-term rate on a new sale.

The real estate purchase agreement—an offer to purchase your home

I believe it will be beneficial for you to become comfortable working with a purchase agreement form long before one is formally presented to you or you go to fill one out with your buyer. By knowing what to expect in a purchase agreement before you are faced with receiving an offer from a real live buyer or before filling it out cold turkey, you will be better prepared and more able to avoid making mistakes. Being organized should help remove any anxiety you might have previously held regarding the paperwork.

A purchase agreement form typically contains boilerplate information that documents and assists in the purchase and sale of real estate. As I mentioned before, the California Association of Realtors (CAR) has a purchase agreement form that most real estate brokers and agents believe is the only acceptable one they can use. They are wrong. As long as a form contains the basic elements of a real estate contract, it is enforceable. (See Form 157)

The process is easiest whenever a published form is used. Forms from different sources may include different clauses, or the focus of the language used can be different as long as the basic elements are included. The purchase agreement, Form 157, works like a checklist for the necessary elements and contains clauses for:

- the identities of the parties;
- the location of the real estate sold, leased or encumbered;
- the price and financing;
- the time for acceptance and performance;
- the physical condition of the property;
- the property's natural hazards and environmental conditions;
- title conditions and vesting;
- the time for opening and closing escrow;
- tax planning;
- the brokerage fee (if any); and
- signatures.

Some of these categories are fairly straightforward and self-explanatory. Others need more discussion. However, I break down those areas that I feel need to be more thoroughly explained below. A later chapter will cover disclosures and their accompanying forms.

The seven major parts to your purchase agreement, Form 157

1. Document identification:

The first section contains the date and location when the contract was prepared, and thereby serves to identify the agreement. It also contains the buyer's name and provides a receipt provision for their "good-faith deposit" towards the purchase price. Naturally, the property is identified by the legal description or the common address, along with the city and county. In this section, you will also list any personal property to be included, like refrigerators, washers and dryers, barbecues, etc. (See Form 157 §1)

Lastly, note the total number of pages in the agreement so that nothing gets left out. (See Form 157 §2)

2. Price and terms:

This second section contains the downpayment amount and the common variables for payment of the remaining balance that the buyer will owe the seller on the property, such as a new fixed rate loan or an adjustable rate loan. Blanks are provided to fill in an approximate payment amount as well as the maximum interest rate that is acceptable to the buyer. (See Form 157 §§3 to 6)

Where does this information come from? Hopefully, your buyer has met with a loan officer and has already been pre-approved for a loan before coming to you. If not, send them to a lender immediately to establish their ability to borrow enough to purchase a home in your price range.

As a matter of fact, I would recommend that you not accept any offer from a buyer until they have taken that critical step. We will cover this later in greater detail when we talk about the buyer's financing, but remember that unless a buyer has cash or can get a loan that will allow them to purchase your property, you do not have a buyer. Do not be afraid to request this most basic of conditions. Then, on the purchase agreement form, there is a place in this section where you can indicate how many days you will give the buyer to provide you with written confirmation that they have the ability to obtain a loan in the amount necessary to buy your home.

DATE:_____, 20_____, at_____, California.

Items left blank or unchecked are not applicable. References to forms includes their equivalent.

FACTS:

1. Received from Buyer(s)_____
    the sum of $ _____, evidenced by ☐ personal check, or ☐ _____,
    payable to _____,
    to be held undeposited until acceptance of this offer as a deposit toward acquisition of property situated
    in the City of _____, County of _____, California, described as:
    Real property: _____
    Personal property: _____

2. This agreement is comprised of this four-page form and _____ pages of addenda/attachments.

TERMS: Buyer to pay the purchase price as follows:

3. Cash payment through escrow, including deposits, in the amount of . . . . $_____
    3.1 Other consideration paid through escrow _____ . . . . $_____

4. Buyer to obtain a ☐ first, or ☐ second, trust deed loan in the amount of . . . . $_____
    payable approximately $_____ monthly for a period of _____ years.
    Interest on closing not to exceed _____%, ☐ ARM, type _____.
    Loan points not to exceed _____.

    4.1 ☐ Unless Buyer, within _____ days after acceptance, hands Seller satisfactory
         written confirmation Buyer has been pre-approved for the financing of
         the purchase price, Seller may terminate the agreement. [ft Form 183]

5. ☐ Take title subject to, or ☐ Assume, an existing first trust deed note held by
    _____ with an unpaid principal balance of . . . . $_____
    payable $_____ monthly, including interest not exceeding _____%,
    ☐ ARM, type _____, plus a monthly tax/insurance impound
    payment of $_____ . _____.

    5.1 At closing, loan balance differences per beneficiary statement(s) to be adjusted
         into: ☐ cash, ☐ carryback note, or ☐ sales price.

    5.2 The impound account to be transferred: ☐ charged, or ☐ without charge, to Buyer.

6. ☐ Take title subject to, or ☐ Assume, an existing second trust deed note held by
    _____ with an unpaid principal balance of . . . . . $_____
    payable $_____ monthly, including interest not exceeding _____%,
    ☐ ARM, type _____, due _____, 20 _____.

7. Assume a tax bond or assessment lien with an unpaid principal balance of . . . . $_____

8. Note for the balance of the purchase price in the amount of . . . . $_____
    to be executed by Buyer in favor of Seller and secured by a trust deed on the property
    junior to any above referenced financing, payable $_____ monthly, or more,
    beginning one month after closing, including interest at _____% from closing, due
    _____ years after closing.

    8.1 This note and trust deed to contain provisions to be provided by Seller for:
         ☐ due-on-sale, ☐ prepayment penalty, ☐ late charges, ☐ _____.

    8.2 A Carryback Disclosure Statement is attached as an addendum. [ft Form 300]

    8.3 Buyer to provide a Request for Notice of Delinquency to senior encumbrancers.
         [ft Form 412]

    8.4 Buyer to hand Seller a completed credit application on acceptance. [ft Form 302]

    8.5 Within _____ days of receipt of Buyer's credit application, Seller may terminate
         the agreement based on a reasonable disapproval of Buyer's creditworthiness.

    8.6 Seller may terminate the agreement on failure of the agreed terms for priority
         financing. [ft Form 183]

    8.7 As additional security, Buyer to execute a security agreement and file a UCC-1
         financing statement on any property transferred by Bill of Sale. [ft Form 436]

9. **Total Purchase Price is** . . . . $_____

10. ACCEPTANCE AND PERFORMANCE:

10.1 This offer to be deemed revoked unless accepted in writing ☐ on presentation, or ☐ within _____ days after date, and acceptance is personally delivered or faxed to Offeror within this period.

10.2 On failure of Buyer to obtain or assume financing as agreed by the date scheduled for closing, Buyer may terminate the agreement. _____.

10.3 Buyer's close of Escrow is conditioned on Buyer's prior or concurrent closing on a sale of other property, commonly described as _____.

10.4 Any termination of the agreement shall be by written Notice of Cancellation timely delivered to the other party, the other party's broker or Escrow, with instructions to Escrow to return all instruments and funds to the parties depositing them. [ft Form 183]

10.5 Both parties reserve their rights to assign and agree to cooperate in effecting an Internal Revenue Code §1031 exchange prior to close of escrow, on either party's written notice. [ft Forms 171 or 172]

10.6 Should Buyer breach the agreement, Buyer's monetary liability to Seller is limited to $_____, or ☐ the deposit receipted in Section 1.

11. PROPERTY CONDITIONS:

11.1 Seller to furnish prior to closing:

    a. ☐ a structural pest control inspection report and certification of clearance of corrective measures.

    b. ☐ a home inspection report prepared by an insured home inspector showing the land and improvements to be free of material defects.

    c. ☐ a one-year home warranty policy:
       Insurer:_____
       Coverage: _____

    d. ☐ a certificate of occupancy, or other clearance or retrofitting, required by local ordinance for the transfer of possession or title.

    e. ☐ a certification by a licensed contractor stating the sewage disposal system is functioning properly, and if it contains a septic tank, is not in need of pumping.

    f. ☐ a certification by a licensed water testing lab stating the well supplying the property meets potable water standards.

    g. ☐ a certification by a licensed well-drilling contractor stating the well supplying the property produces a minimum of _____ gallon(s) per minute.

    h. _____

    i. _____

11.2 Seller's Condition of Property (Transfer) Disclosure Statement (TDS) [ft Form 304]

    a. ☐ is attached; or

    b. ☐ is to be handed to Buyer on acceptance for Buyer's review. Within ten days after receipt, Buyer may either cancel the transaction or deliver to Seller a written notice itemizing any material defects in the property disclosed by the statement and unknown to Buyer prior to acceptance [ft Form 269]. Seller to repair, replace or correct noticed defects prior to closing.

    c. On Seller's failure to repair, replace or correct noticed defects under §11.2b or §11.3a, Buyer may tender the purchase price reduced by the cost to repair, replace or correct the noticed defects, or close escrow and pursue available remedies. [ft Form 183]_____.

11.3 Buyer to inspect the property twice:

    a. An **initial property inspection** is required on acceptance to confirm the property's condition is substantially the same as observed by Buyer and represented by Seller prior to acceptance, and if not substantially the same, Buyer to promptly notify Seller in writing of undisclosed material defects discovered [ft Form 269]. Seller to repair, replace or correct noticed defects prior to closing; and

    b. A **final walk-through inspection** is required within five days before closing to confirm the correction of any noticed defects under §11.2b and §11.3a and maintenance under §11.11. [ft Form 270]

11.4 Seller's Natural Hazard Disclosure Statement [ft Form 314] ☐ is attached, or ☐ is to be handed to Buyer on acceptance for Buyer's review, and within ten days of receipt, Buyer may terminate the agreement based on a reasonable disapproval of hazards disclosed by the Statement and unknown to Buyer prior to acceptance. [ft Form 182 and 183]

11.5 Buyer acknowledges receipt of a booklet and related seller disclosures containing ☐ *Environmental Hazards: A Guide for Homeowners, Buyers, Landlords and Tenants* (on all one-to-four units), ☐ *Protect Your Family from Lead in Your Home* (on all pre-1978, one-to-four units) [ft Form 313], and ☐ *The Homeowner's Guide to Earthquake Safety* (on all pre-1960, one-to-four units). [ft Form 315]

11.6 The property is located in: ☐ an industrial use area, ☐ a military ordnance area, ☐ an airport influence area, Other _____.

11.7 On acceptance, Seller to hand Buyer the following property operating information:

    a. ☐ Property Operating Cost Sheet for Buyer's review within ten days of receipt; Buyer may terminate the agreement during the review period based on a reasonable disapproval of the information received. [ft Form 352 or 562];

    b. ☐ See attached _____ addenda for additional conditions. [ft Forms 250]

11.8 If an **Owner's Association** is involved, ☐ Buyer has received and approves, or ☐ Buyer on acceptance to be handed, copies of the Association's Articles, Bylaws, CC&Rs, collection and lien enforcement policy, operating rules, operating budget, CPA's financial review, insurance policy summary and any age restriction statement.

    a. No association claims for defects or changes in regular or special assessments are pending or anticipated. Current monthly assessment is $_____.

    b. Seller is not in violation of CC&Rs, except_____.

    c. Seller to pay association document and transfer fees.

    d. Buyer to approve Association's statement of condition of assessments and confirm representations in §11.8a as a condition for closing escrow.

    e. Within ten days of Buyer's post-acceptance receipt of the association documents, Buyer may terminate the agreement based on a reasonable disapproval of the documents. [ft Form 183]

11.9 Smoke detector(s) and water heater bracing exist in compliance with the law, and if not, Seller to install.

11.10 Possession of the property and keys/access codes to be delivered: ☐ on close of escrow, or ☐ as stated in the attached Occupancy Agreement. [ft Forms 271 and 272]

11.11 Seller to maintain the property in good condition until possession is delivered.

11.12 Fixtures and fittings attached to the property include, but are not limited to, window shades, blinds, light fixtures, plumbing fixtures, curtain rods, wall-to-wall carpeting, draperies, hardware, antennas, air coolers and conditioners, trees, shrubs, mailboxes and other similar items.

11.13 Notice: Pursuant to Section 290.46 of the Penal Code, information about specified registered sex offenders is made available to the public via an Internet Web site maintained by the Department of Justice at www.meganslaw.ca.gov. Depending on an offender's criminal history, this information will include either the address at which the offender resides or the community of residence and ZIP code in which he or she resides.

12. CLOSING CONDITIONS:

12.1 This transaction to be escrowed with _____.
Parties to deliver instructions to Escrow as soon as reasonably possible after acceptance.

    a. ☐ Escrow holder is authorized and instructed to act on the provisions of this agreement as the mutual escrow instructions of the parties and to draft any additional instructions necessary to close this transaction. [ft Form 401]

    b. ☐ Escrow instructions, prepared and signed by the parties, are attached to be handed to Escrow on acceptance. [ft Form 401]

12.2 Escrow to be handed all instruments needed to **close escrow** on or before _____, 20_____, or within _____ days after acceptance. Parties to hand Escrow all documents required by the title insurer, lenders or other third parties to this transaction prior to seven days before the date scheduled for closing.

    a. Each party to pay its customary escrow charges. [ft Forms 310 and 311]

12.3 Buyer's title to be subject to covenants, conditions, restrictions, reservations and easements of record.
_____.

12.4 Title to be vested in Buyer or Assignee free of encumbrances other than those set forth herein. Buyer's interest in title to be insured under a policy issued by _____
as a(n) ☐ Homeowner(s) policy (one-to-four units), ☐ Residential ALTA-R policy (vacant or improved residential parcel), ☐ Owner's policy (other than one-to-four units), ☐ CLTA Joint Protection policy (also naming Carryback Seller or purchase-assist lender), or ☐ Binder (to insure resale or refinance within two years).

    a. Endorsements: _____

    b. ☐ Seller, or ☐ Buyer, to pay the title insurance premium.

12.5 Buyer to furnish a new fire insurance policy covering the property.

12.6 Taxes, assessments, insurance premiums, rents, interest and other expenses to be **prorated** to close of escrow, unless otherwise provided.

12.7 Bill of Sale to be executed for any **personal property** being transferred.

12.8 If Seller is unable to convey marketable title as agreed, or if the **improvements** on the property are materially damaged prior to closing, Buyer may terminate the agreement. Seller to pay all reasonable escrow cancellation charges. [ft Form 183]

13. NOTICE OF YOUR SUPPLEMENTAL PROPERTY TAX BILL:

California property tax law requires the Assessor to revalue real property at the time the ownership of the property changes. Because of this law, you may receive one or two supplemental tax bills, depending on when your loan closes.

The supplemental tax bills are not mailed to your lender. If you have arranged for your property tax payments to be paid through an impound account, the supplemental tax bills will not be paid by your lender. It is your responsibility to pay these supplemental bills directly to the Tax Collector.

If you have any questions concerning this matter, please call your local Tax Collector's Office.

14. _____

I agree to the terms stated above.	I agree to the terms stated above.
Date:_____, 20_____	Date:_____, 20_____
Buyer: _____	Seller: _____
Buyer: _____	Seller: _____
Signature: _____	Signature: _____
Signature: _____	Signature: _____
Address: _____	Address: _____
Phone:_____	Phone:_____
Fax: _____	Fax: _____
E-mail:_____	E-mail: _____

FORM 157   12-06   ©2007 **first tuesday**, P.O. BOX 20069, RIVERSIDE, CA 92516 (800) 794-0494

How do you calculate the exact loan payment amount to be included in the contract? Most real estate agents carry either a loan calculator or a laptop computer to figure this out. You, however, can go on the Internet to any website that does mortgage calculations. Just search for "mortgage calculator" and you will be given dozens of options. When the page comes up, type in the loan amount and the going interest rate, and you will be given a payment amount. Fixed loans are normally for 30 years (although 40-year loans are slowly being introduced).

You can search for current rates easily online. However, make sure that you check the whole range available. Avoid selecting an interest rate for the contract that is unlikely to be obtainable except in very unusual circumstances. The rate used in the contract should be high enough to accommodate adjustments in the market which might occur before escrow is scheduled to close and while you are going about all the tasks you have to complete before closing.

I actually recommend that you search the Internet and look at some of the lending options currently available. Then, when you do have a buyer, you will know whether the interest rate they are proposing is even possible. Plus, the more comfortable you get checking on these websites, the easier it will be once a bona fide offer is presented to you.

Also included in this section is a place where you address whether the property has any special assessments against it. These are neighborhood improvement bonds (for sidewalks, sewers, or school improvements) and if you have one, you probably know about it because it appears as an additional amount due with your property tax bill. Most of the time, a new buyer will assume the special assessments and continue to make payments on them after they buy your house, but you need to disclose them on the purchase agreement form and make sure the buyer agrees to assume them, or you will have agreed to pay them off on close of escrow. If you are unsure whether any special assessments exist, ask your title or escrow company. (See Form 157

Finally, this is the section where any seller carryback financing terms and conditions would be included, if it is a part of the transaction. Should you be willing to finance part of your equity as a "loan" to your buyer, this section of the form contains the details. Again, we will discuss this later in more detail, but know that an area of the contract that covers seller carryback financing particulars exists.

3. Acceptance and performance periods:

In order for there to be an actual contract between two people, there must be both an offer and an acceptance. If someone offers you something, but you never accept it, you have no agreement—and that is what entering into a contract is all about. The acceptance connection must be made in order to form a binding agreement. Providing for acceptance, the purchase agreement form spells out how and when this happens.

There are also provisions in this section that provide for delays in closing escrow or excuses for nonperformance, with guidelines for termination if all the conditions of the agreement are not met. It even addresses liability limitation to avoid the misleading and unenforceable forfeiture of the buyer's deposit in the event the buyer fails to perform without a legal excuse.

4. Property condition:

Every seller of property in California is required to disclose the condition of the property to prospective buyers. The seller must disclose anything about the property that he knows could negatively affect the value or use of the property. Disclosures include such things as the physical condition of the property, natural hazards, safety, environmental hazards, and operating costs, among many. Because property disclosures are such a large topic, they will be covered thoroughly in the next chapter. Also in this section of the contract is a discussion of how the property will be maintained until closing.

In addition to the full range of disclosures, this part of the contract also covers the timing for when each disclosure must be completed and then communicated to the buyer. It provides for a thorough inspection soon after the contract is signed, and then another one right before escrow closes, called the Final Walk-Through. (See Forms 269 and 270)

Finally, this section dictates when the buyer will take possession of the property.

5. Closing conditions:

To fully transfer title in California, it is customary for all the details to be handled by a neutral third party, called "escrow." Escrow is considered neutral because it has both your and the buyer's interests to fulfill. Unlike real estate agency where a broker owes a duty to care for and protect either you or the buyer, escrow has a duty to accurately follow instructions from each of you separately, but equally.

Escrow is handled in California in several ways. Legally, escrow can be carried out by:

- an independent escrow company;
- a department within a title company; or,
- by a real estate broker who represents either the buyer or the seller in the transaction.

Not only is escrow usually managed in any one of these three ways, different areas within the state of California handle escrow in traditionally different ways. Lenders also occasionally have an escrow division, but they are primarily there for the closing of loans. In addition, attorneys can perform escrow duties, but are seldom used under ordinary sales situations in California.

In Northern California, the majority of escrows are closed by escrow departments within a title company. Although independent escrow companies do exist in Northern California, in this part of the state they are usually used for more complicated escrow transactions, like property exchanges and business escrows.

In Southern California, it is likely that you would select either an independent escrow company or a title insurance escrow. You might also use an escrow company that is owned and managed by one of the brokers in your transaction. The costs for each of these escrow providers are very similar and are normally divided between both the buyer and seller as per the contract.

Which should you choose? Independent escrow companies are the only one of the three that are actually licensed and heavily regulated by the Department of Corporations (DOC) and insured against the loss of escrow funds. They must post bonds for each of their escrow officers, are audited regularly, and have rules that dictate who runs the office and their qualifications. They are usually smaller and offer a more local connection. Because they are privately owned and operated, the owners often provide exceptional service to their clients. They rely largely on referrals and know that they must compete with large title companies for your business.

Title company escrow offices are owned by the large corporations they serve. Each is controlled as a function of the insurance industry, and they offer some protection against losses, but not through the DOC as with independent companies. Their greatest advantage lies with the fact that you will need Title Insurance as a part of your transaction, and it is often easiest to purchase their services all under one roof.

Of the three, an escrow operating under a real estate broker license is the least regulated. There is less protection from the loss of your escrow funds and less regulation by their governing body (the California Department of Real Estate) on the broker and those who work for him. Normally, when you list your property with a real estate agent, they recommend an escrow company that the agent works with on a regular basis. If their broker owns an escrow company (either an independent company or one operated under the broker's license), they are often required by their broker to steer clients to that office as part of their employment with the broker. However, unless the broker-owned escrow is also an independent escrow company licensed under the DOC, I would recommend against using that particular escrow company.

Every homeseller has the complete freedom to select any escrow company with which they feel the most secure, regardless of which company an agent recommends. If you are not sure, always ask if an escrow company is broker-owned, independent, or a part of a title company. They not only handle your documentation, they handle your money; so select carefully.

Even before you find a buyer for your property, you might want to start asking around to see which escrow companies in your area are the most recommended. When you are interviewing real estate agents for a Comparative Market Analysis (CMA), ask them who they suggest. When you go to Open Houses, ask the agents there who they use regularly. Be sure to ask your friends and neighbors if they would recommend a company before you make your final selection.

Escrow companies provide a very complex and specialized service to you as a homeseller. The best of them do a proficient job. What you want is an experienced escrow officer with a reputable company, someone who will go the extra mile to help speed your transaction through to closing.

6. Brokerage information:

Most likely, you won't need to address this provision in the purchase agreement form except to put a big "n/a" (not applicable) in the empty blanks. However, in the event that a real estate agent becomes a part of your sales transaction, we'll discuss it here. Chances are good that if an agent finds a buyer and brings you an offer, it will not be on the form provided in this book's Forms CD. It will likely be on a CAR form instead. However, just as with the purchase agreement form included, when an agent has already placed an amount in the blank where it suggests a fee, know that you have every right to change it. Nothing in an offer is written in stone and cannot be countered.

7. Signatures:

This final section is where both the buyer and seller place their signatures and a date, one for when the offer was made and another for when it was accepted, to assure the existence of both the offer and acceptance. There is also a provision should the seller reject the offer (remember, it is the buyer who usually writes the offer), which conveys the message that the seller is no longer interested in dealing with this buyer.

Do you have to use a contract at all?

No. Legally, you do not need to use a purchase agreement form to sell your house. However, if you and your buyer have any sort of disagreement about the terms of the sale, any sort of oral agreement you have made will be unenforceable, unless you have a written contract signed by all parties.

Let me repeat that. In order for you to have a binding agreement with your buyer, it must be in a writing signed by the buyer and yourself. That is because a law called the Statute of Frauds requires "a writing" in order for the agreement to be enforceable in a court of law. The key word is *enforceable*. Any agreement to sell property (or lease for longer than one year) must be in writing.

So, although it might appear easiest to just shake hands on what you have talked out and agreed to and then open escrow to proceed toward closing, until you have it in writing and signed, you have no way to legally enforce your agreement. By the same token, not only can the buyer back out of the agreement at any time until it is agreed to in writing, so can you. Chances are, this type of loose arrangement is unacceptable to you or any serious prospective buyer. So I recommend you put it in writing!

There is another reason that I recommend that you work together to write out and create your purchase agreement with your buyer. The purchase agreement form acts as a checklist and will help you address issues that you might not realize are necessary. For example, when do you give possession to your buyer? Is it the day the grant deed is recorded by the county recorder? Or is it a couple of days later so that you know without a doubt that you have indeed sold your home? Sometimes these issues become huge if you haven't come to an understanding about them in advance. Even though the buyer might be extremely agreeable and seem incredibly easy to work with, that could change. A signed purchase agreement form helps you and the buyer should a disagreement or dispute arise.

On the other hand, I would personally avoid trying to force a buyer to purchase your property just because you have a written contract that says he will. For example, if you've signed a purchase agreement form with a buyer who later discovers something about your home that is completely unsatisfactory to him, even if you may be legally able to force him to close escrow when he clearly does not want to, you will be required to file a lawsuit to do so. A lawsuit is seldom in your best interest.

Or consider what happens if the buyer backs out because they cannot afford your home. Let's face it; you cannot force someone without sufficient financial resources to buy your home. Actually, any time you are in a legal or no-win battle, you waste valuable time, energy, and resources, rather than moving on to market your property to someone who is willing to close the deal.

The good-faith deposit

Who keeps the deposit if the transaction goes bad? Many sellers, and even some real estate agents, believe that if the buyer backs out of a transaction after a purchase agreement has been signed, then the seller keeps the deposit. Unfortunately, it is relatively rare for the seller to legally retain a deposit when the buyer refuses to close. Regardless of how it is worded in the purchase agreement, the only time that you as a seller are legally entitled to any portion of the deposit made by a buyer is when you can verify that you suffered "actual money losses" as a result of his cancellation.

That is why, if the buyer backs out after a very short period of time, it is usually in your best interests to just agree with the buyer to cancel the agreement and get your property back on the market. If you decide you want all or a portion of the buyer's deposit should he cancel, and he disagrees and you refuse to release the deposit, you might end up in a lawsuit. Unless you can show that you have verifiable money losses, he will get his money back even though he backed out, and you both will end up paying attorney fees and court costs. No one wins in that situation.

Later, in the "Trouble-shooting" section of this book, we will talk about the necessary specifics for money losses should you need or want to cancel the purchase agreement. In the meantime, when getting comfortable with the form, just remember that when you ask for a deposit, you are doing it to reinforce the agreement between you and your buyer. A vast majority of the time, a prospective buyer will not give you a deposit unless they are reasonably sure they want to go through with the transaction. That is why it is called a "good-faith or earnest-money deposit."

Naturally, you want the deposit to be significant enough to be relevant, but your primary motivation is to arrive at a meeting of the minds concerning the transfer of the property. As for amount, I recommend that the deposit be at least 1% of the purchase price. A personal check made out to the escrow company you will be using is the best way to handle the deposit.

Remember, the good-faith deposit does not belong to you at this point. It is a deposit towards the purchase price of your property and only becomes yours on closing.

Counteroffers

Should a buyer present you with an offer to purchase your property and you agree with some of the terms, but not all, you can use a counteroffer form to provide the terms you are willing to agree to. Blank copies of the counteroffer, Form 180, are available on the Forms CD. The most common items changed by the use of a counteroffer would be:

- price;
- the terms of a loan;
- contingencies; and
- the time frames for the opening of escrow, disclosures, and the date for closing.

Remember, what makes a contract is a meeting of the minds between a seller and a buyer. If that happens on the first draft of a purchase agreement, nothing more is necessary to form a binding contract. However, if you wish to change any of the terms or conditions made by the buyer in his signed offer, do not sign the original purchase agreement form. Instead, propose your changes through a counteroffer. Only when the buyer accepts your changes on the counteroffer form will you then finally have a meeting of minds and a binding agreement to sell your property.

If the buyer does not agree to your new terms on the counteroffer form within the time frame for his acceptance, then you do not have an agreement. By your not signing the purchase agreement form as originally proposed by your potential buyer, and instead making him a counteroffer, you have effectively rejected the buyer's offer to purchase your property and no sale will proceed.

If you do not want to use a counteroffer form, you may make minor changes on the purchase agreement form presented to you from the buyer. Just realize that by changing any terms on the purchase agreement form by crossing things out or writing new things in, you have rejected the original offer made by the buyer and restarted the negotiations. If you initial all your changes and sign the purchase agreement form, you have in effect made a counteroffer to the buyer's original offer. The buyer must then initial all of your changes before the agreement will be considered accepted by him. Because changes can be missed or overlooked, and confusion can occur when initialing, I recommend you use a counteroffer form when making changes or corrections to the original offer.

Acceptance

In order for there to be a valid contract between two parties, there must be both offer and acceptance. Acceptance goes beyond mere signing and includes the returned communication of that acceptance. If a buyer writes you an offer and then has a real estate agent bring it to you, you don't have an agreement until you have signed, indicating your acceptance, and then the agent either tells the buyer of your acceptance or gives the buyer a copy of your signed agreement. Once communication happen, an agreement exists.

As I mentioned above, if a buyer submits a written offer to you and then you decide to write a counteroffer, there is no agreement until the buyer agrees to your counter and his acceptance is communicated back to you.

This is important to know because, until your buyer knows you have accepted his offer, he is free to withdraw it. Likewise, if you write a counteroffer to a buyer's offer, you are free to withdraw your counteroffer if you do so before he communicates his acceptance to you.

What terminates an offer?

The buyer's offer is terminated if the buyer withdraws or revokes his offer prior to your acceptance. Again, until the communication of your acceptance is delivered to the buyer, he can withdraw it and no agreement is formed. Alternatively, you as the seller on receiving an offer from a buyer can reject it without a counteroffer, indicating no further desire to continue the negotiation process.

If, as a seller, you submit a written counteroffer or change any pre-printed or filled-in text on the buyer's purchase agreement offer, you have technically rejected the buyer's offer and have indicated further negotiations are necessary. From that point forward, the buyer's original offer cannot then be accepted, and a new or revised agreement is the next alternative.

Other events that can terminate an offer are:

1. The time for acceptance passing beyond the stated time.

2. If no acceptance time is stated, the passing of what is considered a reasonable amount of time without an acceptance.

3. The death of either the buyer or the seller.

4. The destruction of the real estate before acceptance.

5. A prior sale of the property to another buyer (even if this occurs during the acceptance period for the seller's counteroffer).

Making changes to an offer

As stated above, if you receive an offer from a buyer and make any changes to the offer whatsoever, then you have terminated the offer as it stands. Your next step would be to then have the buyer re-agree to (accept) the terms of his offer with the changes you have made.

The challenge for anyone selling their property is determining whether making a change to the buyer's offer will result in losing the buyer altogether. That is always a possible outcome when you make changes. The question you will have to ask yourself is, how far apart are you and your buyer from an agreement? If the issue in question is minor in the scope of the transaction, you may want to let it go. But, if there are a number of major issues that need to be resolved, then it is usually vital for you to counter to include them. In that event, until you are in closer agreement, you are not actually losing out if the buyer backs out because you don't have much in common agreement anyway.

Contingencies

"Contingencies" is a catch-all word that covers the various terms and conditions that need to be addressed or fulfilled before escrow can close and the property can change hands. Contingencies include:

- **activities** to be performed by either the buyer or seller, or both, prior to specific times; and
- **events** which must occur during the transaction process for the property to close escrow.

Typical **buyer contingencies** or activities include:

- obtaining a new loan;
- selling their existing home;
- approving the home inspection reports;
- approving of the different disclosure reports on the property; and
- delivering closing documents to escrow.

Typical **seller contingencies** or activities include:

- providing the buyer with the necessary disclosures;
- making the home available for appraisals;
- making the home available for inspection;
- ordering title insurance for the buyer; and
- providing all homeowners' association materials and information to the buyer.

In most purchase agreements, specified events as stated in the contract must occur in order for the transaction to unfold and eventually close escrow. These events usually rely on the activities of either the buyer or the seller. Events often fall into a sequence with other activities, and as time passes, if the events do not occur, then the buyer or the seller for one reason or another has the right to terminate the agreement. Depending upon the necessity of the event and the attitude of the person affected by its failure to occur, the contingency in question can be extended or the contract terminated.

Ultimately, contingencies are eliminated in one of two ways:

- by the occurrence of the activity or event, or the approval of the activity or event; or
- the waiver of the activity or the event.

Once a required event or activity has occurred, the contingency has been satisfied, which then leads to further events or activates and eventually to the close of escrow. If items that were supposed to happen do not, the person who was to benefit from the activity or event can either waive the requirement or cancel the transaction.

For example, if you have granted the buyer of your home the right to sell his previous home as a contingency in your purchase agreement before he must buy your home, and his sale does not occur, he has three options. First, if his home has not sold by the time spelled out in the purchase agreement, he can seek to extend the time limit on your agreement. Second, he can cancel the purchase agreement altogether, or finally, he can waive his contingency and proceed to buy your home without selling his own. What you do will depend upon how anxious you are to sell, as well as how likely it is that the buyer's property will sell.

On the other hand, if your sale is contingent upon your repairing or making some improvement to your property, you may have breached your agreement if you are unable to deliver as specified. At that point, the buyer could waive the requirement, agree to extend the date for compliance, force you to close escrow, or cancel the purchase agreement and escrow.

Because contingencies have the ability to delay or even terminate your contract, it is usually desirable to avoid them if possible. If that is not possible due to the available buyers at any given time, then eliminating them as quickly as possible is advised. If you know or suspect that you will be required to fulfill certain activities or events related to disclosures or defects, and your escrow is subject to cancellation until they are fulfilled, you may want to take care of them prior to locating a buyer so that they are not even part of your contract.

For example, if you know that you have a "cloud" on your title, then you should work to eliminate it right away. A "cloud on title" is a potential problem when obtaining title insurance on your transfer. One possible "cloud" could be that the property was vested in your late father's name. Even though you might legally own the home, his name must be removed from title before it can be transferred. If there is a delay in closing because of it, you would be in breach. An issue like this must be taken care of before you can ever transfer title, so don't wait until you have an offer to begin the process of eliminating and correcting them.

In the end, if a contingency is not met, the person who was to benefit from the contingency has the right to cancel the agreement. More contingency issues that could affect your transaction will be addressed in the "Trouble-shooting" section of this book.

Getting comfortable with the purchase contract

As a real estate broker, I admit to being challenged by the purchase agreement form approved by CAR. That is dramatically different from when I first entered the real estate field back in the '80s, when the form used was an uncomplicated two-page document. Last time I checked, the CAR form had ballooned to 12 pages with tiny type. Every six months or so, the legal department at CAR includes more clauses, adds more disclaimers, or changes more wording to try to cover every possible outcome. Unfortunately, that is a nearly impossible task.

I am very pleased with the enclosed forms provided by *first tuesday*. The direct and straightforward language used in their forms eliminates ambiguities and uncertainties as to how you should proceed. While they cover all legal necessities, they avoid creating paranoia and use plain words instead of legalese. Real estate transactions are complex, but they don't have to be complicated or difficult to understand.

I suggest that you print out a couple of copies of the purchase agreement, Form 157, from the accompanying CD and fill them out as though you were a buyer for your home. By answering the questions and filling in the forms, you will gain confidence and feel much more comfortable when a real buyer presents you with the need to prepare your first offer.

Paperwork is a necessary aspect of selling your property and one you must learn. But it doesn't have to be difficult. By educating yourself in advance and looking over the details of the included forms and directions, you will be adequately prepared to receive or help prepare your first offer.

CHAPTER SEVEN
Disclosures—why they are important

Disclosure is a significant aspect of the paperwork process involved in selling your home. Long, long ago, it was perfectly acceptable for a home to be sold under the notion of "buyer beware." In those times, sellers took for granted that buyers would accept the property in the condition they found it. "What you see is what you get," was assumed, or even worse was, "You're stuck with whatever you get."

Not any more. That idea has now been completely reversed. Instead, as the level of marketplace sophistication rises, the buyers and the legislature are demanding that buyers be fully informed of anything and everything known to the seller that might adversely affect the value of the property. And when buyers don't get what they expected at the time they signed the purchase agreement, the courts are far more likely to resolve the dispute in the buyers' favor. Not only is the seller liable in the case of most nondisclosures, so too are any real estate agents involved who knew, or should have known, about any problems.

As a result, there are now a large number of disclosures that are required to be made by every seller with every real estate transaction. When an agent is involved, there is even more.

Remember, the present perception behind disclosures is to help keep you, as a seller, free from disputes with the buyer and out of court. By covering everything that adversely influences the value of the property in advance of entering into a purchase agreement, a buyer can then reasonably assume that they are paying a fair price for a home in a condition of full disclosure. If you become a buyer yourself, you too are entitled to and will want these same assurances.

In this chapter, we will discuss the disclosures covered in the Condition of Property (COP) form. Other disclosures will be discussed in Chapter Eight.

The owner's COP disclosure

A seller's COP disclosure is an important part (if not the heart) of every home sale. Throughout the state of California, sellers are required to complete and deliver to a prospective buyer a form called a Transfer Disclosure Statement (TDS). This form, also called a COP Disclosure Statement, is a statutory form created by sections 1102(a) and 1102.3 of the California Civil Code. Naturally, there is one included in the accompanying Forms CD.

One of the few times a seller is exempt from this disclosure is when passing the home from parent to child. It is also not necessary to use a TDS when property is transferred through foreclosure, trustee, tax, court order, probate, or estate related sales. As a homeowner and a For Sale By Owner (FSBO), it is almost certain that you are required to deliver one.

The TDS must be completed by the seller with full honesty and in good faith. Any known or suspected problems that might exist in the property must be communicated. In other words, anything that the seller believes may adversely affect the value or use of the property is vital information and must be disclosed.

A disclosure is not a warranty

Although a seller is required to disclose any and all known defects of the property, there are limitations. The key word is *known*. Legally, if a seller does not know of, or should not be aware of, a defect or problem, he obviously cannot disclose it. That is why the TDS states that the form itself "may not be relied on by a buyer as a warranty of any kind." The form also states that even if it is attached to a purchase agreement form, it is not part of the terms of the contract itself. In all actuality, the TDS is a statement of what the seller is willing and/or able to disclose about the property at that particular point in time. Naturally, the buyer deserves to know about any defects the seller is aware of, but the buyer should go beyond the seller's awareness and call for a complete inspection in order to either approve of the property's condition for himself or cancel the transaction.

Selling "as is" is not an option

In the past, some sellers hoped to avoid trouble with undisclosed defects in the property by selling their property in an "as-is" condition. This supported the "buyer beware" mentality of the time. Unfortunately for sellers, the as-is disclaimer is no longer a valid excuse to avoid disclosing defects. Even if a buyer agrees to purchase your home "as is," you are still completely liable for any undisclosed defects you are aware of that adversely affect the property's value.

Even, and especially, if the buyer could not discover the defect for years, you must disclose it if you know about it. An excellent way to think about the disclosures of today is not "as is," but "as disclosed." The only way you can legally avoid letting your buyers know about anything detrimental on your property is if you don't actually know about it.

When is the TDS given to the buyer?

Ideally, the TDS should be given to all serious prospective buyers before they write out an offer. That way, they at least know what you know about the property at the time they set the price they believe represents the property's value. If they do not receive the form before you arrive at a written agreement, the contract is still valid. However, you as a seller are liable to the buyer for anything you knew about, but did not disclose, which results in a money loss. A money loss includes overpayment to you when the home is purchased.

If the seller delivers the filled out TDS to the buyer after the written purchase offer has been accepted, the buyer has three options.

1. The buyer can cancel the purchase agreement if the TDS contains a previously undisclosed defect that is unacceptable to the buyer. In this case, the buyer actually has three days to cancel the purchase agreement. The three-day statutory right to cancel follows the day of the in-escrow delivery of the TDS. In other words, if you didn't give it to him in advance, he will have three days after you deliver it to him or escrow to cancel.

2. The buyer can demand that the seller correct or cure the previously undisclosed defect before escrow closes.

3. The buyer can close escrow and then demand that the seller pay the costs the buyer needs to cure the defect or the lost value in the property.

Should the TDS not be given to the buyer before the acceptance of the purchase agreement, it should be done as soon as practical. It is considered "delivered" to the buyer if it is attached to the purchase offer made by the buyer or to a counteroffer made by you, the seller. As a last resort, it should definitely be done before closing.

Obviously, as a seller, you want to avoid anything that will result in a future expense or possible lawsuit. Even if a potential buyer does nothing more than back out of the transaction, you will lose by having lost time marketing your property. By completely filling out the TDS form before you begin marketing your home for sale, you will be able to turn it over to any interested buyer prior to final negotiations and entry into the purchase agreement.

The value of a home inspector

One thing I encourage you to do is to hire a professional home inspector as soon as you have made up your mind to sell your home. A home inspector will allow you to use the inspection for a couple of very important things. First, you can use the professional to pinpoint anything that needs repair before you even put a "For Sale" sign in your front yard. By proactively doing any repairs or maintenance easily detected by a home inspector, you will avoid any delay or confrontation that might happen once you have a ready buyer.

Secondly, by having a home inspector provide you with a report at such an early stage, you can then use that material to fill out your own TDS. At that time, you will have the option to tell all prospective purchasers that you had the inspection done. Once you have the report in hand, you can either repair or cure any defects, or disclose to a potential purchaser that you intend to sell with the problems in place.

As long as you exercise a degree of care in the selection of a home inspector, you can then rely on their reports regarding the condition of your property. When hiring, you want to look at the following when choosing an inspector:

- his education;
- his length of time in business and the quality of his experience;
- if the inspector has adequate errors and omission (E&O) insurance to cover his business liability;
- his references; and

- any memberships in professional home inspector organizations.

Should you decide it is sensible to hire one, it is very important that you tell the inspector that you intend to use this report to notify all potential purchasers about the condition of your property. As long as he knows you are relying on it for such a purpose, he is liable to your buyer for any defects he fails to catch. As a matter of fact, even if the home inspector's contract says his liability is limited, that provision is unenforceable in court. Legally, any buyer who discovers an error in a home inspector's report that he relied on when buying a house has up to four years after the date of inspection to pursue recovery.[1]

Home inspectors typically charge in the neighborhood of $250 to $500. Price may play a part in which one you decide to use, but make sure they score highly in other qualifications as well. In some ways, the charge can be viewed as a sort of premium paid to cover errors in your disclosures to the buyer.

The inspection done by a professional home inspector is a physical, non-invasive examination. That means that it does not intrude into the "components of the structure," that is, the plumbing, electrical, or foundation of the house. If the home inspector suspects there is a need for a more invasive inspection, they might recommend it. In that case, you may need to hire further, more specialized inspectors to decipher irregular conditions.

Additionally, be aware that because their inspection is non-invasive, not every defect may be uncovered. After all, every property is filled with thousands of components, and it would be virtually impossible to inspect every single one. However, a home inspector is another line of defense for you as a homeseller when it comes to negotiations with a buyer. The more that you know about the property you are selling, and that the buyer knows about what they are purchasing, the less of a potential problem in the future and the better the outcome.

The most important thing for you to remember as a seller is that you can be held responsible for those things that are not disclosed to a buyer prior to going under contract. That is because the price the buyer willingly offers is based upon what he believes is a used, but defect-free home. If he later finds out, through the use of his own home inspector, that there are defects to your home, then that knowledge clearly affects his willingness to pay a particular price.

Do you have to cure the defects?

The simple answer is no. You don't have to do anything except disclose that the problem exists. However, should you choose not to repair the defect, that will most certainly affect the market value of your property. Remember, market value is what a willing and able seller will sell for, and what a willing and able buyer will pay. Defects can take things out of the ordinary and make them unusual—thus, price is affected.

Regardless of whether you choose to pay to repair or cure defects to the property, you always come from a stronger negotiating point if you fully disclose the problem in advance. Remember, if you withhold the information, you are in for potentially big trouble. In that case, the buyer has the upper hand and can either cancel or require you to fix it.

You will have the greatest negotiating power if you hire a professional inspector upfront to objectively inspect and report to you on your property. Then, assuming you provide your potential buyers with a copy of the report along with your TDS, you may freely decide to either correct or pass on the defect in the transaction.

What if the buyer wants another inspector?

Even if you choose not to hire a professional property inspector, the buyer probably will. The likelihood of this happening increases if the buyer is working with a real estate agent. That is because the agent recognizes that her liability is much greater when there is no professional property inspector involved.

If you do not hire an inspector and the buyer's inspector finds defects in the property, the buyer can cancel the contract, demand that you correct or eliminate the defects, or close escrow and hit you with a bill for payment. If you previously hired an inspector with the understanding that you will use their report to give to the buyer, and the buyer's inspector finds defects that your inspector did not find and you did not know about, then your inspector is responsible, not you.

Of course, if the repair or defect is minor, it is usually advisable to make the repair and move forward with the transaction. On the other hand, if the buyer is overly obsessive about the details of the property condition, and there are several conditions you are asked to eliminate before the property can close, you may have a difficult buyer on your hands. As I said earlier, forcing someone to buy your home is usually not in your best interest. What might seem like a delay (letting go of one buyer to find another) can actually be for the best. There is little to be gained by pushing someone into doing something they do not want to do, including buying your home.

Disclosures regarding safety standards

Property safety standards also must be addressed through a TDS or the purchase agreement form. As a seller, you are required to disclose them to prospective buyers. Several safety standards that are commonly recognized in the state of California are:

1. **Automatic garage doors:** All automatic doors installed after January 1, 1991 are required to have an automatic reverse safety devise. Those installed after January 1, 1993 must have a sensor that prevents the door from closing or when there is a problem with the alignment. When serviced, a repairman must run safety checks. If the door doesn't pass, the repairman must put a warning sticker on the door to alert others about the problem.

2. **Child resistant pool barriers:** Single-family homes built after 1997 have a number of barrier options available to them before they can get a permit to build a pool. They need one of the following:

    *   a fence 60 inches tall blocking access to the pool from the house;

    *   an approved safety cover;

    *   exit alarms on all doors accessing the pool;

    *   doors that access the pool to be self-closing, self-latching and with a release mechanism higher than 54 inches; or

    *   some other means of protection deemed acceptable.

Hot tubs and spas with locking safety covers are exempt. Condominiums and apartments do not have the same regulations because they are not single-family residences. They do, however, have their own set of safety rules.

3. **Water heaters:** All existing water heaters are to be anchored, braced, or strapped to prevent them from falling over or breaking loose during an earthquake.

4. **Residential security bars:** All security bars on residential properties must have release mechanisms if they are the sole windows for escape purposes.

5. **Building codes or permits for home improvements:** If you or any previous owner performed improvements on the property that was done without a permit or does not meet current building codes, you must disclose this to your buyers.

6. **Others ordinances unique to your city or county:** When I lived in Palm Springs, CA, it was necessary for me to have someone from the fire department come and inspect my smoke detectors to insure they worked properly. Once approved, an inspection report was given to me to hand to escrow before we could close escrow. Each city and/or county has unique safety ordinances like this. The best way to discover if there is anything like this in your area is to talk to a local title insurance company, escrow company, or real estate agent.

What happens if you don't comply? As long as you fully disclose the problem, defect, or lack of compliance on the TDS, and give a copy to the buyer, the buyer can agree to accept the property in that condition. However, if a local ordinance has a specific requirement for elimination of a problem, like my smoke detector example, then you are required to correct the situation before closing.

Basically, if you have properly disclosed all defects on your TDS to the buyer prior to his signing the purchase agreement, and the purchase agreement does not state something to the contrary, then you, the seller, are under no obligation to remedy the situation unless required by local ordinance.

Again, for any questions you may have about what is necessary and how it is to be reported, check with your local escrow or title insurance company.

What about problems you don't know about?

What happens if the buyer discovers a defect in the property that you did not know about and therefore did not disclose? If you hired a home inspector as advised above, and the inspector's report also does not include the defect, then you have a case against that company regarding repairs. However, if it is a minor restoration, you may want to go ahead and repair it to show good will towards your buyer.

In the homes and investment properties that I have owned and sold, I find that it is frequently best to make the effort to work with the buyer when you are able to do so. Instead of seeing your buyer as an adversary, it might be beneficial to think of him as your partner in achieving the goal of selling your home. You are getting what you want if he buys your house, and he is getting what he wants—a new home to live in. It is in both of your best interests to make the transaction go smoothly and with the most satisfaction possible. If a minor defect is brought to your attention by the buyer, even if you are not liable, fixing it may make the difference in smoothing the way for further issues that are bound to arise.

Other disclosures on your TDS

While a home inspector is a great help when it comes to identifying physical defects or deferred maintenance in and around your property, you are still required to disclose any you know about, even if his report does not cover them. The defects that you must disclose include any and all that you are aware of, which the occasional or casual observer might miss.

For example, in the last house we sold, we were aware of traffic noise coming from a major street some distance from our home. That was a concern some people may not have noticed or cared about when viewing our home. We certainly didn't hear any noise until we lived there. But knowing about it, we felt we owed it to the new buyers to tell them. It affected us so we must assume it would affect them as well. We also disclosed that we lived close to a small airport, and that train tracks were approximately a half mile away. Both of these items occasionally caused noise. We wanted our new buyers to know in advance of signing the purchase agreement what it would be like to live in our home.

The same is true if you live next door to neighbors that have a dog that barks continuously. If the barking has you sufficiently irritated, then it is wise to disclose a barking dog exists. Other issues needing disclosure would be any pending lawsuits concerning the property or any neighborhood changes you know are coming. At one time, my husband and I almost purchased a home that backed up to a vacant lot. Luckily, we found out that a grocery store, with its noisy loading docks, was scheduled to be built within 50 feet of our location before we made an offer on the house. If there is anything that is extremely annoying or disturbing about your neighborhood, or something is scheduled to happen in the future and you know about it, you are required to disclose it.

Of course, I don't like to downgrade my property any more than you will, but it is always better to disclose early and eliminate any surprises later. Remember, the true value of your house is what a willing and able seller will sell for, and what a willing and able buyer will pay. If you hide a significant detriment to your property, then you are essentially deceiving the buyer into paying more than a reasonable representation of what your house would bring you today.

Sure, a nuisance may go away. We all hope they do. But until they do, a new buyer has the right to know about them—before they make an offer on your home. That is why you want to disclose anything which might be an irritant to a future owner on your TDS and deliver it to prospective buyers before they decide on what they want to offer as a price.

Disclosing deaths on your property

Do you have to disclose if you know someone died on your property? Yes and no. You are not required to disclose a death on the property that happened over three years ago unless you are directly asked about it by the buyer or his agent. Still, if you know that someone was violently murdered or died dramatically on the property, even if it was more than three years ago and that knowledge would likely affect a buyer's desire to live there, then it should be disclosed.

To further complicate things, disclosures surrounding the AIDS virus are highly controlled by law. In an attempt to avoid discrimination against someone afflicted with AIDS or the HIV virus, there is actually a California law that absolves homesellers and agents from such disclosure.

It is generally believed that if a buyer asks you directly whether someone was either killed or died on the property for any reason, however long ago, you are duty bound to disclose it. Just as with other nuisances, if you know about something and do not disclose it, you are being deceptive. For obvious reasons, that practice must be avoided.

HOA or common interest CC&Rs

Separate from a TDS, you are required to let potential owners know about any Covenants, Conditions and Restrictions (CC&Rs) or Homeowners' Association (HOA) policies that affect your property and your neighborhood. Disclosures of such use restrictions are normally disclosed in their respective areas of the purchase agreement form. There, you state that you will provide the buyer with a copy of the CC&Rs and HOA information. Plus, if you know of anything that is out of the ordinary regarding your CC&Rs or HOA that is particularly restrictive, be sure to note it separately on your TDS.

If you are normally billed by an HOA, you should already know whether one is operating in your neighborhood. If not, another way to locate information is to go back to that file that contains all of the paperwork from when you first bought your home. Usually, somewhere within that packet normally given to you by the title company, is the information you need. If you are unable to locate it easily, this is another thing that your local title company can help you uncover. Most CC&Rs are usually routine. In that case, the escrow company will deliver them to the new buyer as agreed in the purchase agreement and escrow instructions, and you will not need to do so yourself.

Be advised that HOAs charge fees for providing documents and statements used for these disclosures. If you call and request documents yourself to provide to prospective buyers before signing the purchase agreement, the HOA will probably want to charge you a fee upfront. Just verify that you will be able to use those documents in escrow to fulfill all of your disclosure and transfer requirements. You would not want to be charged twice for this information.

What about maintenance?

Your purchase agreement states that you will maintain the property in the same condition it was in when the buyer made his offer. In other words, if something breaks after you have signed the purchase agreement, then you will need to fix it. If the air conditioning stops working, you are responsible for repairing it. If the dishwasher floods the kitchen, you need to call the repairman. You don't need to buy a new one, unless the existing one cannot be repaired to as good, or better, condition than when you entered into your purchase agreement.

There is nothing more disappointing than having something break before you sell your house. But it is your responsibility to keep everything in working and satisfactory condition. If you don't, you will be liable to the buyer for his cost of repairs after he moves in, so make the effort and repair it before closing.

I have observed some sellers who obviously stopped taking care of their lawns after reaching an agreement with a buyer. Yet, even if they get away with something that minor, every seller should know that they could be held accountable if the buyer decides to press the issue. It is always advisable to make the effort and maintain the property in even better condition than when you sold it, that is, the moment you signed the purchase agreement.

Other considerations

Whether or not you choose to make repairs or upgrades to your property probably depends upon your own personal circumstances, as well as the real estate market at the time. If you are low on cash and short of time, you may offer your property for sale "as disclosed" with all defects passing to the buyer. Just remember that a buyer will set the price of his offer with that in mind. If you really want top dollar for your property, presenting it in the best condition possible will make a difference.

The market will also influence how little you do and how much you ignore defects or deferred maintenance on your property. If it is a hot Seller's Market with a low inventory of available properties for sale and lots of buyers, then a buyer will generally be more receptive to buying your home with disclosed defects included. If the reverse is true, and there are lots of homes for sale and very few buyers making offers, then they will be picky and you might want to be more generous in your willingness to make repairs.

Another option regarding repairs and maintenance is to suggest that you share the cost with the buyers or perhaps agree to do some repairs, but not others. Depending upon the price you received and the cost of the requested changes, who pays for them is subject to negotiation.

Disclose everything

My best advice is to tell your potential buyers more than they want or need to know. Usually, they will be impressed with your willingness to share details and most will not see those disclosures as insurmountable blocks to owning your home, especially if the buyer knows about them before making an offer. Remember, if a prospective buyer is overly concerned about something you disclose, then they are probably not the best buyer for your property at any price. I've learned that if you attempt to talk someone into doing something they are hesitant to do or simply don't want to do, it often comes back to haunt you. Better to send them packing right upfront and face the fact that your home will not be the right one for everyone. Then you can spend your time and energy focused on people who will appreciate and buy the house for what it is—as fully disclosed.

CHAPTER EIGHT
Other required disclosures

The Transfer Disclosure Statement (TDS) discussed in the last chapter regarding the basic condition of the property is the most important disclosure for you to focus on and prepare. However, there are a number of other disclosure forms that are also required.

The good news about these disclosures is that most of them can be fulfilled by going on the Internet and paying a company to do the work for you. Not only is it easy, it usually costs less than $100. But before I tell you how to do that, let's discuss what is needed and why they are needed in the first place. If you don't care, simply skip ahead.

> Don't let these disclosures intimidate you! There is a very easy and inexpensive solution available.

Natural hazard disclosures

Every seller of a single-family home is required to provide a Natural Hazard Disclosure (NHD) to every buyer. Ideally, just like the TDS, they should be given to every prospective buyer before an offer is made on your home. These disclosures originally became necessary after a series of natural disasters occurred, along with the state's ability to map potential danger zones for future disasters. (Anyone remember the Northridge Earthquake or the Eureka Tsunami?)

Now that the state knows about them, you as a seller are required to know about them and disclose them to prospective purchasers. By making it your responsibility to notify buyers of your home, the state hopes that residents are better prepared for potential problems in the future. More importantly for a buyer, they can now make an offer on a property based upon what natural hazards may affect the property during their ownership.

The six disclosures in the NHD category include:

- earthquake fault zones;

- any seismic hazard zones, that is, property that could be damaged due to very severe shaking from earthquakes because of soil liquefaction, landslides, collapse of buildings, etc.;
- special flood hazard areas (Zone A or Zone V as designated by the Federal Emergency Management Agency)
- any potentially damaging flood or inundation areas, that is, areas which lie downhill of a dam that could potentially flood;
- very high fire hazard severity zones; and
- wild land fire areas, which are under substantial forest fire risk or hazard.

In this area of disclosure, the seller must notify the buyer if any of these potentially dangerous problems exist, as well as anything concerning them that the seller could locate in public records. To address the issue, the California State Legislature created a statutory form called the NHD Statement. Naturally, this disclosure form, Form 314, is included in the accompanying Forms CD.

It is believed that natural hazards have the potential to affect property in the same way that undisclosed defects might, especially in the value of the property to a buyer. Therefore, as with the TDS, every seller is required to disclose natural hazards on an NHD form. If you are unable to determine by reading the state map whether any of these hazards affect your property, then a "yes" must be indicated on the form just to alert the buyer.

Should you not fulfill your investigation and disclosure requirement to your buyer, just like with the TDS, they will then have the right to terminate the purchase agreement before closing. If they don't find out until after the property closes, the buyer has the option of completely rescinding the transaction. In some cases, you could be liable for all his monetary losses in the future as a result of such nondisclosure. Not a good option!

Again, it is advisable for you to provide an NHD Statement as soon as you know a prospective buyer is going to make an offer. That way, they will be able to determine an appropriate price before they make an offer on your property. However, if not done in advance, you can have it ordered and delivered in escrow. Just be aware that if there is anything in the report that is unexpected to the buyer, he has three days after he receives the NHD to cancel the entire purchase agreement.

Remember, even though this may sound difficult to you, I will offer a simple solution later in this chapter.

Other environmental hazards

In addition to the standard TDS discussed in the last chapter and the NHD discussed above, there are other hazards related to the property that must be disclosed.

These hazards are any man-made environmental hazards with the potential to affect the health of humans or interfere with their use and enjoyment of the property. These hazards may either be located on the property or may originate elsewhere.

Typical hazards that originate *on or within* the property are:

- asbestos-containing materials;
- formaldehyde used in construction materials;
- radon gas concentrations;
- hazardous waste from drug manufacturing;
- mold;
- hazardous waste from materials or substances;
- smoke from the combustion of products, supplies or materials;
- restrictive security bars that might stop one from exiting during a fire; and
- lead.

Typical hazards that originate *outside* of the property are:

- military ordnance sites within one mile of the property;
- industrial zoning in the neighborhood of the property;
- airport influences; and
- ground transportation arteries. (See Form 157 §11.6)

Unfortunately, there isn't a statutory form that specifically covers all of these particular hazards. Until one is developed by the legislature, the standard TDS, along with the purchase agreement, is where you will disclose any of these items if you know they exist on or around your property.

The main reasons that you will want to fully disclose these items as quickly as possible are because:

- the presence of any of these items could delay closing;
- they could result in the cancellation of your purchase agreement and escrow if they are discovered when the buyer conducts his due diligence inspection;
- they might result in your having to renegotiate the price or offset repair costs due to the discovery of such items after signing the purchase agreement;
- they could shorten the time the buyer has to do his own inspections; and
- they could cause you to lose control over the costs and expenses you might anticipate incurring during the sale of your property.

The good news is that you are not required to hire an expert to investigate their existence or what any of these hazards mean or represent—only to disclose the environmental hazard if you know it exists. Unless you agree in the purchase agreement or any counteroffers to fix or eliminate a particular hazard previously disclosed, your obligations end with full disclosure.

On-site hazard disclosures in more detail

1. Lead-based paint hazards:

This disclosure is only required for homes built before 1978. Before then, many homes were painted using paint that contained a lead base. Lead-based paint was found to deteriorate into contaminated flakes and dust and to be extremely hazardous to the health of young children. Should a child ingest lead-laced chips of paint or dust, it was found to often result in behavior disorders, learning disabilities, and delayed development. The use of such paint was banned in 1978, but some older homes still contain the potentially hazardous material.

Once outlawed, the federal government required all owners of residential dwellings built before 1978 to disclose to both buyers and tenants of the possible or known existence of the pre-existing hazard. The properties affected are mainly single-family homes, and although there are a few exceptions, most For Sale By Owners (FSBOs) are required to disclose the hazard if their home was built before 1978.

There is a Lead-Based Paint (LBP) Disclosure, Form 313, in the accompanying CD. Be sure to fully fill out the form if the construction of your property pre-dates 1978. In addition to your signing the form, the buyer is also required to sign for their receipt. As part of the disclosure, the buyer has a number of days (ten or less) to inspect the property or to have an expert inspect the property in order to evaluate whether any potential hazard exists.

Naturally, if you know anything regarding the use of lead paint on the property, you will disclose it to your buyer on the LBP disclosure sheet. It is then up to the buyer to determine what that means to him. You might also want to provide information about lead paint in the form of a pamphlet entitled, "Protect Your Family From Lead in Your Home," available online at:
www.epa.gov/opptintr/lead/pubs/leadpdfe.pdf.

Once you give them the LBP disclosure form, be sure to get them to sign for their receipt of it. Once the time period for inspection has passed, your disclosure effort is fulfilled.

2. Structural pest control inspection and certification:

An inspection for structural pests, such as termites, is one of the only disclosures that does not need to be done prior to transfer of title. However, if you know or suspect that your property has a termite problem, don't wait. Someone is going to have to fix the problem, and if you know about it and don't tell the buyer in advance, it is probably going to be you.

Actually, if you suspect there might be a problem, I recommend that you hire a termite pest control person as soon as you know you want to sell your home and before you begin marketing. Just like with a professional home inspector, the pest inspector will then provide you with a report. If he finds any infestation or similar problems, he will tell you what needs to be corrected.

Once you have the report, you can then spell it out on the TDS and give it to any potential purchasers before they make an offer on your property. Then the purchase offer they make you will be based upon the true condition of the property from the information you have disclosed. Or better yet, if the report indicates that repairs are needed, just go ahead and make them in advance. Then, after the repairs are made, your pest control inspector can come back and certify the property is free of structural pests. That will allow you to present your prospective buyer with a full report and obtain top dollar for your property's condition. (See Form 157 §11.1)

3. Mold:

Mold is another one of those issues that began to affect property transfers in the early 2000s. It was determined that some people, especially those with respiratory illnesses, were susceptible to mold spore inflammation, allergy, or infection. With this announcement, mold problems became the issue *du jour* and caused a great deal of concern in the real estate community, especially in the area of disclosure.

Mold tends to consume whatever it grows on, so not only are the spores that are released a potential problem, but so too is the damage. Another telltale sign of mold is a musty or off-smelling odor. If you smell something funny, be sure to check it out. Another sign of concern would be black or gray discoloration in a damp area of the home. For more information about mold, you can search the Internet for a California Department of Health Services Pamphlet entitled, "Mold in My Home: What Do I Do?", available at:

www.dhs.ca.gov/deodc/ehib/EHIB2/PDF/MOLD_2001_07_17FINA L.pdf. The Environmental Protection Agency (EPA) also has information at: www.epa.gov/mold/moldresources.html.

As far as you as a homeseller are concerned, if you know or suspect you have a mold problem, you must disclose it. Mold typically appears when there has been water damage, usually from flooding, broken water pipes, leaking air conditioners, sprinklers, or other water features gone awry. If you know or suspect you have a mold problem, you may want to make necessary repairs just for your own good health. At a minimum, you must disclose any problems to all possible buyers.

Here's something else you may want to note and disclose. If your property has had any water damage in the past and you have claimed it on your property insurance, your insurers now have a record of that damage. Not only will they keep a file on the fact that mold could exist as a result, but it is possible that your new homebuyers will face a higher property hazard insurance premium when they purchase your home. Insurance companies are attempting to cover any future problem that your water damage may have caused, even though repairs were made to eliminate the damage.

4. Methamphetamine contamination:

As of January 1, 2006, local health officials must assess any property that law enforcement agencies say may be potentially contaminated by methamphetamine laboratory activity. If the local health officials determine that contamination exists, they must issue a report prohibiting the property's use or habitation. If any property has this type restriction, a seller is required to notify any buyer of the problem in writing and provide him with a copy of the report. The buyer is then required to provide a written receipt of the disclosure.

5. Radon:

Radon is a radioactive gas that is odorless, tasteless, and invisible. It is created in the natural breakdown of uranium deep in the soil, rock, and water beneath a particular property. When it breaks down, it gets into the air, and according to the U.S. Surgeon General, it is a leading cause of lung cancer.

The good news is that radon gas is rare in California and appears in less that 1% of housing in our state.[1] However, should you have any suspicions about elevated levels in your home, you must disclose it to a potential buyer. More information about radon is available at: www.epa.gov/iaq/radon/pubs/hmbyguid.html.

6. Asbestos in construction materials:

Back in the 1940s, asbestos was commonly used in all sorts of building materials in order to insulate and provide stability to the product. Unfortunately, when products containing asbestos are destroyed or disturbed, such as during removal or renovation, many of its microscopic particles become airborne. These airborne particles can easily become lodged in the lungs and cause significant health problems.

Asbestos use is commonly found in the following household materials or products:

- acoustic popcorn or ceiling tiles;
- vinyl floor tiles or sheet flooring;
- thermal insulation on pipes and hot water heaters;
- joint and spackling compounds; and
- heating and electrical ducts.

The major danger with asbestos is when it becomes airborne. This usually occurs during renovation or demolition. If the building material containing asbestos is in good condition and not deteriorating, then leave it in place to avoid the problem.

Sellers are not required to investigate or have a report issued on whether or not asbestos is present. Also, sellers are not required to remove or clean it up. The only requirement is to disclose it if it is known to exist in the home. For more information, go to: www.epa.gov/oppt/asbestos/index.html.

7. Formaldehyde gas emissions:

Formaldehyde is a gas that results from certain solvents that were used for paints, resins, plastics, and fiberboards. Popular in the 1970s, it was banned from use in residential property constructed after 1982. Because formaldehyde is suspected of being hazardous to human health, its known presence must be disclosed.

8. Hazardous waste on site:

Anything that has the potential to be harmful to human health is considered a hazardous waste. Therefore, any product, material, or substance that is considered toxic, corrosive, ignitable, or reactive, which exists on the property, must be disclosed.

For example, if you know motor oil was routinely disposed of in your yard, that is hazardous waste and you are required to disclose its existence to potential buyers. Anything containing oil, gas, or medical waste that has been dumped or leaked into the ground on your property must be disclosed, especially if any part of your property housed a petrochemical industry, dry cleaner, or printer shop.

Off-site hazard disclosures in more detail

1. Military ordnance disclosure: This is a notification of whether your property is located within one mile of a former federal or state military related location that may contain potentially explosive munitions (See Form 157 §11.6)

2. Industrial disclosures: This disclosure calculates distances based upon maps and public records as to whether your property lies within one mile of such a zone. Industrial property can affect your property in a variety of ways, including noise, traffic, airborne particles, and odors. You must disclose any known nuisance created by industrial activity near your property. (See Form 157 §11.6)

3. Airport proximity disclosures and airport influence areas: Is there an airport nearby? This disclosure has nothing to do with noise levels and everything to do with map location. It leaves any judgment about the location solely in the hands of your buyer. As I mentioned earlier, I personally disclosed that there was occasional noise coming from a local airport when I last sold my home. Not only did I disclose the noise, but the NHD covered the fact that the airport was located there. (See Form 157 §11.6)

4. Sex offenders notification: You as a seller are merely required to notify your buyers that they can go online to see if any of their potential neighbors are registered as sex offenders. The disclosure for the sex offender website is made in the purchase agreement form as provided on the accompanying CD. You are not required to provide any more information beyond the wording in the purchase agreement, unless placed on direct inquiry by the buyer. (See Form 157 §11.13)

Mello-Roos and special assessments

Off-site public improvements in neighborhoods and subdivisions are allowed to be paid for by creating bonds. The bonds are secured by a lien on every property in the area that benefits from the improvement. Examples of these types of improvements are new curbs and gutters for your neighborhood. Naturally, because your neighborhood benefits, only properties in your neighborhood are required to pay an annual assessment to pay the bonds. The total amount owed by you and your property is calculated based upon an allocation of the value of the benefits your property receives from the improvements.

As a seller, you must disclose whether your property lies within one of these districts and whether or not there is a special assessment lien on your property that the buyer will be required to pay in installments, unless you pay it off as a condition of the sale. The installments due on this lien are billed and paid for with your property tax bill and is called a "special tax." But it is not a tax—it is a bonded indebtedness secured by the property.[2] And while automatically assumable by any buyer, it still is a lien that a buyer is responsible for and

Pamphlets and booklets you must provide to your buyer

Earthquake safety: Once you have disclosed what you know about being in a geologic or seismic area, you eliminate all further earthquake related liability by providing your buyer with a copy of a booklet entitled, "Homeowner's Guide To Earthquake Safety." This guide is available online at: www.seismic.ca.gov/pub/CSSC_2005-01_HOG.pdf or by calling (916) 263-5506. Once this booklet has been given to the buyer, you are not required to provide further information. I suggest you go online and print out a copy to give to your buyer.

Lead-based paint: If your home was built prior to 1972 and/or you suspect lead-based paint may have been used, you must disclose as explained earlier in this chapter. You are also required to provide your buyer with the pamphlet entitled, "Protect Your Family From Lead in Your Home", which you can find at the following website:
www.epa.gov/opptintr/lead/pubs/leadpdfe.pdf.

Environmental hazards: If you have reason to believe, and have disclosed, that any of the above explained environmental hazards exists on your property, you must provide them with the pamphlet entitled, "Residential Environmental Hazards: A Guide For Homeowners, Buyers, Landlords and Tenants." If the buyer receives this pamphlet, then you are not required to provide any more information concerning such hazards other than your disclosure of its existence. You may print out a copy of the pamphlet at:
www.dhs.ca.gov/childlead/pdfs/ResEnviroHaz2005.pdf.

will pay during their ownership unless you prepay it. Technically, you will be asking any buyer to buy your home with this existing loan in place. Naturally, this amount is included in the fair market value of your home and it will decrease the amount of equity in your property, just like any existing loan. (See Form 157 §7)

The purchase agreement form included on the Forms CD provides for the amount of the special assessment bond to be assumed by the buyer as a partial payment toward the purchase price when buying your home. It is part of the purchase price and is treated accordingly. (See Form 157 §7)

In addition to stating the amount as part of the purchase price, you must also disclose the terms for repayment of the bonded indebtedness. In order to do this, you must obtain and deliver to your buyers a notice prepared by the Improvement District Office entitled either "Notice of Assessment" or "Notice of Special Tax."[3] Simply contact your improvement district office by phone, fax, or mail. They must provide you with the information within five days and charge no more than $10. To find out the address and/or phone number of your District office, either search the Internet or contact your local city or county office for aid.

If this type of assessment exists on your property, you are advised to contact the District office right away and ask for this report before you put your property on the market. Then, you can hand the notice to any potential buyer upfront, along with the TDS and other disclosures. If you do not provide the improvement district report prior to signing the purchase agreement, the buyer who is assuming the bonded indebtedness has a statutory right to cancel the agreement within three days after you finally do. Should the buyer want more information than your statutory report delivers, then it will be up to him to get it with a little help from you.

Supplemental tax bills

Every seller must disclose to his buyer that property is re-assessed on sale in the state of California, resulting in early payment of increased taxes. The way this is handled is that, until the county assessor makes the adjustments automatically through the tax rolls, every buyer is required to pay a "supplemental tax bill." There may be one or even two supplemental bills, depending upon what time of year the property closes escrow.

These supplemental tax bills will not go to the lender. They will be sent directly to the buyer of the property sometime within their first year of ownership. They will receive these bills even if they are paying an escrowed amount in their monthly payment towards future tax bills. Because far too many buyers were surprised and unprepared to pay these temporary billings, you as a seller are now required to let them know to expect them in advance. (See Form 157 §13)

Documents and financial statements for CIDs

One of the disclosures mentioned in the last chapter had to do with Conditions, Covenants and Restrictions (CC&Rs) and Home-owners' Associations (HOAs) for your property. A very similar disclosure is also necessary for homes located in subdivisions, called a Common Interest Development (CID). Examples of these are condominium projects, planned developments, or stock cooperatives. If you know your property is a part of a CID, you must give to your buyers:

1. A copy of all the governing documents, including the rules and regulations, and the articles of incorporation.

2. Notice of an age restriction not consistent with Section 51.3 of the California Civil Code.

3. A copy of the financial documents of the association, including a financial statement, operating budget, and reserve and assessment accountings.

4. A written statement specifying the amount of dues and assessments, along with unpaid amounts, late charge amounts, interest, and how late payments are fined and/or levied.

5. Notice of any alleged violations on the property not previously resolved by the owner and the association.

6. A list of any construction defects that might exist and when they would be repaired.

7. Notice of any settlement agreements between the developer and the association.

8. Notice if any assessments or dues will be changed in the near future.

Disclosures in CIDs or Condominium Associations are critical because so much of the condition and use of the property is tied to an HOA. Before a buyer can realistically arrive at a price and make an offer, they must be able to see all the variables that affect price and usage. As a seller, it is in your long-term best interests to gather all of the above information together and have it ready to hand to prospective purchasers before they make an offer. Then, when you do receive a purchase agreement or work together with a buyer to prepare one, you can be more assured that your buyer's expectations are met.

Also, as mentioned previously concerning HOAs, there is usually a fee charged by the HOA for any of the above information they provide. Sometimes, the HOA requires the fee to be paid upfront—other times it can be paid through escrow. Double check to make sure that if you receive copies of these disclosures from your HOA before you find a buyer and open escrow, that the documents you have obtained can be eventually used by escrow to fulfill your disclosure requirements. You would not want to have to pay twice for this information.

Another thing for you to note is that some HOAs will not process the transfer of the property to the buyer until they receive a copy of the grant deed and the transfer tax receipt. This is normally handled through escrow, but you will want to ensure that it will be done to relieve yourself of future liability to the HOA.

The simplest solution for fulfilling most hazard disclosures

Some of the above listed hazards may seem very complicated and difficult to disclose, but there is actually an easy way to meet all your NHD requirements. Again, if you know of any specific hazard, you must always disclose it in writing on the TDS or on the purchase agreement. However, in most cases, you will be able to easily fulfill the disclosure by contacting a residential disclosure company.

Normally, when a real estate agent is involved, they will suggest that you use a particular company that they regularly use. However, if no agent is involved, you can easily locate a company through the Internet. Simply search for a "California Natural Hazard Disclosure" and many different companies will appear. A company that I have used personally is LGS Reports. You can also ask your local real estate agents, title company, and escrow companies for recommendations. As long as the company has the experience and credentials to be labeled an "expert," they assume the liability for preparing an NHD. The costs range from $35 to $100, and cover most of the above-mentioned disclosures.

If you want to prepare the disclosure yourself, a statutory form (just like those used by all NHD companies) is included as Form 314 on the accompanying CD. Just remember, if you do complete the form yourself, you must contact the county offices where you live for a printout of the NHD information on your property, and then fill out the form based upon that information.

Even if you do rely on one of the expert companies to provide the NHD, their disclosure will not excuse you from noting conditions you are aware of that the NHD does not include. Then, prior to handing the NHD report to your buyers, you must sign it.

Seller financing disclosure statement

One other disclosure exists that you are required to make as a seller, but only if you decide to carry part of the financing for your buyer. Because California is worried that you and your buyer might not have an understanding of carryback trust deed law, they require this disclosure so the public is well informed of their rights, obligations, and risks in such an instance. The disclosure is unnecessary if you do not include a finance charge and do not collect more than four payments before you are paid in full.

If the idea of carrying back part of the financing is too complicated to imagine just yet, just know that you have what you need on the accompanying CD if you want to help the buyer finance the price. In a later chapter, I will discuss some of the ramifications of seller financing and why you might want to consider it. (See Form 300)

Even more disclosures

Yes, there are even more disclosures in some real estate transactions, but the above are all that are necessary for you as a seller of a single-family home. Buyers have disclosures they must make, but those are handled by escrow as part of their services. Also, further disclosures are required of any real estate agent who may be involved in your sale.

Hopefully, after explaining all of these disclosures and the way to fulfill your obligations to your prospective buyer, you are no longer intimidated by the disclosure process. As stated in the last chapter, you are never required to guarantee that your property has no defects—only to disclose what you know. Your basic obligation is to sell your property and carefully document any factors that might affect a prospective buyer's use or enjoyment of the property. Selling a property "fully disclosed" is the best course of action in today's litigious world.

CHAPTER NINE
Your partners in selling your home

There is good news for everyone who wants to sell a home in California. That news is that you are not alone when you sell your property—even if you are a For Sale By Owner (FSBO). A number of different businesses routinely help sellers and buyers all the time. Of course, you must pay for their services. But because you pay them to help you, you have a right to expect good service in return. However, if you don't know what to expect or what to ask for, you are at a serious disadvantage. In this chapter, we review your selling partners and what they can do to help maximize your efforts to locate a buyer and close a sale.

The escrow officer

I mentioned in an earlier chapter that escrow is a "neutral" third party, bound by written instructions, to help both you and your buyer to close a transaction. Normally, this third party will either be an independent escrow company or an escrow division of a title company. However, the actual person you deal with will hold the title of "escrow officer." The vast majority of escrow officers in California are individuals who perform their obligations with a very high level of proficiency.

Just as there are good real estate agents and some who are not so good, the same is true with escrow officers. I happen to have a great deal of respect for most of them because they work very hard and are essential to the transaction. Ask around. Find out who is one of the best in your area. Chances are good that if you ask enough people, the name of one or two escrow officers will continually pop up. That is the person you want to use. I personally choose a specific escrow officer rather than a particular office. Also, avoid selecting your escrow company because its office is closest to your home or the escrow fee is the lowest one in town. Make your selection knowing that a good officer can make the difference between success and failure in getting your transaction closed.

How much do they charge? It is actually fairly standard and usually a percentage of the sales price of your home. In Southern California, the seller traditionally pays half and the buyer pays the other half of the escrow fee. This varies in Northern California, with Kern County considered the dividing line of the state. Although a bit of fee negotiation is possible, remember that quality of service is more important than saving a few dollars.

The contract used by your escrow officer is called escrow instructions. Instructions specify exactly what the escrow officer must do for you and the buyer to fully meet the terms of the purchase agreement you both entered into. Escrow must follow the contract to the letter and is not allowed any self-interpretation. A classic example of escrow instructions is included on Form 401 on your Forms CD.

Because escrow works for the benefit of both the buyer and seller, escrow will never take your side to the exclusion of the buyer or vice versa. Escrow works for each of you equally according to the dictates of the escrow instructions. As a neutral third party, escrow cannot provide you with any legal, accounting, or even real estate related advice. Escrow's sole role is to carry out and complete whatever you have set in motion as spelled out in the escrow instructions.

The primary duties of your escrow officer

The usual amount of time for escrow to complete all of its tasks is 45 to 60 days. This time is necessary because a new loan or loan assumption routinely takes this amount of time to complete, and there are a number of other details to coordinate. A list of the most common tasks escrow must complete before closing include:

1. Reviewing with the seller or buyer, or both, to determine what must be included in the escrow instructions to close the purchase agreement.

2. Preparing escrow instructions.

3. Accepting and holding any good-faith deposit made by the buyer toward the purchase price.

4. Contacting the existing lenders for payoff or assumption information, handling all the details to pay off and clear title of any existing loans, or processing the loan assumption for the buyer.

5. Preparing documents, including the grant deed transferring the property to the buyer.

6. Arranging with the new lender to fulfill all necessary requirements, including receiving the loan package and making sure all loan documents are signed and notarized.

7. Making sure that all contingencies and conditions agreed to in the escrow instructions are fulfilled.

8. Ordering the title search from the title company and communicating issues to the appropriate party should any need to be addressed before closing.

9. Determining the additional funds needed from the buyer and requesting these funds when escrow has all documents needed to close.

10. Calculating costs for recording, prorations, payoffs, buyer and seller charges, and escrow/title fees.

11. Notarizing all documents to be recorded.

12. Reviewing the escrow instructions to verify that all conditions have been met and all funds from the buyer have been received into escrow.

13. Ordering the title company to record the grant deed.

14. Disbursing all funds held by escrow in accordance with escrow instructions.

15. Preparing closing statements for a final accounting of all the funds received into and disbursed from escrow.

16. Communicating constantly with you, the buyer, the lender, and the title company throughout the escrow process, along with any other parties related to the transaction.

The escrow officer will double-check all of your paperwork to assure it is done correctly. If either you or the buyer needs to do something to move the transaction along, escrow will contact the appropriate party to get it done. If you take the time to select a quality escrow officer before you accept an offer to purchase from a buyer, your escrow officer may feel like your best friend during the process of selling your home.

Items left blank or unchecked are not applicable.

Escrow number _____ Dated _____, 20 _____

Escrow/brokerage company: _____

Licensed by the Department of _____, State of California, license # _____

Escrow officer: _____

Address: _____

_____

Phone number: _____ Fax: _____

Buyer: _____

Seller: _____

TERMS OF SALE: (for escrow use only)

$_____   Total Consideration Seller to receive from Buyer

$_____   Assessment Bond paid with property taxes

$_____   1st Trust Deed of Record

$_____   2nd Trust Deed of Record

$_____   Trust Deed to record

$_____   Trust Deed to record

$_____   Cash through Escrow

$_____   Other Consideration_____

1. **You, the escrow officer, are authorized and instructed as follows:**

   1.1   Buyer deposits herewith the sum of $_____.

   1.2   On or before _____, 20_____, the date set for closing, Buyer will deposit with You on your request the additional sum of $_____, to make a total deposit of $_____.

   1.3   Buyer will deliver to You prior to the date set for closing any additional funds and instruments required which You request.

   1.4   You may thereafter use these funds and instruments until such time as You have received written instruction not to do so. Brokers are authorized to extend any performance date up to one month.

   1.5   Close of escrow is the date instruments are recorded.

2. Upon the use of these funds and instruments, You are to obtain the following policy of title insurance, with the usual title company exceptions, in the following checked type and form:

   Title to be vested in Buyer or Assignee free of encumbrances other than those set forth herein. Buyer's interest in title to be insured under a policy issued by _____
   as a(n) ☐ Homeowner(s) policy (one-to-four units), ☐ Residential ALTA-R policy (vacant or improved residential parcel), ☐ Owner's policy (other than one-to-four units), ☐ Joint Protection policy (also naming the Carryback Seller or Purchase-assist Lender), or ☐ Binder (to insure resale or refinance within two years).
   Endorsements: _____

   _____

   2.1   With title insurance in the amount of $_____ covering the following described real property, commonly known as:_____
   and legally described as: _____

   _____

   _____

   _____

   2.2   Showing title vested in: _____

   2.3   Subject to the following only:

       a. All General and Special taxes for the _____ fiscal year, including any special district taxes or personal property taxes collected with the ad valorem taxes.

       b. Assessments and Bonds with an unpaid balance of $_____.

    c. Any covenants, conditions, restrictions, reservations, rights, right of ways and easements of record, or in deed to record, and EXCEPTIONS of water, minerals, oil, gas, and kindred substances, on or under said real property, now of record, or in deed to record.

    d. First encumbrance now of record with an unpaid balance of $_____, payable $_____ monthly, including interest of _____% per annum. ☐ ARM

    e. Second encumbrance now of record with an unpaid balance of $_____, payable $_____ monthly, including interest of _____% per annum, all due and payable _____, 20_____.

    f. Deed of Trust to record in the amount of $_____.
    Execution of loan documents under §2.3f or §2.3g shall be Buyer's approval of their terms. Should Seller carry back under §2.3h, You are to obtain Seller's written approval of the loan terms for any Deed of Trust to record.

    g. Deed of Trust to record in the amount of $_____.

    h. Purchase money Deed of Trust with Assignment of Rents on standard form, executed by Buyer securing a note for $_____ in favor of Seller as their interests appear on the preliminary title report, with interest at _____% per annum from close of escrow, principal and interest payable in installments of $_____, or more, each on the same day of every calendar month, beginning one month from ☐ close of escrow, or ☐ _____, 20_____, and continuing until _____.

    You, as escrow holder, are instructed to prepare the note and Deed of Trust and insert the correct principal amount and correct first payment date, interest accrual date and due date as soon as they can be determined. The address for deliver of note payments is: _____

3. You are to obtain at Seller's expense beneficiary statements on the Deed(s) of Trust (or mortgage) now of record (§2.3d and §2.3e above). If the principal balances shown by the statements are more or less than the amount shown above, You are to make adjustments as checked below:

    ☐ cash through escrow, ☐ total consideration, or ☐ purchase-money Deed of Trust.

    3.1   You are to deliver to Buyer for Buyer's approval prior to close of escrow a copy of the beneficiary statement for each Deed of Trust to remain of record on closing.

    3.2   You are to deliver to Seller prior to close of escrow, any payoff demand necessary to eliminate encumbrances so You can comply with conditions in §2.3 for title insurance.

4. You are to obtain at Seller's expense a UCC-3 clearance on the following described personal property:
_____
_____
_____

    and cause title thereto to be vested in Buyer subject to the following UCC-1 financing statements:

    a. A UCC-1 obligation in the approximate amount of $_____, payable $_____ per month, including an annual percentage rate of _____%, all due and payable _____, 20_____.

    b A UCC-1 form in favor of Seller at Buyer's expense as additional security for any note carried back under §2.3h above.

5. Prior to close of escrow, Buyer is to hand You a sufficient hazard insurance policy. In the event Seller carries back under §2.3h above, then Seller is to be named as additional loss payee. The policy is to be in an amount sufficient to cover all lien balances or the coverage demanded by the new lender if greater in amount.

6. ☐ Prior to the close of escrow and at Seller's expense, Seller to hand You a structural pest control clearance on the subject property.

7. ☐ Prior to close of escrow and at Seller's expense, You are to obtain a one-year policy of homeowner's warranty issued by _____, in favor of Buyer, covering _____.

8. Prior to the close of escrow and at Seller's expense, You are to obtain from the homeowners' association of any common interest development which includes the described property the following checked item(s) for Buyer's approval:

    8.1 ☐ A statement of condition of assessments;

    8.2 ☐ Copies of the association's articles, bylaws, CC&Rs, collection and lien enforcement policies, operating budget, operating rules, CPA's financial review, insurance policy summary and any age restriction statement;

    8.3 ☐ Copies from the association of any notice to Seller of CC&R violations, any list of construction defects, and any assessment charges not yet payable.

9. ☐ You are authorized and instructed to prepare assignments for all existing lease/rental agreements.

10. The following checked prorations and adjustments shall be computed by You on a monthly basis of 30 days as of ☐ close of escrow, or ☐ _____, 20_____, on which date Buyer is to be treated as the owner for the entire day:

    a. ☐ Taxes, based on latest tax statement available and Seller warrants that no reassessment or reassessment activity has since occurred

    b. ☐ Hazard (fire) insurance premium

    c. ☐ Interest on existing note(s) and Deed(s) of Trust

    d. ☐ Rents and deposits based on rental statement handed to You and approved by Buyer and Seller prior to close of escrow

    e. ☐ Impounds, under §2.3d or §2.3e above, together with an assignment of these impounds to Buyer through escrow

    f. ☐ Association assessments for any common interest development which includes the property

    g.   Other _____

  10.1 You are to account for the above prorations and adjustments into the item checked below:
    ☐ cash through escrow, ☐ total consideration, or ☐ purchase-money Deed of Trust.

11. You are to promptly obtain and hand Buyer a preliminary title report on the property from title company for Buyer's approval or disapproval and cancellation of this transaction within _____ days of receipt by Buyer or Buyer's Broker of the report.

12. The Grant Deed to state the tax statements are to be mailed to: _____

_____

at _____ .

13. Escrow is herewith handed a purchase agreement dated _____, 20_____ and (a) counteroffer(s) dated _____, 20_____ and _____, 20_____, entered into by Buyer and Seller regarding the sale of the property which authorizes and instructs escrow to act on the provisions of the agreement as mutual escrow instructions to close this transaction.

  13.1 Any inconsistencies between the provisions in the purchase agreement and provisions in the instructions prepared by escrow shall be controlled by the instructions prepared by escrow.

14. The close of escrow and disbursement of funds can be affected based on the form of the deposit with escrow. Funds deposited in cash or by electronic payment allow for closing and disbursement on or after the business day of deposit with the escrow's financial institution. Funds deposited by cashier's check allow for closing and disbursement on or after two business days after deposit with the escrow's financial institution. All other forms of deposit cannot be disbursed and thus, the closing cannot occur until the funds are made available to escrow by the escrow's financial institution.

15. Buyer is required to withhold 10% of each Seller's share of the sales price for payment of Seller's federal income taxes on this transaction, unless Seller meets one of the following conditions:

  15.1 Each Seller provides Buyer with their taxpayer identification number and declares under penalty of perjury to be a citizen of the United States or a resident alien [ft Form 301];

  15.2 Buyer declares under penalty of perjury the property will be used as their residence and the sales price is $300,000 or less [ft Form 301]; or

  15.3 Seller requests and obtains a withholding certificate from the Internal Revenue Service (IRS) authorizing a reduced amount or no amount be withheld.

16. Buyer is required to withhold $3\frac{1}{3}$% of each Seller's share of the sales price for payment of Seller's California income taxes on this transaction, unless one of the following exemptions exists:

  16.1 Seller executes a real estate withholding certificate, FTB form 593-C, declaring the sale is exempt due to:

    a. The property sold is or was last used as Seller's principal residence;

    b. The property sold was the decedent's principal residence;

    c. The property was sold as part of an IRC §1031 exchange;

    d. The property was taken by involuntary conversion and will be replaced under IRC §1033;

    e. The property was sold at a taxable loss.

  16.2 Buyer is also exempt from withholding $3\frac{1}{3}$% of Seller's share of the sales price if:

    a. The property was sold for less than $100,000;

    b. Buyer is acquiring the property by a deed-in-lieu of foreclosure;

    c. Seller is a bank acting as a trustee under an agreement other than a Deed of Trust.

16.3 On an installment sale, Buyer may agree to withhold on each payment on the carryback note and thus defer withholding. [FTB Forms 593-I and 597]

17. In the event You become involved in litigation between Buyer and Seller arising out of this transaction, Buyer and Seller shall pay a reasonable fee for attorney services which You may be required to incur.

18. You are authorized to use Seller's instruments when You hold and can deliver to Seller the money and instruments to be delivered to Seller under these instructions.

   18.1 You are authorized to pay and charge Seller for the following checked item(s):

     a. ☐ Bonds, assessments, taxes and other liens of record to show title as called for.

     b. ☐ Documentary transfer taxes as required.

     c. ☐ Brokerage fees: $_____ to _____
       $_____ to _____
       $_____ to _____

     d. ☐ Transaction coordinator's fees:
       $_____ to _____
       $_____ to _____

     e. ☐ Title insurance premium on the policy to be issued to Buyer.

     f. ☐ Costs of recording Seller's Grant Deed.

     g. ☐ Escrow fees for your services and any charges incurred by escrow on Seller's behalf.

     h. ☐ Payables submitted to escrow for payment by Seller or Seller's Broker.

     i. ☐ Attorney fees: $_____ to _____

     j. Other _____

19. You are authorized to pay and charge Buyer for the following checked item(s):

     a. ☐ Escrow fees for your services and any charges incurred by escrow on Buyer's behalf.

     b. ☐ Costs of and lender's charges for recording or assuming any Deed of Trust, including a policy of title insurance for any new lender.

     c. ☐ Attorney fees: $_____ to _____

     d. ☐ Brokerage fees: $_____ to _____

     e. ☐ Title insurance premium on the policy to be issued to Buyer.

     f. Other _____

20. _____

I hereby agree to perform all acts called for above to be performed by Seller.

Date:_____, 20_____
Seller: _____
Seller: _____
Signature: _____
Signature: _____
Address: _____
_____
Phone: _____
Fax: _____
Email: _____

I hereby agree to perform all acts called for above to be performed by Buyer.

Date:_____, 20_____
Buyer: _____
Buyer: _____
Signature: _____
Signature: _____
Address: _____
_____
Phone: _____
Fax: _____
Email: _____

How you can help your escrow officer

You can help your escrow officer during the course of your transaction by performing a number of activities. I suggest you keep a folder handy to fill with the papers and reports that come up early on. Many of those documents will be necessary in escrow. (See Form 402)

A few things you should provide your escrow officer with are:

1. A copy of the purchase agreement signed by you and the buyers, including any counteroffers you may have included and signed.

2. Your full legal name, address, and contact information—as well as for any others who hold title to your property.

3. The complete legal name, address, and contact information on the buyers.

4. The complete name, address, phone number, and loan numbers of any lenders who hold a trust deed on the property.

5. Copies of your original grant deed and your old title insurance policy.

6. Copies of any reports you have received, such as the home inspector's report or the termite/pest control report.

7. If your home is in a Common Interest Development (CID) or has a Homeowners' Association (HOA), gather the name, address, and contact information for escrow.

8. If your property is subject to a Mello-Roos special assessment lien, include everything you have obtained from the district office.

9. Provide the name of the title company that you want to use to supply title insurance.

10. Any other paperwork that you think might be important.

Every escrow company has a copy machine, so if you are worried about copies, don't be. Just take your folder containing all your property related information and your escrow officer will make copies of whatever she needs. Also, don't be concerned about confidentiality. Escrow must keep your personal information private and will avoid sharing the details of your sale with anyone who is not a part of the transaction.

However, just because your escrow officer is a wiz at handling details, you will still want to read over the instructions and all the documents you sign or receive to make sure that nothing has been accidentally overlooked, miscalculated, or misspelled. Even the best escrow officer occasionally makes mistakes.

What are prorations and how are they handled?

Other tasks handled by your escrow officer include prorations. Proration is the act of distributing proportionately any expenses or benefits derived from the ownership or possession of property. The dividing point is usually the day that the new grant deed from the seller to the buyer is recorded by the county clerk and recorder. That particular day of recording is considered the first full day of ownership for the buyer.

The exact date of recordation normally follows escrow's orchestration of numerous events involved in your transaction. A few of the most difficult events to coordinate include the new loan funding date, completion and removal of all contingencies, and the date of possession. The date for closing is initially set in the purchase agreement by the seller and the buyer. However, it is the escrow officer who determines if all elements of escrow have been completed for closing and then coordinates the actual recording date to coincide with all the parties and services involved.

Items to be prorated are fairly standard. The most common include property taxes, assessments, mortgage interest on assumed loans, HOA dues, and any rents. Some of these are paid in advance, and some are paid after they have accrued.

Because prorations alter the final accounting by escrow, every payment you do or do not make will affect it. Because of that, I recommend that you let your escrow officer know before making any payments to see how you should proceed. Just be sure to keep copies and receipts of any payments made and give them to your escrow officer. Keep in mind, even if you do go ahead and make payments as due, in most cases, you will receive your prorated share as a credit on the final accounting for the sale.

If you have any questions about what is prorated on your property, just ask your escrow officer.

Using a title company escrow officer

In some cases, your escrow officer will be employed in a division of the title company that you have selected. If that is the case, you will notice little difference from what they do as described above. In some ways, it may be easier to have your title company and your escrow officer in the same building.

Then why bother with an independent escrow office at all? As mentioned in an earlier chapter, there are actually two things to consider. To begin with, I usually advise that you work with an escrow officer who has been recommended. If she works for a title company, fine. If that person works for an independent escrow office, then use an independent office. Always choose recommended personnel rather than one assigned to you, regardless of where they work.

The second reason I often support using independent escrow companies is because they are licensed and regulated by the California Department of Corporations (DOC). They must post bonds for each of their escrow officers, are audited regularly, and have rules that dictate who oversees the office and their qualifications. Most importantly, any money you have deposited with an independent escrow company is insured against loss. This is not true for title companies or broker-owned escrow companies. Independent escrow offices are generally smaller and offer a more intimate connection to buyers and sellers. Because they are privately owned, the escrow officers typically provide exceptional personal service. They rely largely on referrals and know that they must compete with large title companies for your business.

Title-company escrows are normally a division separate from the primary business of providing title insurance to homebuyers. Hence, their escrow division is regulated as a sideline to their major focus and they are considered to be "controlled" since they are not licensed as escrow companies. In Northern California, the escrow officer is almost always a division attached to a title company. Even though independent escrow offices do exist in the northern part of the state, they primarily handle escrows for property exchange, business opportunities, holding escrows, and syndicated investment properties.

Just remember that you always have a choice about the individual you will use as your escrow officer. Regardless of which type of escrow operation you choose, I suggest that you discover who is the best individual officer in your local area, and make sure she is on your team.

Where title insurance fits in

A title company is one of the necessary affiliates you will work with when you sell your property. Even if you do not use an escrow officer in their escrow division, you still benefit by selecting the right title company. To begin with, let's start with why you need a title company in the first place.

Title insurance is issued by an insurance company to cover a loss your buyer may suffer from an unknown defect on the title to your property.

According to Wikipedia.com:

- "It is meant to protect an owner's or lender's financial interest in property against loss due to title defects, liens, or other matters of public record. It will defend against a lawsuit attacking the title, or reimburse the insured for the actual monetary loss incurred, up to the dollar amount of insurance provided by the policy."[1]

An important distinction is that even though they won't fix things that may be wrong with your title, they will pay off any money losses.

How often are there problems with title? The good news is that there is seldom a problem since most title issues are found and rectified prior to close of escrow once the title company gets involved. According to an article by Beth Bresnahan, published by RISMedia.com, a member survey of the American Land Title Association reported that in 2005, initial title problems were up to 36% of all residential transactions.[2] This percentage has increased from 25% in 2000 and is probably due to the booming real estate market in 2004 and 2005. The article went on to say that most of these title irregularities were related to faulty releases or payoffs on previous loans. In other words, because there were so many properties being bought and sold during 2005 and 2006, the number of clouds on title was higher than normal.

In some ways, a title policy is similar to any other company you hire to disclose different aspects of your property to your new buyer. Just as a home inspector alerts the buyer to the condition of the physical property, the title policy process alerts the buyer to the condition of your title.

The first step is to order a preliminary title report. This is routinely handled by your escrow officer and need not be addressed before opening escrow. It is good to remember that the preliminary report is not an actual policy but only an offer to provide the policy; therefore, the preliminary policy can never be relied on for any losses should any losses occur. Unless a policy is paid for and issued, never consider insurance to be in effect.

This is how it works. A preliminary title policy is issued and lists as exceptions the existing conditions of title to the property as disclosed by the common public record. These exceptions include property taxes, as well as any assessments, bonds, loans, and judgments. It also lists covenants, conditions, and restrictions (CC&Rs), easements, and rights of way reflected by the public record. All items listed will pass with the ownership of the property unless the buyer has not agreed to accept them in the purchase agreement and escrow instructions. In that case, the seller will be required to remove or rectify them before escrow can close and the actual title insurance policy is issued.

Of course, just like with any insurance, there are a number of things that are excluded from coverage. Standard title policy exclusions are:

- zoning laws or ordinances affecting the use of the property;
- unrecorded claims known to the buyer but not known by the title company;
- events which occur after closing, and any adverse claims created after the date of the policy;
- claims coming from bankruptcy; and
- police power or eminent domain.

Perhaps the largest exclusion to remember is that title insurance does not cover the physical condition of the land and the improvements on the property. That is because physical conditions are considered to be highly observable, so the buyer is assumed to have agreed to buy the property with any physical conditions present. Examples of physical conditions include highways, canals, and electric poles running through the property, as well as buildings.

So what does title insurance cover? Remember, the primary purpose of title insurance is to assure buyers that their ownership interest in title to a property is marketable and what they anticipated. As stated above, their insurance is actually an indemnification against loss. Common losses could be caused by any of the following:

- claims made against title by others;
- the title being unmarketable for sale or financing;
- having encumbrances not previously known or listed;
- a lack of recorded access to and from the described property;
- forgery and impersonation by someone signing a deed or other document;
- lack of competency, capacity, or legal authority of a party who signed;
- a deed not joined in by a necessary party (co-owner, heir, spouse, corporate officer, or business partner);
- an erroneous or inadequate legal description;
- a deed not properly recorded;
- errors or omissions in the deeds;
- mistakes in examining records;
- undisclosed heirs or missing heirs;
- liens for unpaid taxes; and
- liens by contractors.

Occasionally, the preliminary policy will list conditions that affect title that neither you nor the buyer were aware of. These unexpected issues will usually show up as an exception on your preliminary policy. That means you must rectify or remove the issue before the sale is complete because the title policy cannot be issued with that exception according to your purchase agreement or escrow instructions. These conditions are called "clouds on title." Should a cloud appear on the preliminary report, your escrow officer and title insurance representative should be able to tell you what needs to be done to cure the problem. Most of the time the problem is minor and escrow should be able to cure it without delaying the closing of your property.

Note: When an escrow officer or real estate agent calls and requests a preliminary title report, there is seldom a charge. That is because the title company knows that even if that particular transaction does not go through, the officer or agent will continue to bring in business. Just be aware as a FSBO that the title company may ask you for a deposit if you request the preliminary policy yourself since, if your property doesn't sell or close, they might not be assured a fee for the work involved in preparing the preliminary report.

The three types of title insurance—which type do you need?

There are actually a number of title insurance policies, but you only need to concern yourself with the three major ones. The first and most common policy is called a California Land Title Association (CLTA) policy, which is a basic title policy. Then, beginning in 1998, title companies operating in California adopted a new "standard" policy, called the American Land Title Association (ALTA) Homeowner's policy that offers the buyer expanded coverage.[3] This expanded coverage primarily deals with tract homes in subdivisions. The third major type of coverage in California is the ALTA Lender's policy, which every lender requires to protect their interest before they will originate a loan.

I do not believe it is necessary to explain all the subtleties of coverage offered by various other policies. Unless you have any reason to believe that there might be a problem with the quality of your deed or title, I recommend that you get what is standard in your area. What is commonly used as standard by the California Department of Real Estate (DRE) is the CLTA/ALTA Homeowner's policy as a default policy, unless you select a different kind. This is also used in the purchase agreement included in the accompanying CD. (See Form 157 §12.4)

If you have any specific questions about what is actually covered, I would suggest that you call your local title company representative. They will be able to tell you what each type of insurance offered specifically covers. Then, if either you or the buyer wants more coverage than what is customary in your area, either you or the buyer can agree to pay the additional premium required.

How much does title insurance cost and who pays for what?

Who pays for the title insurance in your sale will be subject to what is commonly called "county custom." In other words, it depends upon what county you live in as to who pays for what. From one county to the next, it may be traditional and customary for the buyer to pay for title insurance. In the next county over, it might be that the seller always pays. In order for you to know in advance, it is best if you call one of your local escrow officers. A good question to ask would be, "I am thinking about selling my house so could you please tell me what are the customary costs that a seller pays in our area?" Have them also tell you what the customary costs for a buyer are in your county. Worksheets for analyzing these costs for both sellers and buyers are included in the accompanying Forms CD. (See Forms 337 and 311)

Of course, just because it is customary doesn't mean you have to pay for something. It may be possible to negotiate a different arrangement with a buyer. But remember, if you make uncustomary financial demands on your buyer that other sellers would not normally make, he may choose to purchase another house. I usually go with what is customary when it comes to selling my own home, knowing that what I pay for on a sale will normally be equalized when I buy my next house and the seller pays the fee for me.

How much does a title policy cost? The price is normally based upon a percentage of the sales price and is fairly consistent amongst all title companies. The quickest way to find out is to go to the California Department of Insurance web site at: interactive.web.insurance.ca.gov/webuser/titw_get_rates$.startup, and do a search. By inputting your asking price and the county you live in, it will list current pricing. As an example, the ALTA/CLTA Homeowner's policy for a $400,000 home will cost approximately $1,500 to $1,700, a $500,000 home will cost approximately $1600 to $1900, and the cost for a $600,000 home will cost approximately $1,900 to $2,100.

However, I still recommend that you call several of your local title companies just to get a feel for how the company responds to you. By calling, you will get their current rate structure for the price of their policies, as well as gain knowledge about their customer service.

How can your title representative help?

No matter where you live in the state of California, title insurance is an integral part of your real estate sales transaction. As long as the organization is supported by the real estate industry, you may as well take advantage of all of the services they provide. I mentioned in the chapter on pricing that you can call your local title company for a list of comparable properties to help you come up with a good asking price for your property. That is just one of the services they routinely provide. Just don't stop there.

Title insurance companies regularly provide real estate agents with all sorts of business enhancement items. What you will want to do is tell your local title representative that you are going to be selling your house. Then ask them what services they can provide to help you. One thing they should definitely be able to provide you with is names and address of all of the neighbors in your local area. This would be very useful if you wanted to send out a flyer.

A good title representative will offer to help you by answering your specific questions about the title process. If you take the time in advance to establish a relationship with a title company, don't be shy about calling them up if an aspect of the process that you didn't expect occurs during marketing or escrow. Even if they don't have an exact answer, they should be able to offer a referral. Consider the title company a partner in the successful sale of your home.

Appraisers, inspectors, and other partners

If you decide to have an appraisal done on your property before you sell it, then consider the appraiser that you select as part of your team. Be sure and accompany the appraiser while he inspects your house, and ask questions if you are unsure of some of his areas of interest.

One thing you can do to help insure that the appraiser's value of your home will come in close to what you expect is to provide the appraiser with any comparable properties you may have located. As I mentioned earlier in the pricing chapter, an appraiser uses the same comparables as everyone else, but that doesn't mean he is always completely up-to-date.

If the appraisal doesn't come in at the amount you expect, ask why. Again, it is possible that the appraiser missed one of the recent comparables or one of the unique and valuable distinctions that your property contains. Or, if the appraiser knows of features that affect the value of your property either positively or negatively, you will want to know about them. It is rare for an appraiser to change the appraisal amount once arrived at, but at least you will understand how they came to their opinion of value.

Your future buyer will normally pay to get an appraisal in order to get a new loan. It is unlikely that the buyer will be able to use any appraisal that you previously acquired because most lenders only accept appraisals from select appraisers that they work with frequently. I recommend that you follow the same procedure with the lender's appraiser by accompanying them, providing them with comparables, and pointing out special features your property may contain. Even if the appraisal is for the benefit of the buyer, it is in your best interest to have the appraisal be at the highest price possible. After all, the buyer's loan depends on it.

You will also want to follow your home inspector through your house. If you have any concerns, be sure and point them out. After all, if you are going to be using his report to fully inform the buyer of any conditions, irregularities, or defects, why not make certain you understand his perspective when making his report.

Treat all of your inspectors the same. They are partners in your transaction and are usually a fount of information if you take the time to make inquiries. Ask them about the market. Ask them about any issues you think might relate to your property. Ask them about title companies and escrow companies that they have worked with in the past.

I also recommend that you enlist the help of all your local real estate agents as well. Most of them are friendly and helpful people and can assist you in unexpected ways down the road. If you run into any that are less than considerate or pushy, then just use that information for future reference. Don't take any of their rejections personally. Just know that there are plenty out there who realize their reputation is too valuable to ever be rude. Besides, they just might have that buyer who will end up buying your home.

In some ways, selling your home yourself is like setting up a temporary small business. Not only can you use the services of everyone you come in contact with, but they might also know of someone who might buy your home. Stay open to input and never be afraid to ask questions!

CHAPTER TEN
Negotiating and receiving offers

At this point, it may seem a bit premature to talk about what to do when you get an offer on your property, but I want you to be prepared to handle it. After all, your goal is to sell your property, and things really get going when you receive an offer.

Before we get into the details of marketing your property, I want you to understand and anticipate some of the issues that you will face once the offers do arrive. By readying yourself in advance for some of the possibilities, you will be more confident and better prepared to concentrate on negotiations.

Purchase offers from buyers without a broker

Once you place a "For Sale" sign in your yard and begin marketing your house, that should eventually lead to locating a prospective buyer. If that buyer comes to you without a real estate agent, then I suggest that you and the buyer work together to prepare a purchase agreement to be signed. (See Form 157)

Except in rare cases, most Buyers Without Brokers (BWOBs) will not have a blank purchase agreement form at their disposal to write you an offer. In that case, I suggest that you make the buyer a copy of Form 157, and if agreeable, go through the contract together, section by section, to help the buyer understand the details of each section. Of course, if he is interested, you could even give him a copy of this book where it explains the different aspects of the purchase agreement.

Actually, you could sit down with the buyer and fill out the offer together. This is not often done, but there is no reason not to do it. As long as you are close enough in agreement on the price before you begin, it should be a natural and comfortable experience. There is absolutely no reason why selling a home needs to be an adversarial experience.

Homesellers and buyers are often portrayed as having opposing views. But when you think about it, they actually have much in common. One wants to sell and the other wants to buy. They both want to feel they either sold at a good price, or bought at a good price. They believe that the property has good value—certainly the homeseller, as one who has enjoyed the home in the past. And the homebuyer hopes to enjoy the home in the future. With so much in common, they should have an easy time working out the details—right?

Unfortunately, when agents get involved, there is often an atmosphere of conflict. Because agents serve as a go-between, that in itself can create misunderstandings and miscommunications. Even without intending to, some agents can create a climate of distrust between buyers and sellers. Let's face it, sometimes the more people you get involved, the more egos there are to be appeased.

The best real estate agents know that and can usually stay out of the way. But I have witnessed numerous times when the agents made everything much harder than it needed to be by asserting their personal opinions instead of working for the best interests of their client. You as a For Sale By Owner (FSBO) have a great advantage because you know exactly what you want to do. No agent is in the middle of your negotiations trying to determine what that might be—nor is there any agent standing in the way of you asking your prospective buyer any question you might want to ask. Not only will limiting the number of people involved save time, it will likely make negotiations easier if you understand the process.

With that in mind, if a buyer comes to you and is interested in your home, then I recommend that you be completely open and honest with him or her. Remember, it is highly advisable that you hand over all your disclosures to anyone who shows definite interest in your property. You want any prospective buyer to know what they may be buying before they make you an offer. In that same regard, everything you communicate to them should be done with an open and helpful attitude.

Right upfront, ask them if they will be working with a real estate agent. If they say yes, then explain that you do not want to pay a real estate commission, but that you are open to all offers. Keep in mind, just because you don't want to pay a commission doesn't mean that you would never pay one—only that their offer must be sufficiently attractive for you to do so. In the following section, we will discuss strategies you can use if they bring in a real estate agent.

If your prospective buyer tells you that they don't have a real estate agent, explain to them that you have done your homework and brought together a team of experts so they have nothing to worry about. Again, offer to share this book with them if they are interested, or suggest that before they sign the purchase agreement they can always run it by an attorney or other advisors to confirm their interests are protected. Naturally, you want them to be comfortable working directly with you, but avoid attempting to pressure them into signing if they appear reluctant.

As a matter of fact, if you do sit down together to work out the details of the purchase agreement, I suggest that you not sign it then and there. If you are both allowed to review the purchase agreement to be certain it contains what you have discussed between yourselves, then you will be much more confident when the actual time arrives.

Don't be afraid of the truth

When you first begin sharing disclosures with your prospective buyers, it may make you a bit nervous. After all, you might suspect that if they see what is wrong with your property, they might not buy it. True. However, in my experience, if people like a home, they realize that every property has both positives and negatives. Then, as long as the property has more positives then negatives, the house has appeal and will sell.

The funny thing about negatives and positives—they look different to different people. Things that you or I might think are huge and detrimental don't matter to others. Things that you adore and think are just amazing—will stop others cold. Because everyone is different, they will find different things appealing. The right buyer for your house will be able to overlook things others perceive as "negative" and be happy with your property. Someone who is obsessed with the negative aspects of your home will never be happy there—so don't attempt to sell them on it!

In every property I have sold myself I have attempted to tell the buyer more than they ever wanted to know. Of course, many lookers pretend to be interested, but it was the ones who really appeared to want the house that eventually bought it. In the end, never trap someone into buying your house. Believe me, even if you can, you don't want to. Someone who considers himself deceived is just a lawsuit waiting to happen.

As long as you disclose the facts about your property that affect its value and do so to your best ability, eventually you will locate a buyer who will see the advantages in owning your home. Then, even when they are aware of its shortcomings, the benefits they see will tip the scale. Once you find that someone, half of all the negotiations have been completed.

Filling out the purchase offer

To begin with, print out a couple of copies of the purchase agreement, Form 157, and then sit down and go through every provision one by one. If you like, use Chapter Six in this book and go through it carefully. I am pleased to say that the purchase agreement provided with this book is one of the least complicated and easy-to-understand contracts available. Use a pencil if you want and don't be afraid to change your entries to get a feel for the differences any particular change makes.

If you come to something that doesn't apply, just write a "n/a" in the blank, meaning "not applicable," or leave it blank. Then, once you have filled out your rough draft, take a blank copy, use a pen, and fill out another copy.

If the buyer needs time to review the agreement with advisors, let him. As I mentioned above, if others are going to dissuade him, then it is best to know about it right away. What if he says he wants to run the contract by a real estate agent or broker? No problem. Just explain that you have agreed in concept with him on a price without a broker. If he wants to bring one in now, and that agent expects you to pay him, then you will need to charge more for the property. When faced with paying more for your property, most will avoid bringing in an agent at the last minute.

Of course, before you begin to fill out the form with the buyer, you will have given him all of the disclosure forms and reports you have. If you haven't already handed them over, make sure that you do when your buyer takes the contract home to review. Remember, you want the buyer to make his offer at a price based upon every little thing you have disclosed. If you don't let him know in advance, he can back out of the transaction later, require you to fix the details you knew about, or ask you to reduce your price even more, so be sure and hand over those disclosures before you sign the agreement, and then have the buyer sign the disclosure forms acknowledging his receipt of the documents.

Once you are both in agreement and the buyer has reviewed the contract with anyone he is comfortable with, you can both sit down and sign it.

What about the good-faith deposit?

A valid purchase agreement does not need or require a good-faith deposit. Many real estate agents believe otherwise and will suggest that it is a legal requirement. They are wrong. Oftentimes, a real estate agent will also imply that the good-faith deposit is yours to keep if the buyer backs out. That is also wrong. Actually, a good-faith deposit is just that—a deposit made by the buyer to demonstrate his offer is made in good faith.(See Form 157 §1)

In certain purchase agreement forms used by real estate agents, the good-faith deposit is sometimes referred to as "liquidated damages." Labeled in this way, the contracts, and often agents themselves, imply that the buyer will award you, as a seller, with the deposit as liquidated damages upon default. However, the law is very clear about the fact that the only money that you can ever legally retain is money that you have verifiably lost due to the breach of the buyer.

What that means is that if a buyer backs out of a transaction, the only portion of the deposit you can legally claim is the amount necessary to reimburse you for any actual money losses that you can prove. Liquidated damages are only recoverable if they are genuine money losses. Liquidated damages, as referred to in more complicated real estate contracts, is merely a ceiling limiting the amount of money you can recover as a seller should the buyer default. (See Form 157 §10.6)

So why collect a good-faith deposit in the first place? The truth is you don't have to. Still, I recommend collecting the amount and turning it over to the escrow officer immediately on acceptance of the buyer's offer to be applied to the down payment at closing. I know that you can't keep it except for the amount of your recoverable

---

Note: Sometimes, an escrow company will require that a deposit be made when escrow is opened, even if the contract does not call for it. This is because the escrow company wants to ensure, should the escrow later be cancelled, that money is available to pay any fees or charges that may have occurred.

losses, but it still represents a commitment on the part of the buyer to pay it in the first place. Should a buyer not have the resources at his disposal to include a deposit with his purchase agreement, I would be suspicious that he may be unable to come up with the remainder of the down payment as well.

The decision is actually yours. If you would feel more comfortable with a deposit, an amount of 1-3% is completely acceptable. Just don't make the mistake of thinking that the money is yours until the transaction closes. That deposit belongs to the buyer until you can prove you actually lost money if he backs out.

Actually, both the seller and buyer have the right to collect their money losses should the other party default. If either one of you pulls out at the last minute, the other person has legal remedies. In certain circumstances, you may choose to go down that road. Just remember, most of the time it will require a court case to recover money and that will likely cost more than you will ever collect.

Purchase offers from a buyer with a broker

It is very likely that once you begin marketing your home, you will receive an offer from a buyer through a real estate agent. Both the National Association of Realtors (NAR) and the California Association of Realtors (CAR) have published surveys that report that close to 90% of all homebuyers use the services of a real estate agent during the buying process. Traditionally, buyers have found it very easy to work with a real estate agent who is paid by a homeseller. Who can blame them? It is usually free and carries a number of benefits.

If you do receive an offer from a buyer who has an agent, the offer will probably be written out on a purchase agreement form published by CAR. This contract is many pages long and much more complicated than the comparable one included as Form 150 in the Forms CD accompanying this book.

Your best bet is to insist on using the *first tuesday* form you have become accustomed to and to tell the real estate agent that you will re-write the terms and conditions of the CAR purchase agreement on Form 150. Of course, the agent will then tell you that you are rejecting the buyer's offer when you do so, which is true. If you do not sign their original offer on their form, then the offer is rejected. If you re-write your offer on your form, then you are effectively countering the buyer's offer, even if all your terms and conditions are exactly the same.

The real estate agent will not want you to do this. Agents are very familiar with their forms and believe it is filled with language that protects them as agents. If you insist on using your form, they will have to read it and re-digest all of the information anew. This puts you in the unusual position of having read and understood what a purchase agreement says and gives you an advantage. By requesting this change, there is a chance that the agent will become so distressed with your taking control that it could get in the way of doing the transaction. However, if the buyer really likes your home, the agent will probably agree to re-write the form since it is in his client's best interest.

Another reason agents want to avoid using your form is that it clearly spells out the amount of commission the agent will be paid for all to see, unlike their usual form where the commission agreement is usually unnoticed by the buyer. It is highly likely that in the original purchase offer made through a real estate agent, you will be expected to pay a commission even though the agent is representing the buyer. (See Form 150 §14)

Do you have to pay a commission?

No. You never have to pay a commission to sell your house. You are only obligated to pay a commission if you sign a listing agreement with a broker beforehand or if you sign a purchase contract agreeing to it. Should you? That is completely up to you. If you do sell to a buyer who brought an agent into the negotiations and you do not want to pay a commission, be certain that the buyer agrees to pay any claim his agent might later make in an attempt to collect a fee.

Personally, if an agent brought me a buyer and a valid purchase agreement and asked me to pay a commission of 5-6%, I would say, "absolutely not!" However, if I had been marketing my property for several months, and this was the first solid offer I received, I would probably be open to consider an alternative and say, "well, maybe." You might be the same.

Remember when I explained how real estate works back in the first section of this book? When a broker lists a property, they typically do it for 5-6% of the sales price. But most of the time, a broker will only receive half of that amount, because he has agreed to split it with another broker who locates a buyer. In other words, the broker with the buyer would get half, and the listing agent would get the other half.

Because you are selling your home yourself, there is no listing broker. Therefore, you should automatically save 2.5-3% of any commission amount. The only amount that any broker with a buyer should be entitled to would be 2.5-3% as the buyer's agent. And then, you only have to pay it if you agree; otherwise, the buyer will pay it as a separate, additional cost of purchasing your property. Of course, the agent is going to assume that you don't know how the commission thing works. The agent may also attempt to convince you that you owe the entire commission amount (6%), and may have even written it into the separate commission agreement they want you to sign. If the offer is prepared on the agent's purchase agreement form, be very cautious and study it privately before signing.

If you are interested in accepting this offer because it is a good price and you do not have other serious prospects on the horizon, you can either re-write the purchase offer on Form 150 or tell the agent that you want to counter the buyer's offer. Not only will you want to counter any terms in the offer that are not acceptable, you will also clarify in the purchase agreement any commission amount and who will pay it.

Avoid getting greedy. If the offer price is a reasonable amount, decide whether a lower commission will still net you a good profit. Most of the time, the agent will know that he is only realistically entitled to half of a standard commission and will simply accept half. If you attempt to go much lower, then know that you must negotiate that with the agent directly or through the buyer. Just keep in mind that an unhappy agent in the middle of your sale, who has failed to control their fee, can sometimes reap havoc on the transaction.

It may sound simple to negotiate the commission with the agent, but always be aware that the agent could influence the buyer away from your property if you don't arrive at a fee arrangement acceptable to the agent. When the buyer has expressed interest in other homes in the area in which those homesellers have agreed to pay a more traditional fee amount, the agent may feel justified in swaying the buyer to those houses just to obtain a larger fee.

Another tactic is to re-write the offer and counter by raising the price enough to cover the commission. Then explain to the broker that it will be up to her to sell the buyer on paying the higher price. Then again, avoid getting greedy. No one is going to pay more for a house than they think it is worth to them, including you.

One way to keep all of these negotiations in mind is to understand that every time you reject an offer—in this case with a small commission to be paid—you are effectively buying your house back from yourself. Are you so attached to your home that you want to own it for the difference you want them to pay? Maybe yes. Maybe no.

What you decide to accept and what you decide to refuse will, in the end, likely depend upon your individual circumstances. If you need to move right away, strongly consider every offer and try to find a compromise. If you have all the time in the world and are very happy living where you live, then you can afford to be picky. Just remember that there is no absolute set price for any home. The market value of a home on any given day is what a willing and able seller will sell for and what a willing and able buyer will pay given time to compare available inventory.

Handling the commission in a new way—make it a single agency agreement

In rare cases, the real estate agent is paid directly by the buyer as a cost on top of the purchase price of the property they want to buy. Called single agency, this type of agreement has been around for some time but is only used occasionally by a handful of agents who specialize in the practice. In some ways, a single agency agent (SAA) can be very advantageous, but until knowledge about it grows, it remains an anomaly. (See Form 151 §10)

One of the best advantages with an SAA is that it is obvious who is working for whom. When a broker represents a buyer exclusively, then he can make offers for that buyer with the complete intention of serving that buyer. In an SAA real estate sale, when a buyer pays his agent's fee, the buyer automatically reduces that amount from the purchase price paid to the seller. Then, at closing, the buyer's agent receives his fee from the buyer, not the seller.

If a broker comes to you with a buyer, you might ask him to look to his buyer to pay the commission. This fee arrangement is always an option for you, although you should realistically know that many buyer's agents are very uncomfortable asking their clients to pay their fee. Most agents are traditionally tied to the standard practice of asking the seller to pay the commission without actually disclosing the fee to the buyer. As mentioned before, they might even discourage the buyer from pursuing the purchase of your home any further rather than face the discomfort of asking the buyer to pay them directly.

Again, you are never forced to pay a commission, but every time you reject an offer, you are effectively buying your home back for just over whatever amount the buyer offered. Remember, in a Seller's Market, you will have the advantage. In a Buyer's Market, each buyer interested in your property becomes much more of an asset. In most cases, if you believe a buyer's offer has any value, work to arrive at a compromise.

What differs when a real estate agent is involved?

If you do come to an agreement with a buyer who is working with a real estate agent, then it is important for you to be aware of a number of other things. If the agent is competent, that agent will work with you to help the transaction go more smoothly. An agent can also help explain things to the buyer that you might find difficult or unfamiliar—and the agent will likely be a source of recommendation for a number of services you may need before closing.

However, if you accept an offer on their purchase agreement form or use the form included on the CD with this book, pay attention to which companies are selected for services. Real estate agents tend to use services that they are familiar with because it is easier for them—not you. If you have gone to all of the time and trouble to find an escrow officer, title company, and other inspectors, realize that you are fully justified in insisting on using your prearranged team. Don't lose control of your sale to individuals who you do not know. Unless an agent can give you a very strong reason why you should use their recommendations, stay with your own.

You will also want to be sure that the escrow officer selected is with either an independent escrow company or a substantial title company. Some brokers set up an in-house, co-owned escrow company and require their agents to use that service since they profit from the fees they receive. Remember how I mentioned that escrow is supposed to be a neutral third party? I believe it is very difficult for a broker-owned escrow to fulfill the "neutral" part of the deal when one of the broker's own agents is working on behalf of the buyer. There are simply too many chances for their conflict of interest to work against you. I personally recommend that you avoid any broker-owned escrow companies unless they are also licensed by the Department of Corporations (DOC).

Just because there is an agent involved, do not assume that they will take care of what details need to be done. Because you are a FSBO and have this book and education behind you, follow up and proceed as though you still needed to monitor the progress of your transaction. The best thing to do in this area is to make sure that your escrow officer is of the highest caliber and will take the time needed to talk to you. Once you've signed the purchase agreement with your buyer, your escrow officer is the one person that will have the most impact on your closing. So, choose wisely!

Comfortably anticipating your first offer

It is my hope that after reading this chapter you will be prepared to receive and even accept the first reasonable offer that comes from a real estate agent. Chances are very high that your buyer will be using one. Remember, if nine out of ten buyers use a real estate agent, then you want access to those prospects.

Naturally, your first priority as a FSBO is to save money when selling your house. But even if a broker does bring you a buyer and you end up paying a fee, you are still substantially ahead in savings if you follow the advice in this book. In addition, if the agent brings a ready, willing, and able buyer who wants your house, the agent ends up being your partner in selling your house. They too want to sell your home if it is suitable to one of their buyers. Just remember, you can negotiate to alter anything they ask for as long as you are secure in knowing the consequences of your demands.

Remember, around 10% of buyers will not be working with a broker. If you find a buyer without an agent, you have all the forms and knowledge you need to prepare a purchase agreement and open escrow. When it comes to negotiating, the best approach is always straightforward honesty. As long as both you and the buyer are willing to work together to achieve your mutual goals, you should succeed.

CHAPTER ELEVEN
Counteroffers, contingencies, and other contract issues

A number of other concerns routinely arise during a real estate sale, but nothing that you can't handle when properly informed. In fact, once you have read through and considered each of these issues, you can always return at a later time and use this and the last couple of chapters as a reference.

Counteroffers

As explained earlier, when you receive an offer from a buyer that contains many items you agree with, but others you want to change, you should prepare a counteroffer on a form specifically for that purpose. (See Form 180) Just remember that whenever you change the terms of the original purchase offer in any way, you are rejecting it by having made a counteroffer to the buyer's offer. Essentially, a counteroffer is similar to making a brand new offer even though it contains all of the terms made by the buyer in his original offer, with your modifications of course.

There are a couple of benefits to using a counteroffer form. The major benefit is that it gives you the opportunity to make all of your disclosures upfront before you sign a final contract. If you have not handed the buyer every disclosure necessary to fully inform the buyer about the property prior to receiving his offer as I recommended earlier, you can counter the offer and include as attachments any remaining documents you have not yet delivered. Then the buyer will be able to review them prior to signing his acceptance of your counteroffer.

Otherwise, if your buyer did not receive all of the necessary disclosures before signing, he will have three days (sometimes more) to review those documents and cancel the transaction to avoid being locked into your contract. You may as well get that taken care upfront, or you will face the possibility of having to renegotiate the purchase price or lose the deal completely should your buyer decide to exercise his three-day period for cancellation.

The other benefit to using a counteroffer form is for you to clarify any terms or uncertainties that the original purchase offer might include. One major uncertainty could be the buyer's ability to close. This might be reflected in how realistic the buyer's terms for obtaining a new loan are spelled out in the purchase agreement offer. The buyer's readiness to produce a pre-approval letter from a lender towards obtaining a new loan also indicates his ability to move forward. Finally, using a counteroffer allows you as a seller to limit the effects any contingencies requested by the buyer may bring to the transaction.

Using a counteroffer is also considered to be more appropriate than the act of crossing out or deleting words on the original purchase agreement. Crossing out or deleting should be avoided even when done with the buyer's initialing to indicate his approval because it causes confusion and misunderstandings. If you want to change something on the purchase agreement, use a counteroffer and keep things clear.

Also, remember that if you start over by preparing another purchase agreement to include the terms you will agree to, you are effectively counteroffering and rejecting the offer originally made to you. If there are a large number of things you want to change or add before you will accept this buyer as your purchaser, it might be easiest to start fresh by preparing another purchase agreement.

The process of counteroffering can go on indefinitely. The buyer can counter your counteroffer, and then you can begin all over again, until you both grow tired. I would recommend that if the buyer does counter your counteroffer, you start fresh with another purchase agreement form to clarify those issues you have been able to agree on up to that point. Starting over will be simpler and easier for you all to follow once you arrive at escrow.

> **Note:** Even if your original offer is on a different form presented through a real estate agent, you can always use the counteroffer, Form 180, on the accompanying CD to counter the offer.

Closing costs

The net cash you receive from your sale is called proceeds. Although your reasons for selling your home are varied, getting your hands on those proceeds is surely a big part of them. Just remember, the market value of your home has nothing to do with how much you hope to generate in net proceeds. Instead, before you can even begin to imagine what your final net proceeds from the sale will be, you must start with a realistic sales price. After that, you should be able to estimate your costs prior to accepting an offer so you can see how the expenses of a sale will affect your bottom-line. Once you know your bottom-line, then you will be better prepared to negotiate when the time comes to work with a buyer.

Form 337 on the accompanying CD is a seller's net sheet. It was originally designed so that real estate brokers could help a seller figure out his anticipated net proceeds from the sale. It works for you as well by clearly listing the costs of just about every expense or fee that might be associated with selling your home. I suggest that you go through and attempt to fill out the form right away. Not only will it help inform you of all the many disclosures and reports you are responsible for, it will also remind you to call and get prices for all the other fees associated with a sale.

Because costs are different all over the state, it will be necessary for you to call one of the local title or escrow companies for help. Better yet, make an appointment and go into their office for a meeting. Explain that you are estimating how much you will net from a sale of your home. They can then tell you how much the typical fees are for the expenses listed on Form 337. You should also ask them if they know of any other charges or obligations not listed. Again, use this as an opportunity to talk to two or three escrow or title companies. This is another way for you to interview them to find out which is the most helpful among them.

When you know in advance the approximate amount of all the fees and expenses you will face when closing the sale of your home, it will help you with all of your negotiations. If you receive an offer that is less than your asking price, you'll know its affect on your bottom-line. Plus, if you receive an offer from a buyer asking you to pay a number of charges not normally paid by the seller, such as the lender's charge for the buyer's new loan, you will be able to determine how those costs will affect your bottom-line.

Taking backup offers, or the "backup contingency"

As you may recall from Chapter Six, a contingency is something that must be either waived or completed prior to transferring owner-

This is an estimate of the fix-up, marketing and transaction expenses Seller is likely to incur on a sale, and the likely amount of net sales proceeds Seller may anticipate receiving on the close of a sale.

This net sheet is prepared to assist the seller by providing an estimate of the amount of net sales proceeds the seller is likely to receive on closing, based on the price set, the estimated amount for expenses likely to be incurred to market the property and close a sale, and any adjustments and prorates necessitated by the sale.

Date _____, 20_____, property _____, prepared by_____.

1. SALES PRICE:
1.1   Price Received . . . . ADD: $_____

2. ENCUMBRANCES:
2.1   First Trust Deed Note . . . . $_____

2.2   Second Trust Deed Note . . . . $_____

2.3   Other Liens/Bonds/UCC-1 . . . . $_____

2.4   TOTAL ENCUMBRANCES: . . . . DEDUCT: $_____

3. SALES EXPENSES AND CHARGES:
3.1   Fix-up Cost . . . . $_____

3.2   Structural Pest Control Report . . . . $_____

3.3   Structural Pest Control Clearance . . . . $_____

3.4   Property/Home Inspection Report. . . . . $_____

3.5   Elimination of Property Defects. . . . . $_____

3.6   Local Ordinance Compliance Report. . . . . $_____

3.7   Compliance with Local Ordinances. . . . . $_____

3.8   Natural Hazard Disclosure Report . . . . $_____

3.9   Smoke Detector/Water Heater Safety Compliance . . . . $_____

3.10 Owners' Association Document Charge . . . . $_____

3.11 Mello-Roos Assessment Statement Charge . . . . $_____

3.12 Well Water Reports . . . . $_____

3.13 Septic/Sewer Reports . . . . $_____

3.14 Lead-based Paint Report . . . . $_____

3.15 Marketing Budget. . . . . $_____

3.16 Home Warranty Insurance. $_____

3.17 Buyer's Escrow Closing Costs . . . . $_____

3.18 Loan Appraisal Fee . . . . $_____

3.19 Buyer's Loan Charges. . . . . $_____

3.20 Escrow Fee. . . . . $_____

3.21 Document Preparation Fee . . . . $_____

3.22 Notary Fees . . . . $_____

3.23 Recording Fees/Documentary Transfer Tax . . . . $_____

3.24 Title Insurance Premium. . . . . $_____

3.25 Beneficiary Statement/Demand . . . . $_____

3.26 Prepayment Penalty (first). $_____

3.27 Prepayment Penalty (second). . . . . $_____

3.28 Reconveyance Fees . . . . $_____

3.29 Real Estate Fees . . . . $_____

3.30 Transaction Coordinator Fee . . . . $_____

3.31 Attorney/Accountant Fees . . . . $_____

3.32	Misc. Expense _____ . . . $_____	
3.33	Misc. Expense _____ . . . $_____	
3.34	TOTAL EXPENSES AND CHARGES . . . . DEDUCT: $_____	

4. ESTIMATED NET EQUITY: . . . . SUBTOTAL: $_____

5. PRORATES DUE BUYER:
5.1	Unpaid Taxes/Assessments . . . . $_____
5.2	Interest Accrued and Unpaid . . . . $_____
5.3	Unearned Rental Income . . . . $_____
5.4	Tenant Security Deposits . . . . $_____
5.5	TOTAL PRORATES DUE BUYER . . . . DEDUCT: $_____

6. PRORATES DUE SELLER:
6.1	Prepaid Taxes/Assessments . . . . $_____
6.2	Impound Account Balances . . . . $_____
6.3	Prepaid Association Assessment . . . . $_____
6.4	Prepaid Ground Lease . . . . $_____
6.5	Unpaid Rent Assigned to Buyer . . . . $_____
6.6	Miscellaneous _____ . . . $_____
6.7	TOTAL PRORATES DUE SELLER . . . . ADD: $_____

7. ESTIMATED PROCEEDS OF SALE: . . . . $_____

7.1 The estimated net proceeds at Section 7 from the sale or exchange analyzed in this net sheet will be received in the form of:
a. Cash . . . . $_____
b. Note secured by a Trust Deed. . . . . $_____
c. Equity in Replacement Real Estate. . . . . $_____
d. Other_____ . . . . $_____

ship. Some contingencies are routine, such as the buyer qualifying and obtaining a new first loan on the property. If the buyer can't qualify or acceptable loans are not available, he may exercise his contingency and back out of the sale by canceling the purchase agreement and escrow instructions.

Sellers generally prefer there be no contingencies, but sometimes they are unavoidable. Much of the time, the standard contingencies in transactions, like one requesting a new loan or the buyer's approval of all reports, are met with little or no problem. A seller's willingness to include an unusual contingency in the purchase agreement is often tied to how slow the real estate market is locally, how few and far between the buyers, and how anxious the seller is to sell. In those cases, a seller is usually willing to take the risk of accepting conditions which create more uncertainty. (See Form 157 §10.2)

When I sold my last home, I accepted an offer from buyers who needed to sell their home before they could buy mine. Naturally, I would have preferred a buyer with all cash and no contingencies, but I had no other offers at the time and fewer prospects. These buyers liked my home and I liked them. I had already located and made an offer on another home, and that seller had agreed to let me sell mine first. So, even though a contingency made things more complicated and riskier, I accepted one from my buyers.

The good news is that even if you do accept an offer with contingencies which carry a risk that the transaction might be cancelled, there are a couple of things you can do to alleviate the potential loss. One thing you can do is accept backup offers. This is where you continue to market your home to find and encourage other buyers to make an offer after you have already received and signed an acceptable purchase agreement offer on your home. (See Form 276)

Unfortunately, backup buyers may not want to make a serious offer on your property if you already have a buyer that you are under contract with. Why? In reality, most backup buyers know that they will be unable to purchase your home, even if you do come to an agreement on the terms and conditions. Most of the time, the original buyers will complete the sale and the backup buyers will be left empty-handed and forced to continue to shop. In some cases, they too might have homes to sell before they can buy yours.

Still, there are ways for you to make it more enticing to backup buyers. One way to do that is to have a backup-offer clause included as an addendum to the purchase agreement with your first buyers. That clause will state that if you receive another offer to buy your property, your original buyers will be given notice that they have a certain amount of time, for example 48 hours or one week, to remove or waive their contingency, or cancel the transaction. If the first buyers don't waive the contingency or cancel, you may cancel the purchase agreement you have entered into with them. You are then free to close on the purchase agreement you have entered into with your backup buyers. (See Form 277 and 181)

Your first buyers may not want that clause as a part of your purchase agreement. However, if you insist that this is the only way you will put in a contingency that allows them to sell their home before buying yours, they may well consent. What a backup clause provides you with is the opportunity to shorten the time period your buyer has to waive their contingency or cancel. At the same time, it allows you to keep your home on the market during the time you wait for the buyer's home to sell. This way, you lose no marketing time locating a buyer who may be in an even better position to buy your home.

SALE OF OTHER PROPERTY WAIVER AGREEMENT
(Addendum to Purchase Agreement)

NOTE: This form, and its provision, is used as an addendum to a purchase agreement which contains a sale-of-other-property contingency provision which gives the buyer the right to cancel if property owned by the buyer doesn't sell prior to close of escrow.

DATE: _____, 20_____, at _____, California.
Items left blank or unchecked are not applicable.

FACTS:

1. This is an addendum to the following agreement:

☐ Purchase agreement   ☐ Escrow instructions

☐ Counteroffer   ☐ _____

☐ Exchange agreement

1.1 dated _____, 20_____, at_____, California,

1.2 entered into by _____, as the buyer, and

_____, as the seller,

1.3 regarding real estate referred to as _____

AGREEMENT:

2. In addition to the terms of the above referenced agreement, the undersigned agree to the following:

2.1 Seller is hereby granted the right to cancel the above agreement and terminate the transaction on expiration of _____ days after Buyer or his agent receives written notice from Seller that Seller has entered into a new purchase agreement to sell the property to another buyer.

a. Seller may not exercise this right if, prior to the expiration of the period following Buyer's or his agent's receipt of the written notice, Buyer, in writing, waives his right to cancel the above referenced transaction as granted Buyer by the contingency provision regarding the sale of other property in the above referenced agreement.

2.2 _____

_____

_____

I agree to the terms stated above.	I agree to the terms stated above.
Date:_____, 20_____	Date:_____, 20_____
Buyer's Name: _____	Seller's Name: _____
Signature: _____	Signature: _____
Buyer's Name: _____	Seller's Name: _____
Signature: _____	Signature: _____

FORM 277   10-07   ©2007 **first tuesday**, P.O. BOX 20069, RIVERSIDE, CA 92516 (800) 794-0494

In the case with the home I sold, no other buyers came along that were serious enough to make a backup offer. But by having that backup clause in my purchase agreement, I was assured that I would not lose any time marketing my property should the buyer's house fail to sell.

If you do enter into a purchase agreement with backup buyers, you would then go to your first buyers with a notice giving them the time agreed to remove their contingency and proceed with the purchase or cancel. If they do not remove the contingency and do not cancel, then you may cancel the purchase agreement and escrow instructions you entered into with your first buyers and open your next escrow with the backup buyers.

Other contingency safeguards

Most contingencies in real estate contracts are routine. Yet, every now and then a buyer will put something in the agreement that is unusual. Sometimes buyers will have a genuine demand that needs to be fulfilled before they will unconditionally commit to buying your house. That need, written as a contingency in your purchase agreement, could be something as simple as an inspection and approval from Great-Uncle Norman. Or, it could be as complicated as obtaining approval from the city to build a new garage. Whatever the contingency, there are things you can do to reduce the risk that they might cancel the transaction should you choose to accept their offer.

As mentioned before, placing a backup clause in the contract will allow you to continue to market your home and locate a backup buyer during the time you must wait to see if your buyer will remove the contingency or cancel escrow. If you use a clause calling for a 48-hour notice to waive or cancel, your first buyers must remove their contingency or cancel the contract within 48 hours of your giving them notice that you have entered into an agreement with a backup buyer. Such a backup clause, with its waive-or-cancel requirement, is your safety net should the further-approval of a report, zoning or condition not be given. (See Form 276)

Another safeguard you should use with any contingency is a time limit to waive it or cancel the purchase agreement. If your buyers want Great-Uncle Norman to inspect the property, put into the agreement that this must happen within a fixed period of time, say five days. Then, if Great-Uncle Norman doesn't like your house, you will lose only those days waiting. If they want something complicated like a zone change from the city, make sure that the time frame is both realistic in length and as short as possible.

Finally, if the buyers insist on a contingency that must be completed before they become obligated to close escrow, make sure that it is written clearly, identifying the activity or event to occur and the deadline to either waive the contingency or cancel the transaction. For example, in the case of Great-Uncle Norman, ask that his approval be put in writing and delivered to you on or before a specific date. In the case of a buyer requesting a contingency to build an addition on the house at an acceptable cost, require that the buyer give you a particular date by which they will have all acceptable bids in place so that they will either waive the contingency or cancel escrow once that date arrives.

Contingencies are common provisions in every purchase agreement. When they come up, be sure to clarify the activity or event behind the request. By placing dates for specific fulfillment requirements to be attained by the buyer as outlined within the purchase agreement, you ensure that the condition will either be waived or the purchase agreement cancelled to terminate the purchase rights of the first buyer and to clear the way to close escrow with the next buyer.

Contingency problems

Most buyers will have a genuine need to place a contingency or two into the purchase agreement. As I said before, just about every offer you will receive will contain a new loan contingency, or an appraisal contingency. Obviously, you can't make someone buy your house if they can't get a new loan. Other contingencies, like the buyer's approval of the preliminary title report, are normal steps in any transaction.

However, you will still want the activity to be clearly stated and the time frame set for approval or cancellation for even the most common contingencies. The greatest problems with contingencies happen when there is vague language relating to the issue or no fixed date for approval or cancellation. For example, if you don't request that the buyer provide you with loan approval documents by a particular date, you might not find out until a month or two later when escrow is scheduled to close that your buyers aren't even qualified for the loan.

Just keep in mind that you don't have an enforceable agreement (even though it is binding) until all of the contingencies have been approved or the time for cancellation has expired. That is why it is of primary importance that you work to eliminate or remove contingencies as quickly as possible. It is also very important that you make sure all of your disclosures are made before you sign the purchase agreement so that there is no way your buyer may use lack of proper disclosure as an excuse to back out of the sale.

If your buyer puts an unusual contingency in the contract, besides asking for specifics, I also advise you to ask the buyer directly why it is important. Don't be afraid to talk about these issues because from the time you open escrow until you close the sale of your property, both of you will be entangled financially and emotionally in the process. Some things that affect your buyers and their ability to buy your house will have a direct effect on you—and vice versa. By asking upfront why your buyer needs something to happen, you should be able to gauge their need as well as their sincerity. If either one seems suspect, you are better off looking for another prospective buyer as soon as possible.

Your right to include contingencies

You may also include contingencies for your benefit. For example, if you need extra time to repair a defect or remove a cloud on the title, it is perfectly acceptable for you to place a contingency in the purchase agreement giving you a specific amount of time to complete the activity or to cancel the sale if it can't be completed.

Contingencies are as varied as the people involved. If there is anything you need to check out or fulfill before you become obligated to complete the sale of your house, writing a contingency in your purchase agreement gives you the option to waive the contingency or cancel the sale if the condition is not met or does not occur. Just remember that every contingency, whether it is yours or your buyers', will be one more aspect of negotiations.

Possession—when do you move out and they move in?

Another area where you and your buyer must reach agreement is occupancy of the home before and after closing. Technically, the new buyer will own the property the day your grant deed transferring title is recorded by the county recorder. In spite of this, the personal situations of both you and your buyer regarding occupancy are often different and require some negotiation.

In most cases, the buyer will want to move in on the day that the deed will be recorded. If not then, the buyer may want to begin any remodeling or alterations they plan to do as soon as they own the property. However, unless you have already rented or purchased a replacement home to move into, you might have other needs.

In the past, the move-in and move-out date was often handled informally. Now, the safest avenue is for you and the buyer to come to an agreement regarding occupancy of the home upfront when you negotiate the purchase agreement. Occupancy decisions must be made for the period before and after the close of escrow. If you, as seller, are the one who wishes to remain after close of escrow, then you will want to use a holdover occupancy agreement.

A seller holdover occupancy agreement form is included on the accompanying Forms CD as Form 272. You will want to fill it out and make it a part of your purchase agreement right from the beginning. If you do not know exact dates, you can write in the blank a specific time that is most advantageous for you, for example, 48 hours, 72 hours, one week, etc. after the close of escrow. The contract calls for rent to be paid and an amount for any security deposit, but actual sums can be low or even waived. Again, every term within a transaction, including occupancy, is subject to negotiation and agreement between you and your buyer.

Something to consider is the benefit of your staying in the property past the close of escrow. When I sold my last house, I was a holdover tenant for two weeks following the close of escrow. I needed that time because the house I was moving into needed to close escrow—which took about a week longer than mine—and then I wanted to have the new house painted inside and out before moving in. It was to my advantage to remain in my previous house, so I paid an amount of rent that covered the buyer's daily ownership costs for the period after closing until I vacated the property.

Another reason why it might be worth it to you to pay to stay longer is that it is a safe bet to eliminate risks involved should the sale not close. Sometimes, a seller will move out on the day that escrow was supposed to close only to discover something came up that either delayed the closing or cancelled escrow altogether. If you aren't absolutely sure that the transaction will go through, you may not want to move out until escrow has received closing funds from the buyer and his lender. By planning to stay put for a few days after closing, you will be assured that escrow has proceeded as planned, your grant deed has been recorded, and your net sales proceeds received.

What if you have already moved out and the buyer wants to move in before escrow closes? Should you agree to the buyer's early occupancy and have arrived at an agreeable amount of rent to charge, you want to use an interim occupancy agreement, such as Form 271 in the accompanying CD. This form acknowledges that the buyer is a tenant and clarifies all the issues that need to be addressed from a landlord's perspective.

As mentioned above, everything is negotiable as far as rental and security deposit amounts go. The advantage to having a written agreement is that if anything unexpected happens to interfere with the scheduled close of escrow, you will have already agreed on a course of action regarding the buyer's occupancy. This form explains that the occupancy agreement will expire on the date that escrow is scheduled to close.

Canceling escrow

What happens if you or your buyer wants out of your agreement and escrow? The cancellation of a sale happens for a number of reasons, but let's assume it happens because the buyers had a contingency to sell their home within 30 days and have not been able to locate a buyer. Of course, they can ask you to extend the time period for cancellation under their contingency. But if the buyer just wants to cancel the agreement and escrow, what do you do?

Form 183 is a form for the cancellation of an agreement to be filled out and signed by both you and the former buyer. This form cancels your original purchase agreement as well as providing you with a cancellation of escrow instructions.

Because the escrow officer of your transaction works equally for you and your buyer, both of you will be required to sign escrow cancellation instructions. While Form 183 provides for the cancellation of escrow, your particular escrow company may also want their own form signed by the both of you as well. Once done, escrow will refund any deposit it holds less any expenses they may have paid on your or your buyer's behalf. The escrow company may also charge a fee to cancel, although this is usually waived if they are convinced you will use them again when you locate another buyer.

Most of the time, when escrow is cancelled due to an unfulfilled contingency, the buyer is entitled to a full refund of his deposit. If the buyer has defaulted on the agreement by breaching it in some way, you as the seller may be entitled to a portion of the deposit for your actual money losses. Just keep in mind that unless the buyer agrees, you may have to go to court to prove your money losses so an award can be made allowing you to collect them. Regardless of what might seem fair, anything that keeps you from canceling escrow as quickly as possible and moving forward with the marketing of your property hinders your goal of selling your property and moving on.

Home warranties

Home warranties are another form of insurance coverage available to homebuyers. This type of insurance covers the risk of repairs to many of the standard components and systems in a home. Most policies cover the first year of ownership and offer reassurance to the buyers against many unexpected repair costs. In the past, sellers have agreed to pay the premiums for these policies as another incentive for buyers, especially in older homes. (See Form 157 §11.1)

Fortunately, basic coverage includes things like hot water heaters, stoves, microwaves, plumbing and heating systems, and other items. Unfortunately, there are a number of other important elements that are only covered by additional endorsements and for an increased fee. Those add-ons are air-conditioning units, pool and spa motors, and refrigerators. Even worse are a number of small things that are not covered because they are considered to be outside the standard policy. Just be aware that even though home warranties provide buyers with a degree of comfort, they are not all inclusive.

The normal cost for a home warranty is usually around $500 for a policy that covers most of the important appliances and systems in a home for one year. On top of that, there is an approximate $50 service fee for every repair call made, which is paid by the buyer as the new owner of the house.

Should you decide to pay the premium for a home warranty policy, there are many available through the Internet. Many title insurance companies also offer a home warranty plan through a subsidiary company they control. I would shop around for prices and ask others for referrals before selecting one.

A home warranty is another negotiable point in a sales transaction. Should a buyer be particularly nervous about the age or condition of your property, you may want to mention you would be willing to include a policy as a benefit for the buyer in your sale. In some cases, if you find yourself negotiating with the buyer's real estate agent regarding fees, don't be shy about asking them to pay, or to help pay, for the home warranty.

Homeowners' associations, CIDs, or condominiums

Many property owners in California belong to a Homeowners' Association (HOA) that manages a Common Interest Development (CID) which includes the owner's property. HOAs are often in charge of the landscaping and the architectural review of a member-owner's improvements and activities. They are also frequently responsible for the repairs, replacement, and management of the structures, grounds, and property. Articles of association, bylaws, and other rules and regulations give them the authority to carry out their work. If your property is within a CID and subject to an HOA, then you should have received all the pertinent information about these rules when you purchased your home. Regardless, you must provide your buyer with reports of all of the HOA's or CID's governing forms, financial statements, and management policies. (See Form 157 §11.8)

If you live in a CID project where the HOA has little involvement, then most of it can be handled through your escrow officer. Escrow will order the information and make sure that it is delivered to the buyer. Once received, the buyer will have ten days to review the documents and may cancel the contract if something troubling about the information is discovered. Most of the time, such neighborhood restrictions are so vague or non-evasive that the majority of buyers will have little to find objectionable.

However, if you live in a condominium or another apartment-style housing arrangement that carries considerable use restrictions, then the urgency to disclose information to your buyer is greatly increased. Prospective buyers must be made aware of all use and operating restrictions covering such items as parking, pets, guests, structural alterations, use of the pool, leasing conditions, and many others. Because the use restrictions and the financial status of many condominium HOAs can be very intrusive, as well as financially influential, your disclosures will take on heightened significance that suggests you should make these CID disclosures upfront with all other disclosures as part of the purchase agreement.

CIDs require HOA members to fund them in order to pay the expenses of present and future repairs, maintenance, and the eventual replacement of all components owned in-common. Such expenditures are funded by assessments paid by the members, which are collected on a regular basis, monthly or quarterly for example, and can be collected as a lump sum, called a special assessment. Special assessments are initiated when regular assessments are inadequate to cover the expenses, especially in extraordinary circumstances.

The only way that a prospective purchaser can reasonably ascertain if the regular assessments will be increased significantly in the future, or special assessments may be billed them in the near future, is to carefully analyze the pro forma operating budget of the HOA. Clearly, it is mandatory that you provide a prospective buyer with all of the information and disclosures regarding the financial status of the HOA as soon as the buyer expresses interest in the property. How else will the buyer be able to evaluate the property and set a price, unless he is able to consider all the financial obligations that they will undertake with a purchase?

If you live in a condominium project or other restrictive HOA, I suggest that once you decide you want to sell your property that you immediately contact your HOA and tell them what you are doing. Request all the documentation needed to fully disclose the restrictions on use and the financial condition of the HOA. If they offer to send a summary, indicate that you want the full package. Once requested, your HOA has ten days to supply you with the information. HOAs may charge a service fee for this information, but they are limited to charging a reasonable amount to cover their costs. A checklist of all the HOA/CID disclosures are contained in provisions in the purchase agreement forms in the accompanying CD. HOAs may also charge a fee to transfer ownership of the property to a new buyer, but are limited to their actual out-of-pocket costs incurred.

Without a doubt, the more restrictive your community, the more imperative it is for you to disclose full details regarding all the use restrictions and financial conditions to all prospective buyers before entering into a purchase agreement.

Personal property

Occasionally, you may want to sell some of your furniture or other items of a personal nature to your buyer. These items are often included in the price as part of the overall sales price of your home. At closing, they are transferred under a bill of sale. (See Form 434)

You need to understand that if the buyer is putting a new loan on the property and the purchase agreement price includes personal property, that the lender will want to know the dollar amount of the sales price allotted to personal property. It is also likely that the lender will then require the buyer to pay cash for that amount and adjust the purchase price downward to reflect the separate price paid for the real estate. This is because they won't loan money on personal property and are treating its value as lowering the purchase price actually paid for your home.

What's included?

When you sell your home, you are selling everything that is considered attached, even if you do not list it. Things like draperies, window blinds, light fixtures, and ceiling fans automatically pass to the new owner as real estate fixtures due to a provision in the purchase agreement. (See Form 157)

If you have a favorite fixture that you do not want transferred to the buyers, you must be very clear to identify it in writing in the purchase agreement as an item you are removing and taking with you so it is excluded from the sale. If there is anything you are taking which you are not sure is a fixture, then clearly state that fact in the purchase agreement. It is better to be very specific with your buyer to avoid any misunderstandings.

This disclosure of personal items also includes statues or other items in your yard. Fountains or decorative yard art can sometimes appear to be a fixture. Barbecues that are attached to a building or the ground are also questionable as possibly being a fixture since they could be considered part of the real estate. Just list the items to be excluded and you will be safe. If you receive a purchase agreement offer that does not list the items, you will want to write a counteroffer with a provision excluding them from the sale. If there is any doubt about an item, list it!

Final walk-through inspection

Another section of your purchase agreement contains the buyer's right to a final walk-through. This has become common practice because, without a final walk-through provision, many buyers were not allowed to see the property again until after escrow closed and they owned the property.

The primary purpose for the final walk-through is to allow the buyer to verify that any changes or corrections the seller was to have completed have been done as agreed to in the purchase agreement or as a result of disclosures or discoveries. The buyer also wants to verify that you have maintained and kept the property in substantially the same condition it was in when he contracted to buy it.

Once the buyer has performed the final walk-through inspection, you will want to have them sign Form 270 from the accompanying CD, which verifies that the buyer has completed the inspection and has found the property acceptable as observed.

Counteroffers, contingencies, and the other contract issues talked about in this chapter are all part of most real estate transactions. Most are subject to negotiation and compromise. Although these issues and provisions are not usually difficult to understand and, when discussed upfront, not detrimental to negotiating the transaction, they do require a working understanding of them, along with reasonable compliance by you.

CHAPTER TWELVE
Financing the sales price

In early 2005, a national mortgage company interviewed consumers nationwide to find out what they considered to be barriers to homeownership. Nearly one quarter of those surveyed felt that a lack of financial security was a primary obstacle to buying a home, while another quarter said that it was saving for a down payment. Taken together, these obstacles show that nearly half of the available buyers at any given time are more concerned about financing issues than finding the right house.

In other words, going into debt and then figuring out how to pay for that debt intimidates a significant number of buyers who may be interested in buying your home. So, even though the major task of locating a lender and qualifying for a new loan rests with your buyer, make no mistake, the financing of your home will likely be an issue that affects you both. In this chapter, I will explain the basics of financing as well as how different types of loan programs may impact your sale.

How financing is affected by the current market and vice versa

Home loans and the real estate market are tied closely together. One affects the other and then back again. It is important for you to realize the interwoven nature of sales and loans because if you notice what is happening with either the real estate market or the lending market, you will be able to anticipate changes before they occur.

One reason why the real estate market was so hot during 2004 and most of 2005 was that interest rates were very low compared to prior years. Money to loan was also readily available. Because numerous lenders were willing to loan on real estate, the competition intensified and the loans that were available were the result of more and more creativity by the lenders. These unusually creative loan programs allowed people who had never before been able to qualify to suddenly be able to borrow money and buy a home. Too often, people with very bad credit were able to borrow money, even though it was highly unlikely they would ever be able to make the payments, let alone repay the entire loan.

Low interest rates combined with extremely creative loan terms caused large numbers of people to flood the real estate market. Extra buyers, hoping to take advantage of the new lending terms, resulted in a shortage of available properties. With more buyers and fewer homes available, prices rose. Then other people with good credit jumped in as speculators to gamble on buying and flipping properties in the rising market. Using the creative lending options available, they too purchased homes with practically no money down and low interest rates, intent on buying property solely to make a profit on an immediate resale. With more people buying, the higher the prices rose.

Then, when interest rates began to rise and money tightened up beginning in August of 2005, lenders became less creative and loans become less available. Fewer buyers qualified, and even fewer were willing to gamble on loans with little or no equity and potentially high payments. Eventually, prices stopped rising and as we saw in 2007, prices actually dropped from prior months.

Interest rates, the types of loans, and the number of buyers willing to borrow all affect the real estate market. Market prices for homes rise when money is cheap and readily available. Then, as money gets tight, real estate prices soften and eventually decline. Knowing where the real estate market is and what loans costs are at any given time will help you as you sell your home. As stated in Chapter One, when the market is very active and there are few homes available, it is a Seller's Market and prices are high. When the market is slow, loans for the same amount are harder to qualify for, inventory is high, and buyers will have the upper hand in negotiating everything.

How mortgage loans work in California

When you take out a loan on a home in California, two major documents are involved. One document is a note stating the loan amount and its terms with a promise to repay the lender. The other document is a deed of trust. A deed of trust is recorded as a lien on the property you are buying which secures your repayment of a loan. A deed of trust allows a lender to foreclose without going to court. A deed of trust securing your loan is made out to a third party who then serves as a trustee until you pay off your loan. If you don't pay the loan as agreed, the trustee will be instructed by the lender to foreclose and sell your home at a trustee's sale.

Once you pay off your loan, either by making payments for the life of the loan or prepaying it when you sell the property, the trustee will record a reconveyance deed releasing the trust deed from the property. Normally, your escrow officer completes the payoff and the title company handles the reconveyance as part of your property sale.

If you have a second loan on your property, this is also probably secured by a trust deed as is each other loan against your property. Unless the buyer assumes these loans, each loan that is a lien on your property must be paid off in full before the property is transferred and escrow can close.

Another aspect of nearly all loans in California is that the monthly payments, which include interest, are paid in arrears. Arrears is a real estate word that means "paid after" an accrual period rather than paying before such a period begins, like rent under a lease agreement. In other words, when you make your mortgage payment, usually around the first of the month, the interest amount you are paying accrued and was earned by the lender during the previous month, not the current month. This is important to remember because when escrow asks for the final payoff, the amount will include the accrued and unpaid interest for the days of the month preceding your closing, plus the days of the current month as well.

Loan payoff amounts also include any prepayment penalties agreed to in the note or deed of trust. Many loans, especially a number of them made in 2005 when loans were extremely creative, contained a prepayment penalty. Why? The lender wanted to make sure that their money brought them a minimum return on investment. If you pay off the loan prior to the expiration of the prepayment provision, that changes the investor's annualized return and they will want to penalize you for their making less money than they anticipated.

Prepayment penalties are based on a percentage of what you owe and can be several thousand dollars. The maximum that can be charged is six months' worth of interest on the remaining loan balance after deducting 20% of the original loan amount. The penalty is harshest during the first couple of years of your loan and none can be charged after five years.[1] If you want to see whether your loan contains one, take out the copy of your note and read it.

I mention both interest payments in arrears and prepayment penalties so that when you are using the seller's net proceeds sheet you can anticipate these costs beforehand. When you know your bottom-line, you will be in a better position to negotiate the price and terms.

Loan assumptions

Prior to 1985, it was common for the buyer to assume, or take over, an existing loan on a property. However, when interest rates dropped to their lowest levels during 2004 and 2005, and lenders were so creative, few people wanted or needed to assume an existing loan.

That could change. When interest rates rise or financing is less available, and it becomes more and more difficult for buyers to qualify for or obtain new loans, then loan assumptions could become popular once again. What does that mean for you?

Most of the loans made today contain a clause in the trust deed making them fully due on a sale of the property. Lenders have the option to allow their loans to be assumed, but the buyer will be required to submit an application and go through a review process. Of course, if the property is transferred to a spouse due to divorce, on death to a spouse or child living in the property, or into a living trust vesting, an exemption bars the lender from calling the loan.

If you fail to get the lender's approval when you sell your home and allow the buyer to take title on the condition he will make your loan payments, the loan can be called as due in full, forcing its prepayment. If your buyer is unable to qualify for or get refinancing, you are still responsible as the original borrower.

Fortunately, if the loan was one you originally obtained to buy the property as your principal residence (called a purchase-assist loan), the loan is non-recourse. That means you are not personally liable for any shortfall in property value on a foreclosure, but as the original borrower, your credit would definitely be affected. However, if the loan is a refinance of a prior loan you had on the property, whether or not the buyer assumes it, it is then a recourse loan. In the case of a recourse loan, you could be held liable for any lender losses for lack of property value if the lender proceeds with a judicial fore-closure sale or it is a second trust deed loan which is wiped out by the foreclosure of a first trust deed.

Sometimes, the lender will allow a buyer to assume the loan and waive their right to call the loan under its due-on-sale clause. However, the lender will likely make the buyer submit paperwork for approval, charge an additional fee, and raise the interest rate to reflect the current market rate. Should you and the buyer consider this option, it will probably not be any less expensive, nor offer better terms, than a brand new loan.

New purchase-assist loans

When you sell your property, the buyer will usually offer to make a down payment and obtain a new loan to pay the balance of the purchase price. This funding essentially provides you with an all cash sale of your property. Out of that cash, you must pay off any existing loans encumbering the property in order to transfer title as agreed. Then, after paying off your loan and the other costs of the sale, the remaining money is your net proceeds from the sale.

Certainly, applying for and obtaining a new loan falls on the buyer to fulfill, but as mentioned before, it is to your benefit to know what is happening with new loans as well. To begin with, it is important that you realize how easy or difficult it may be for any buyer to get a loan. If interest rates are high or loans become hard to qualify for, that will affect the number of buyers who will be able to afford your home. If loans are cheap and easy to qualify for, then you may be able to price your house higher and realize more profit.

How do you find out the rates and charges for new loans? Read the paper and go on the Internet. Just about every local newspaper will list current rates for loans and the lender's fees. If you notice rates going up—especially going higher than the rate on your current loan—take note as this tends to drive real estate values down. If you notice rates going down, note that this is a trend that boosts property values. Usually, what you see advertised is the interest rate a lender will offer the most qualified homebuyers. Only buyers with the highest credit rating and the largest down payment will be able to qualify for those rates.

You might also want to notice the term for amortization of the loans being advertised. The standard term for home loans has long been 30 years. A 15-year payment option is also available from most lenders. Recently, creative lenders have begun advertising loan programs for 40 or 50 years. What a 40-year or 50-year loan offers is slightly lower payments by adding ten to twenty years to the life of a loan. Unfortunately, the payments aren't that much lower, and the total amount of payment to be made during the additional time period is dramatic. Yet, the 40-or 50-year loan allows buyers who can't qualify for a traditional 30-year loan to still purchase a home. As interest rates rise, lenders are still attempting creative ways to make loans.

Besides charging interest rates, the lender collects fees just to make the loan. This loan fee is usually called an origination fee or "points." A point equals one percent of the loan amount. For example, a $500,000 loan with two points charged as the lender fee would cost $10,000. When shopping for loans, it is necessary to inquire about both the interest rate and the points charged to obtain the loan. The blended rate of those two figures equates to what is called the Annual Percentage Rate (APR). The APR is the rate that you are actually paying in interest over the total life of the loan, if it is a fixed-rate loan.

So, by paying attention to what lenders are offering by way of rates and charges, you may be in the position to refer your buyer to a particular lender and better assist him in his purchase of your house. Beyond that, it is also beneficial to know which type of lender best fits the needs of you and your buyer.

There are three major types of lenders in California:

1. **Banks and Savings & Loans (S&Ls):** These are the large institutional lenders that we are most familiar with. Wells Fargo Bank, Bank of America, and Downey Savings are some of the most common. It is easy to go online and check their mortgage rates at any given time. One thing to note is that the more competitive the interest rates and costs, the more receptive the lender is to making loans at any particular time. Lenders go through cycles of having more or less available cash that they have available to lend out.

2. **Direct lenders:** Most banks and S&Ls are direct lenders, but a growing number of direct lenders sound less institu-

tional and are mortgage bankers. Probably the largest direct lender in the United States that is not a bank is Countrywide Funding. Direct lenders, sometimes called mortgage bankers, provide loans directly from their own pool of investors. Besides that, direct lenders usually have specific guidelines for loans they want to make. When you bring them a loan that fits their investment guidelines, they can easily make a decision and fund the loan. That can save you time and the buyer money.

3. **Mortgage loan brokers:** The best way to spot a mortgage loan broker is to watch for ads that say, "We can get a loan for anyone." What a loan broker does is shop all the lenders looking to loan money and then fit a buyer to the lender to make a loan happen. Mortgage brokers are particularly good when a buyer has unusual circumstances or the property or sale is not typical. That is because they work with a wider lending pool and can find lenders who take nonconforming situations. The downside is that loan brokers tend to charge higher interest rates and fees for their services than a direct lender would charge your buyer, and the time it takes to obtain approval and loan funding can be longer than the other options.

I always recommend that if you have a buyer with good credit and a good job, then make sure that they go to a direct lender or a bank. How do you know which is which? Ask them. There is usually no need to bring in a mortgage broker, who may charge more, when a well-qualified buyer can get a loan just about anywhere. In some cases, a mortgage banker may be a direct lender. In that case, you have the best of both worlds.

If your buyer has credit problems or has little job history, then a mortgage broker is probably your best option. Even then, I would still start with a bank or a direct lender to get their rates and possibly a loan commitment. Then, if they will not grant the loan, use them to negotiate comparable rates and charges when shopping a loan through a mortgage loan broker.

Types of common loans available

Fixed rate amortized: The most common loan is a fully amortized fixed rate loan for either 15 or 30 years. Amortization means that the loan will be fully paid out in monthly installments of interest and loan principal during the 15-or 30-year life of the loan. As most of you know, during the first few years, the loan payments contain mostly interest. Then, when the loan is older, even though the payments stay the same, more is applied to principal and less to interest. It is easy to track a fixed rate loan to see how much is paid each month on interest and principal.

As mentioned above, lenders are now introducing 40-and even 50-year fixed rate loans in an attempt to qualify buyers for payments and loan amounts they otherwise couldn't afford. Just keep in mind that a 40-or 50-year loan doesn't lower the monthly payment by much.

What are the payment differences? The easiest way to discover what a payment would be on a loan is to go online and type in "mortgage loan calculator." (An easy one to use is RealEstateabc.com.) You might have to look around on a couple of web pages, but look for a calculator where you type in an interest rate, the length of the loan, and the loan amount to get the monthly payment the buyer would have to pay.

For example, on Bankrate.com, I went to their mortgage calculator and typed in $500,000 for 30 years with an interest rate of 6.32%. The payment came back around $3,100 per month. At 40 years, the payment is approximately $2,683. The difference between these payments is $417. So, while a buyer may get somewhat lower payments, he would be required to pay $2,683 each month for an additional 10 years for a total extra amount of $322,000! In the end, some people accept the trade-off of an additional 10 to 20 years of loan payments just to own a more expensive home. Ultimately, you are better off knowing the cost of such a luxury.

Adjustable loans: Another type of loan available from all lenders is an adjustable rate loan. Adjustables come in many varieties and anyone who is willing to consider them should compare the terms for calculating the interest adjustment very carefully.

The lengths of these loans tend to be for a fixed period of time, but the interest rate adjusts periodically (monthly or semi-annually) according to an agreed on timeframe. Often, the first year of an Adjustable Rate Mortgage (ARM) is at a fixed percentage rate, and then the rate adjusts semi-annually based on interest rate movement within the financial world. If interest rates are rising, so will the interest rate on the ARM. When it adjusts, your monthly payments will also change, rising when rates rise, falling when they fall. Unfortunately, the change is nearly always an increase.

The frequency that adjustments occur is different according to agreement. Some adjust every single month, others only once a year, some every three years. ARMs usually adjust according to a financial index that is spelled out in the note signed by the buyer at closing. Normally, an ARM includes a cap on the interest rate so a buyer can anticipate the maximum interest rate his loan could rise to, as well as the maximum payment amount he could be charged.

What ARMs typically do is offer a very low initial rate for the first month, six months, or year. That way, although the rate will rise to the current market rate after the initial term expires, a buyer is only required to qualify for the initial rate. Many buyers obtain these loans in this way so they can qualify for a larger loan or become able to buy a much more expensive house than they could otherwise afford. If your buyer is having trouble buying your house with a fixed rate loan, then an ARM loan with a low initial rate is always an option.

Unfortunately, many people who qualify for the low initial rate often cannot afford to make payments when they increase the following month or year. When that happens, they can lose their home to foreclosure. Again, it is beneficial to understand the consequences of an ARM loan, even if you are a seller and would not yourself finance the purchase of a home in this way.

Government loans: Two common government backed loans are Federal Housing Authority (FHA) loans and Veterans Administration (VA) loans. Both of these types of loans are designed to benefit borrowers and are easier to obtain than a conventional loan. However, not everyone is eligible, and sometimes the paperwork can be just as onerous as with any other type of loan.

VA loans are only available to those buyers who are veterans of our country and are usually offered with little or no down payment. On the other hand, FHA loans are available to most citizens. Unfortunately, both the FHA and the VA have strict maximum loan amounts that are often too low to buy a house in most areas of California.

In 2005, it was frequently easier to obtain a conventional loan in California than one of the government backed loans. However, the lower qualifying standards for FHA and VA loans continue to be attractive to those who are eligible. Should interest rates rise and mortgages become even more difficult to obtain, these types of loans will once again be important to pursue.

Other loan types and terms to know

Conforming loans: A conforming loan is a standard loan that easily fits within most direct lender guidelines. These types of loans are easy for a lender to package and resell in the bond market because the property is standard and the sales prices do not greatly exceed the median price of a home in the region. These types of loans usually offer the lowest rates and loan charges at origination.

Nonconforming loans: If you are selling a home that is in an unusual location or has unusual features, it can fall into a category requiring a nonconforming loan. Lenders tend to like a home in a subdivision where a number of other homes look and price the same. That way, they can easily identify their risk when lending on that property. If the property is unusual, it is harder to appraise and could be more difficult to resell in order to recover their loan amount if they were forced to foreclose. What a nonconforming loan means to you or a buyer is that the loan will probably have a higher interest rate, require more fees, and be offered by fewer lenders.

Jumbo loans: Once a property becomes higher-priced than the averages for an area and requires a higher loan amount to finance the purchase price after a 20% down payment, the loan for that property is considered a jumbo loan. Similar to a nonconforming loan, investors view these types of loans as out of the ordinary, and therefore more risky. Because lenders consider them more risky, they charge a slightly higher interest rate and more fees to cover their additional risk of loss.

Balloon payments: A balloon payment is a fixed lump-sum payment on a loan that is due before the standard 15- or 30-year loan term. The loan itself is usually amortized over a longer 15- or 30-year period, but rather than paying out over that time, the remaining balance becomes due and payable at an earlier date along the way. That lump payment is much larger than a standard payment, and that's why it is called a balloon payment.

Some balloon loans allow for a rollover of the loan balance when the balloon payment is due so that the borrower doesn't have to come up with the huge lump-sum payment at the time. Although these loans may help a borrower buy property, they should only be used by those with the means to take care of the balloon when it comes due and payable.

Negative amortization loans: Some types of loans actually allow the principal amount to grow with each payment rather than reduce it. This happens in an ARM loan when the payment is capped rather than the interest rate. Think about it—if your payment remains the same, but the interest rate charged on the loan increases so that the monthly amount of interest which has accrued during the prior month exceeds the payment amount, then the portion of interest you have not paid and that you still owe is tacked on to your loan amount. This type of loan was promoted in 2004, 2005, and 2006 as a way for buyers to qualify for a loan, but it is extremely risky. After all, if the loan amount increases, but the value on the home does not appreciate, the buyer will soon owe much more on the property than it is worth.

These negative amortization loans usually give the borrower several options, one being to pay larger payments to cover the increased amount of interest so that there will be no unpaid interest added to the loan balance. But unless people are highly disciplined and able to pay exactly the amount necessary on the loan to avoid the interest buildup, they will find that the loan balance has grown considerably in a short time.

Private mortgage insurance: Another term you might want to acquaint yourself with is private mortgage insurance (PMI). This is loan default insurance that lenders require whenever a loan amount is more than 80% of the home's value. For example, if your buyer makes a down payment of 10% to buy your house and obtains a new loan, his lender will require that the 10% spread between the down payment and the 80% standard loan amount be covered by PMI. Then, should the buyer default and the lender foreclose, the PMI protects the lender's losses for the excess over the standard 80% loan amount.

PMI allows a buyer to purchase a home with a smaller down payment and a lender to cover his increased risk of loss on default. The premium the buyer pays for PMI is sometimes paid in a lump amount at the time of loan origination. At other times, the premiums are included as a part of the monthly loan payment. Another option, called single payment, is when the entire PMI amount charged is added on to the loan amount, increasing the total amount borrowed and then paid along with the loan payment.

Because the PMI premium can be paid in different ways, buyers need to be aware that it will either increase their cash deposit to cover loan charges and close escrow, or their monthly payments during their initial years of ownership. Still, if PMI allows buyers to purchase homes with a lower down payment, it can be highly beneficial to a seller since it supports a buyer's purchase of a higher-priced home.

100% financing: Prior to the 2007 real estate recession, many lenders offered loans for 100% financing through a scheme called piggyback loans. To obtain a piggyback loan, a buyer begins by arranging an adjustable first loan for 80% of the price. He then arranges financing of some sort, typically with the same lender and often as a home equity line of credit, for the remaining 10%, 15%, or 20% of the price. Together, both loans finance nearly the entire purchase. Besides the benefit of near 100% financing, the buyer is also not required to have PMI because the first loan has a loan-to-value (LTV) ratio of less than 80%, and the second loan does not require it.

For your buyer to qualify for this type of loan, the buyer must have excellent credit. After all, the buyer has nothing invested in the property through a down payment, so he has nothing to lose if the loan defaults except for a blemish on his credit. The second loan, because it is in a far riskier position, is usually at a much higher interest rate with a shorter repayment period.

Due to the terms of any creative financing, the buyer should be educated about the consequences of his choices. While piggyback loans are initially beneficial, borrowers may soon find themselves in a situation where they become unable to repay the loans.

Seller buy-downs: Whenever a seller agrees to prepay a portion of the interest on behalf of his prospective buyer for a short period of time, this is called a seller buy-down. Although loan buy-downs haven't been used much recently, they are incentives that sellers may offer to help make the transaction work. Besides serving as an incentive to the buyer, a buy-down may also lower the cash requirements buyers have at closing and best of all, they usually allow a buyer to qualify for a larger loan than they might otherwise be able to obtain.

A common form of a seller buy-down involves the seller prepaying some of the buyer's interest for the first one to three years of his new loan. This type of interest rate buy-down allows the lender to reduce the interest rate the buyer will pay during that period of time and lower the buyer's monthly payments for that same period.

How much do buy-downs cost the seller? Normally it takes 1% of the loan amount, or one point, to buy down the interest rate 1/8th of a percent for one year of the loan. For example, if you paid 2 points on a loan amount of $500,000, that equals $10,000. If the fixed interest rate for the life of the loan were 7%, the buy-down rate for the first year would be 6.75%. After the first year, the interest rate would return to 7% for the remaining 29 years of the loan.

Of course, there are a variety of loan buy-down programs and a few of them extend over the first couple of years of the loan. If you think this type of incentive might be an option for you in order to sell your home, you may want to check online or talk to a local lender about the many alternatives.

As interest rates rise, you will notice buy-downs offered more and more as an alternative to ARM loans. Large new-home developers are usually the first to make them available to move their house inventory without reducing the price in a rising interest rate market. Just keep in mind that buy-downs are something that any seller, you included, could offer should it be the only thing standing between your buyer qualifying for a necessary loan amount to buy your home.

The timeline for the lending process

When a buyer comes to you and offers to purchase your home, a number of things routinely take place. To give you an overview, here is a list of the main activities required of most buyers to obtain a loan:

1. Select a lender.

2. Fill out a loan application.

3. Provide work history and wage verification (W-2s, tax returns, etc.).

4. Provide copies of bank statements.

5. Provide verification of down payment.

6. Provide copies of any current mortgage statements.

7. Provide copies of the purchase agreement.

8. Provide the names and contact information of the escrow officer and the title company.

9. Make a selection of the loan to use (fixed, adjustable, etc.).

10. Order an appraisal.

11. Provide a copy of the preliminary title report.

12. All of the Truth-In-Lending and Real Estate Settlement Procedures Act (RESPA) Disclosures are to be received by the buyer.

13. Sign and return loan disclosures as required by the lender.

14. The loan is to be approved, subject to the appraisal and final loan committee approval once the financials on the buyer are complete.

15. Make sure that the appraisal is done and that it has been communicated to the lender.

16. Final loan approval by the lender.

17. Paperwork prepared and sent to the escrow officer.

18. The buyer goes to escrow and signs all the loan documents.

19. Lender funds (wires) the money to the escrow officer.

20. The escrow officer sends the deed to be recorded.

21. The escrow officer prepares final prorations and disperses funds.

22. The seller (you) picks up his check along with the final paperwork.

Don't let this list overwhelm you or your buyer! The lender and escrow officer do much of the work.

As you can see, getting a new loan requires a number of steps. If any one of these is delayed or forgotten, then it can slow the entire process down by a week or so. The more you stay on top of these steps, the more likely the closing will happen as you plan. Just remember that if you remain removed or uninformed about the steps, you may be partially responsible for any delay in your closing.

Form 338, called Tracking the Loan Origination Process, is on the accompanying CD. Review each event with a loan representative and then with your escrow officer to set the schedule for when each should occur so you can keep track and monitor the buyer's loan activities. Then, should any delay or problem occur, you will know about it immediately.

Two essentials for a smooth closing

As a seller, there are a couple of things you can do to make sure that the new loan process goes as smoothly as possible. Even though these tasks are not usually your responsibility, neglect could affect you and your sale. By scheduling and staying on top of these activities, you will be able to anticipate problems, avoid others, and bring your sale to a close faster than otherwise.

1. Require your buyers to be preapproved:

Preapproval for a loan is better than being prequalified. If a buyer wants to make an offer on your home and says they have neither, then tell them to call a lender and get preapproved for a loan amount before returning to negotiate a price or fill out a purchase agreement. If your buyer hasn't talked to a lender, then you have no indication that the buyer is able to afford your home. It is nice to know someone wants to buy your home, but it's worthless if they can't pay for it.

A lender prequalifies a buyer by telling him how much he should qualify for if, and the if is a big one, everything the buyer has told the lender is correct and complete. That lender then provides a letter stating the buyer is qualified to borrow a particular amount, subject to verification and clarification of the information the buyer has given the lender. This type of qualification gives you an indication that the buyer can afford your house, but only an unsubstantiated one.

TRACKING THE LOAN ORIGINATION PROCESS

NOTE: This form is prepared and used by a seller, buyer or owner of real estate to assist in policing the events and activities which typically occur during the process of originating a real estate loan. On a review of the form's content with a loan representative, enter the date each itemized event or activity is anticipated to occur. With this information, performance deadlines can be scheduled.

Date prepared _____, 20_____, by _____

1. SELECTION OF LENDER AND TYPE OF LOAN:

1.1 Identify Lender _____(bank, mortgage banker, loan broker, credit union)

    a. Back-up Lender under second application:_____

1.2 Type of loan chosen _____ (conventional/conforming; FHA/VA/Cal Vet; jumbo; Alt-A or subprime)

    a. Fixed rate or adjustable rate _____

1.3 Pre-approval Letter of Commitment _____

2. LOAN APPLICATION:

2.1 Good-faith costs estimate received from loan representative _____, 20_____.

    a. Needs to conform with Federal Regulation Z Truth-in-Lending Disclosure.

2.2 Application to Lender for loans on FNMA Form 1003:

    a. Prepaid, signed and submitted _____, 20_____.

    b. Payment of fees and charges for credit investigation and appraisal costs _____, 20_____.

2.3 Receipt of Lender's Federal Reg Z/RESPA Truth-in-Lending Disclosure Statement _____, 20_____.

    a. Does it conform with good-faith costs estimate.

2.4 Receipt of Lender disclosures signed by Borrower and returned to Lender _____, 20_____.

2.5 Escrow and title company given Lender identification and contact information _____, 20_____.

2.6 Statement of identification from Buyer prepared and submitted to escrow _____, 20_____.

    a. Escrow orders preliminary title report _____, 20_____.

    b . Copies of driver's license and social security cards (and any military ID or alien registration card) _____, 20_____.

3. LOAN PROCESSING ACTIVITIES:

3.1 Copies of purchase agreement, escrow instructions, TDS and NHD handed to Lender _____, 20_____.

3.2 Request for Verification of Employment prepared and signed by Borrower and handed to Lender _____, 20_____.

3.3 Request for Verification of Rent or Mortgages prepared and signed by Borrower and handed to Lender _____, 20_____.

    a. Documents for last 12 months of mortgage or rent payments made by Borrower.

    b. Some Lenders also request cancelled checks for payments of recent mortgage statement or rental agreement.

3.4 Copies of statements for the recent three months of all checking and savings accounts handed to Lender _____, 20_____.

3.5 Request for Verification of Deposit (downpayment) prepared and signed by the Borrower and handed to Lender _____, 20_____.

3.6 Credit Report Authorization prepared and signed by Borrower and handed to Lender _____, 20_____.

3.7 Copies, if applicable, of bankruptcy discharge (with list of creditors) and divorce papers handed to Lender _____, 20_____.

3.8 Borrower to coordinate inspection of property by Appraiser.

    a. Lender orders appraisal _____, 20_____.

    b. Appraiser to inspect property _____, 20_____.

    c. Borrower must request a copy of appraisal to receive one.

    d. Copy of appraisal report received from Lender _____, 20_____.

3.9 Preliminary title report received and reviewed by Borrower and returned to Escrow _____, 20_____ .

3.10 Lender approves the property as qualified to be security for Borrower's loan _____, 20_____ .

4. FINALIZING THE LOAN:

4.1 Loan approved on Borrower's receipt of RESPA three-day right to cancel _____, 20_____ .

4.2 Borrower makes arrangement for Homeowner's insurance on the property _____, 20_____ .

    a. Coverage will be required by Lender on closing.

4.3 Loan documents from Lender are received by Escrow or title company _____, 20_____ .

    a. Borrower signs loan documents _____, 20_____ .

4.4 Escrow prepares closing (settlement) statement for Buyer's approval _____, 20_____ .

5. FUNDING AND CLOSING ESCROW:

5.1 Escrow makes a demand on Lender and Buyer for funds needed to close _____, 20_____ .

5.2 Escrow forwards deeds to title company for recording when Escrow can close _____, 20_____ .

5.3 Lender wires funds to Escrow or title company _____, 20_____ .

5.4 Buyer deposits funds in Escrow as needed to close _____, 20_____ .

5.5 Deeds are recorded by title company on telephonic instruction from Escrow _____, 20_____ .

5.6 Escrow issues check to Seller for net proceeds from the sale _____, 20_____ .

FORM 338   05-07   ©2007 **first tuesday**, P.O. BOX 20069, RIVERSIDE, CA 92516 (800) 794-0494

Once the lender has the buyer's loan application and the other documents needed to verify the buyer's representations, only then will the lender put in writing that the buyer is preapproved to borrow up to a specific loan amount. Obviously, if you know in advance that your buyer can afford to buy your house, you have already advanced to step #7 on Form 338 covering the lending process. Unfortunately, if you do not ask for a preapproval or prequalification letter right upfront, you could easily be wasting your time talking to people who cannot afford to buy your house. Also, keep in mind that even if the buyer is working with a real estate agent who may tell you that his buyers are qualified, unless you see a preapproval letter from a lender, you can never be sure.

For this reason, I strongly recommend that you ask for a copy of your prospective buyer's loan preapproval letter before accepting any offer from them. If you don't do it upfront, then be sure that your purchase agreement contains a contingency that requires your receipt of the buyer's preapproval letter within as few as seven days after acceptance or you have the right to cancel the sale. (See Form 157 §4.1)

No matter how friendly or convincing your prospective buyer might appear, your best protection for avoiding a false start and time lost with a buyer on a canceled purchase agreement is to insist on a preapproval letter from a lender. A preapproval letter demonstrates to you that your buyer not only qualifies, but that the lender is prepared to proceed quickly to fund the loan and close.

2. Require weekly loan progress reports:

Because a number of steps must take place before the loan can be funded and escrow closed, I recommend that you ask for weekly loan updates from the lender. The best way to get these is to get the name of the loan officer that the buyer is working with and contact that person to set out a schedule on the loan progress worksheet and regularly receive updates. Tell the buyer you want to make sure that the loan officer has everything they need at the earliest moment. Just realize that the loan officer will not be able to disclose anything confidential to you. However, by asking the loan officer on a weekly basis what still needs to be done, you can help facilitate many actions that might otherwise go unattended and drag out the time for closing. Most importantly, if there are going to be any delays or failures, you will know that immediately.

Both of these steps seem simple enough, yet it amazes me how often they don't happen. Even if you are represented by a real estate agent, I would recommend that you either do it yourself or make sure your agent reports to you weekly without you having to chase them down. Policing the loan process is critical and will greatly aid you in closing your sale on schedule.

Seller financing

Another option you have as a seller is to provide all or some of the financing. If your home is free and clear of a loan, or if you are willing to carry a second loan behind the buyer's new first loan, you can help the buyer with the financing they need to purchase your property. (See Form 157 §8)

Typically, as interest rates rise and the loan amount that buyers can qualify for reduces, seller financing becomes more predominant. A seller who is in the position to carry some or all of the financing can sometimes entice a buyer who, even though he has excellent credit, may not have the full down payment to buy. This can be a rewarding option, especially if the property requires a loan that is nonconforming or if the buyer has unusual circumstances. If you don't require all of the cash from the sale of your home, then offering to extend credit to the buyer can sometimes result in your receiving a higher price for your property. If not, at least you might be able to sell when others can't.

Another seller benefit is in the the area of taxes. When a seller provides financing to sell the property, the sale is treated as an installment sale for tax purposes. Installment sales allow you to only pay tax on the profit in the cash you receive rather than the total amount of profit your sales price may have generated. Although there are very favorable tax benefits for homeowners that we will discuss in a later chapter, if there is profit in excess of $250,000 for each owner on a sale of a home, then the tax on the windfall of that excess profit is delayed until years later with an installment sale.

Should you decide to carry the financing, you will want to minimize your risk of loss. The first thing you need to do is print out Form 300 on the accompanying CD called the Seller Carryback Disclosure Statement. Once printed, you will fill it out and attach it to the purchase agreement as an addendum whenever you agree to carry a note. You will sign it and so will the buyer. The sooner you can get the disclosure signed the better since the buyer will have the right to cancel the transaction upon receipt unless he received the disclosure before you accepted his offer.

One of the benefits of using this disclosure form is that it acts as a checklist for the risks you must consider before making a decision to carry some of the financing. Plus, it serves as a notice to the buyer of everything you are legally required to communicate to him.

California law requires the seller carryback disclosure in a number of other situations. Any time a land sales contract, lease-option, all inclusive trust deed (AITD), or a purchase agreement coupled with interim occupancy is used, then a disclosure of this type must be included. Bear in mind that if there are interest and finance charges, or five or more payments beyond one year, then use of the form is mandatory.

If the form is not signed and included with the purchase agreement, and it states anything other than what the buyer reasonably expected from your negotiations, the buyer may cancel the transaction until he signs the disclosure. Obviously, rather than risk the buyer's cancellation, this disclosure, like others that are required, should be included with the purchase agreement right from the beginning.

An important issue addressed in the seller's carryback disclosure is the seller's review and approval of the buyer's ability to repay the loan. Naturally, you will want the buyer to fill out a credit application so you can check out his credit by obtaining a report from a credit agency. The carryback disclosure then allows you to cancel the purchase agreement and escrow if you find something about the buyer's financial history that makes him an unacceptable credit risk for you. Mortgage lenders often accept credit risks that a carryback seller should not take. (See Forms 302 and Form 157 §8.5)

You will want to also inspect and approve the terms of any new loans the buyer will be placing on the property that will have priority to yours. This is because, if those loans are risky, they put you at additional risk. In addition to the terms of the new loans, you must pay attention to the total amount of the loans. For example, if the buyer wants to put a new 80%-of-value loan on the property (and avoid paying PMI), and then asks you to carry 20% as a second, then the property will be 100% financed and the buyer will have no equity. As mentioned before, if the buyer has little or no capital invested in the property, it is much easier for him to allow his loans to go into default. Should that happen, you would then need to foreclose and assume the buyer's first loan in order to save your equity position. Keep that in mind should you choose to carry any part of the financing. You can always insist on a lower loan amount so that your LTV percentages are better protected.

The length of the payoff on a carryback note is another consideration. Although the loan term is always subject to negotiation, few sellers carry financing for a full 15 to 30 years. It is very normal to call for a balloon payment at the end of three, five or ten years. At the end of that time, the buyer would be required to pay you off either out of his pocket or by obtaining a new second loan, refinancing, or selling the property. (See Form 157 §8)

Even if you are not interested in providing a portion of the financing, it may be beneficial for you to review the form and recognize its potential value in a tight money market. One other financial advantage for sellers is that a carryback note provides a seller with an income stream at a potentially better-than-market interest rate. If you only intend to put your net proceeds in a bank and draw interest, perhaps you would be better served by being the lender in your transaction. Your challenge is to insure the creditworthiness of the buyer and that the value of your home supports the payment schedule and principal amount of your carryback.

How to check a buyer's credit

If you do decide to provide part of the financing on your sale, then you must check the credit of your buyer. There are three major companies, and numerous small ones with records on prior tenants, who provide credit reports, and they are all available on the Internet. Naturally, you will need the buyer's permission to check his credit. That is why you will want him to fill out Form 302 on the accompanying CD as it gives you authorization.

Not only do I recommend that you check the buyer's credit, you may also want to collaborate with a financial advisor or someone in the lending industry to help analyze the data on the credit report. If you are going to be extending credit to the buyer, it is in your best interest to get comfortable with his past credit history and present ability to repay his debts.

Preparing the documents

If you do decide to assist with financing, your escrow officer has the notes and trust deeds available and will prepare them for closing as a normal part of escrow services. If you or your buyers would like to review the documents in advance, you may ask your escrow officer to provide the blank forms. Also included on the accompanying CD are a standard note and trust deed that you may use. (See Forms 420 and 450)

Loan closing costs

The good news is that, as a seller, you have little or no closing costs due to the buyer getting a new loan. Your primary loan closing cost will result from paying off your existing loan(s), which include charges for drawing up the reconveyance deed and recording it. Also, escrow will charge for their cost to wire transfer the payoff to your lender, but these expenses and others like them are small compared to what the buyer must pay his lender.

Also remember, because interest is paid in arrears, you will likely have to pay up to one full month's interest at payoff, based upon the days of the month until closing. Additionally, you may be charged for a prepayment penalty as well. Of course, you don't have to write a check for these amounts, since escrow will merely reduce the total sales proceeds you will receive on closing.

If you provide seller carryback financing, most of the costs related to the loan will be passed to your buyer. Besides the fees for drawing up the documents and recording them, you will also want to have the title company issue what is called a joint protection (JP) title policy for your loan. This title policy insures that your trust deed is second only to the buyer's new first as described in an earlier chapter where I talked about title insurance. The JP policy is the same policy issued by the title company to insure your conveyance of the property to your buyer, as well as the recording of the second trust deed you carried back. (See Form 157 §12.4)

Normally, you are not required to pay any of the many closing costs that your buyer may incur due to his new loan. However, there might be a time when you agree to do so. For example, if the buyer gets a loan guaranteed by the VA, then the VA requires that the seller pay most of the loan closing costs. It is also quite normal for the seller to pay many of the lending fees with an FHA loan as well since these buyers typically have less savings, are generally first time homebuyers, and are greater credit risks than buyers obtaining conventional financing.

Lenders allow a seller to pay any closing cost for a buyer that is considered to be a non-reoccurring closing cost. These costs include most lender fees, appraisals, surveys, or even the lender's separate title insurance policy. On the other hand, a lender will usually not allow a seller to pay buyer costs that are reoccurring, such as property insurance or taxes. If needed, your escrow officer can provide clarification on this issue.

No matter the type of loan, a buyer can negotiate that you pay all or some of his loan fees. Although not normal in a Seller's Market, it might make the difference between selling your home or not selling in a Buyer's Market. Sometimes, it may actually be to your advantage to charge more for your home and offer to pay the buyer's loan fees, than to accept less and make the buyer pay them. With so many variations as to who pays for what in a real estate sale, it is critical that you fill out your seller net sheet's in advance so that you know your bottom-line before you begin to negotiate the price and terms you will accept. When you are clear about the amount of your potential net proceeds, you can work with your buyer to structure a transaction that works for the benefit of you both.

Financing—an important part of your sale

Back in the early 1990s, when interest rates were high and the market favored buyers, it was normal for an owner to carry part of the financing to help sell property. I have sold homes where I carried part of the financing, and I bought homes where the previous owner extended financing to me. Each time, I believe it benefitted the both of us in the transaction.

Naturally, every seller hopes that a buyer will come along with the cash in the bank to pay for the property in full, but that seldom happens. By understanding the lending process and paying attention to changes in the real estate and loan market, you can use these to your advantage when necessary. After all, even if you find someone who loves your home, they most likely won't be able to buy it unless they can get a loan. Anything you can do to help your prospective buyers find a loan they can arrange and live with is an important step toward selling your home.

PART THREE

Marketing, trouble-shooting, and other final considerations.

CHAPTER THIRTEEN
Marketing your property

I purposely included the marketing of your property in the final section of this book. While other For Sale By Owner (FSBO) books focus on marketing, I believe a major reason some FSBOs are unsuccessful is because the idea of talking with buyers and dealing with contracts becomes overwhelming. Hopefully, if you have read and absorbed the previous sections of this book, you now feel comfortable enough to proceed with some basic ideas about promoting your property and locating a buyer. Just bear in mind that how you market your house will dramatically affect your success, so stay with it.

Who are homebuyers and what do they want?

One of the best ways to promote your property is to anticipate what attracts buyers in the first place. A great place to start is to analyze recent surveys that show where, how, and why buyers have purchased in the recent past. This section includes a number of statistics that I find significant to the selling process.

In 2005, the National Association of Realtors (NAR) mailed out an 8-page survey to 90,000 buyers who had purchased homes during the previous year.[1] Out of those mailed, they were able to tabulate nearly 8,000 responses. Naturally, the questions were geared toward the promotion of their organization and the value of NAR membership, but the survey provides other insights that anyone can use. Most especially, the survey provides insights into the actions of buyers in the early part of the 21st century.

What are the highlights and how do they benefit a FSBO?

1. According to the survey, 40% of the buyers who responded were first-time homebuyers.[2] You can reasonably expect that a little over one-third of the prospective buyers for homes in the medium to lower price ranges are buying for the first time. If your home falls in that range, then your buyer could be a first-time buyer and would likely need more assistance and coaching than someone who has been through the buying process before.

2. Most repeat buyers (79%) purchased single-family detached homes. Fewer first-time homebuyers did the same (69%).[3] Therefore, nearly 30% of first-time homebuyers purchased condos, townhouses, or duplexes because of their lower income levels.

3. The size of the home was also different for repeat vs. first-time homebuyers. The average size for repeat buyers was 2,015 square feet. First-time homebuyers purchased homes with 1,546 square feet.[4]

4. In the west, nearly 50% of all homes sold were in the suburbs. One quarter were urban, and 16% were in small towns. Only 9% were in rural areas, and 2% were in resort/recreation areas.[5] The survey goes on to show that most people from the suburbs stayed in the suburbs, or in whatever type of neighborhood they lived in before.[6]

5. The single most important factor of the location where buyers purchased their property was neighborhood quality (68%). The second most important factor was that it was close to their job or school (43%). After that, being close to friends and family, popular schools, shopping, parks, and other features entered into the equation.[7]

6. The survey asked buyers what feature they would sacrifice in order to buy the house they eventually purchased. The characteristic most forfeited was the size of the property (16%). Only 13% compromised on neighborhood quality, and only 11% sacrificed on planned expenditures or distance from work/school.[8] This shows that although most people prefer larger homes, they are willing to accept less square footage if need be. Far more important to most is the quality of the neighborhood, the cost of the property, and the distance to work or school.

How do buyers find property and how long does it take?

The NAR survey reports that the typical homebuyer in the Western U.S. spent six weeks actively searching for a home. Repeat buyers typically viewed ten homes before purchasing. First-time homebuyers considered only eight.[9]

This statistic illustrates how important it is for your house to be shown to its greatest potential each and every time it is viewed by a prospective buyer. Don't waste time showing your property before it is in its best possible condition, both inside and out. Even though some will be lookers with no intention of buying, anyone who is a serious buyer will probably decide to make an offer to purchase very quickly (after seeing only eight to ten houses). If yours isn't top-notch, or you aren't willing to offer a measurable price reduction, it will be thrown out of the competition.

Next, the survey points to how buyers *first* learned about the home they eventually bought. The number one source was through a real estate agent (36%).[10] Interesting enough, this percentage has gone down every year since 1997 when it was 50%. That is good news for FSBOs because it shows how other resources are being developed to match sellers with buyers.

The Internet was the second source buyers used to first find the home they eventually purchased. It rose to 24% in 2005, from a low point of 2% back in 1997. This demonstrates how critical the use of the Internet is for promoting your property.

Next, 15% used a yard sign as a method to locate buyers. The survey reported that most buyers move less than 12 miles from their last location, so they are probably looking for homes by driving through neighborhoods where they would like to live.[11] This too is good news for FSBOs because a very nice "For Sale" sign is so easy to place in the front yard.

After that, their friends, neighbors, or relatives serve as a source for finding a home. This provides justification for holding an Open House and inviting your friends and neighbors. You never know who might be the one to buy your house or lead you to that perfect buyer.

Other sources initially used to locate a home for sale was the newspaper at 5% and home books or magazines at 1%.[12] These figures reveal that while real estate agents have a large impact on how buyers find homes, that is changing for enterprising FSBOs.

What resources do buyers use when searching for a home? Primarily, they use a real estate agent (90%). This is understandable since an agent doesn't cost the buyer a thing.

The second resource used was the Internet at 77%. Actually, first-time homebuyers use the Internet even more than average (79%), probably because they are younger and more computer literate. This clearly suggests that anyone wanting to sell their home in today's world must have a presence on the Internet to maximize their exposure to buyers.

Other means used by buyers to gather information was the yard sign at 71%, an Open House at 51%, newspaper advertising at 50%, home books or magazines at 38%, a home builder at 36%, the television at 25%, billboards at 19%, and a relocation company at 15%.[13] Keep in mind that these resources were used for the purpose of gathering information about the process and the purchase of property. These tools are valuable to FSBOs because they provide insight about how to promote yourself to buyers. For example, don't bother with television advertising because, in relation to cost, it isn't that important to buyers. In addition, these tools also represent other resources you can use to gather information about "selling" your home.

Website statistics from the NAR survey

The features that were rated to be the most valuable for any real estate website were photos (84%), detailed property information (83%), virtual tours (59%), interactive maps (44%), neighborhood and community information (36%), and real estate contact information (29%).[14] One website that buyers viewed when searching for property was Realtor.com at 42% in the Western U.S. Buyers also searched local multiple listing service (MLS) sites (55%) or went to a specific real estate company's site (33%). Local newspaper websites drew 17%, while real estate magazine websites drew 5%. Other sites (10%) that buyers viewed were likely the personal websites of real estate agents or perhaps even FSBO sites.[15]

Seller statistics—who used a real estate agent and who sold it themselves?

The NAR survey reports that in the Western U.S., 92% of homesellers sold property by using a real estate agent or broker. Three percent of those first attempted to sell it themselves, but eventually listed with a broker.

The national average of homes sold by a FSBO was 13%, but the survey says that in the west, it was only 7%. Of the 7% in the Western U.S., 1% first listed with a broker and then ended up selling it himself.[16] I believe this shows that FSBO sellers have been those traditionally within the lower priced home market.

It is simple to understand that when properties are selling quickly and easily at high prices, like those seen in California in 2005, then sellers are more forgiving and willing to pay high brokerage fees. Then, as the market slows down and money is more difficult to come by, I believe more homeowners will choose to sell their home themselves.

During the high appreciation rate period of 2005, the number of people wanting to sell their home themselves fell to the lowest rate ever (13%). A high period of FSBO activity was in 1991, when it was 19%, and during 1997 when it was 18%.[17] These were years when the country was coping with a long, drawn-out real estate recession and sellers wanted to keep more of the profits in their own pockets.

What do real estate agents do to market homes?

There are a number of routine things that most successful real estate agents do to sell homes. According to the NAR Survey, here is a list of activities practiced by agents in the Western U.S. to sell homes in 2005:[18]

- placed properties on the Internet — 81% (89% listed on a local MLS);
- placed yard signs — 79%;
- held Open Houses — 57%;
- placed newspaper advertisements — 43%;
- placed ads in real estate magazine s— 27%;
- sent direct mail (flyers, postcards, etc.) — 25%;
- placed television ads — 3%; and
- other — 11%.

Every one of the above listed activities is something that you can do as a FSBO. There are also other activities that I recommend you do if you want to sell your house in the shortest time possible for the highest price possible. Below are what I consider to be the fundamentals for successfully marketing your home.

Get on the MLS

One of the best ways to gain exposure for your property is to use the MLS. Even though getting listed carries the greatest cost, it remains the single most important way to promote your property available. As the statistics quoted above demonstrate, of the 81% who sold their property through the Internet, 89% of those were through an MLS. That means that although there are a number of FSBO Internet property databases, they are not nearly so successful or viewed as MLSs.

Your local MLS is compiled by all the real estate brokers who list and sell homes in your area. That complete inventory is held within the MLS database and accessed by all the local agents though the Internet. There has been talk of a major overhaul to make the MLS a regional or national database, but it is impossible to guess when that might happen. So, because most buyers continue to work with real estate agents, and most agents use the MLS to find available properties, it remains an expensive but valuable resource. By offering your home on the MLS, you will be exposing your property to hundreds of local agents who are working with the vast majority of buyers available at any given time.

What does MLS exposure cost? As you may recall from an earlier chapter, the price to be placed on your local MLS varies. Some flat-fee agents will work with you solely through the Internet. Also, many local discount brokers offer MLS exposure at a reduced fee. One way to locate such brokers would be to read the newspaper for ads. Remember that local discount brokers usually charge either a very small percentage or a flat fee for their services. Then, in addition to that fee, you have the option of paying a commission to a buyer's agent if published in the MLS. That fee is usually a percentage, and the amount you offer to pay is set upfront when you choose to be listed in the MLS.

The percentage that a buyer's agent charges in your local area varies. Except in extreme cases, it should be no more than 3%. In some situations, you might be able to offer as little as 2% or 2.5%. Just realize that, if you offer below what is "standard" in your community and the market is slow, some agents may avoid showing their buyers your property. If an agent can make 3% elsewhere, they may steer their clients to those sellers willing to pay more.

Whether or not you go the MLS route probably depends upon your motivation. If you have all the time in the world, or it is a Seller's Market, you may not need the exposure to locate a buyer. On the other hand, if it is a Buyer's Market and you need to move quickly, then I recommend it highly.

It is actually my preferred way of selling property. The last three homes I sold I listed with the MLS and offered to pay the buyer's agent his half of a full fee. I did it because I had already found the house I wanted to move into and needed a fast sale. I could have sold my home solely by myself—but it would have taken much longer without exposure of my property to buyers through the local MLS. Plus, I saved myself the standard 2.5-3% commission that would have been paid to a listing broker. Knowing I didn't want to wait, I paid the buyer's agent's commission and moved quickly.

Keep in mind, if you do list your property in the MLS, be sure to include as many photos as is allowed. Besides detailed information, buyers want to see photos of the properties to know whether they are interested.

What if your property doesn't photograph well? Submit photos anyway. When a property doesn't have many photos, I usually assume that it is either too messy or in such a bad condition that the owner doesn't want me to see it. Just know that if you don't include photos, others might think the same thing.

You may also want to consider a virtual tour. A virtual tour is a short video of your home's finest features—usually room by room. The MLS allows real estate agents to post a virtual tour along with the listing. They are a nice feature, and I believe buyers use them to gather more information, but I just don't think they actually make a sale. Therefore, I doubt that the expense of a virtual tour is justified for a FSBO. Unless you have the means to do it inexpensively, don't bother. On the other hand, if you ever decide to traditionally sell your property by listing it with a real estate agent, I would insist on it since the broker should arrange and pay for it.

Some FSBOs will see the option of listing through the MLS by using either a flat rate or discount broker as just another less expensive way to list with a broker. True, it does require you to work with real estate agents and pay a buyer's agent's fee. Still, I believe it is such a viable marketing arrangement that I strongly recommend you consider it as a great way to get the job done and still save a great deal of money. It offers the advantage of exposing your property to ready and able buyers in the marketplace, and it still saves you money on a standard fee. In a slow market, it could be one of the best decisions you make.

Free listing with Zillow.com for homesellers

Zillow.com has been making tremendous progress with helping sellers and buyers access homes for sale in California. If you have decided to sell your house yourself, be sure and go to Zillow.com and "Post For Sale" your home. You can even upload photos. Be sure to also carefully list all of your home's amenities so the "Zestimate" offered by Zillow is close to, or below, your asking price. If you decide to list your home with a real estate broker, you will also want to insure that your home is offered through Zillow for the extra exposure it provides.

As Zillow continues to improve and offer more benefits, it is likely that MLS exclusiveness will diminish. As the buying public begins to study inventory on Zillow.com, it will become less necessary to agree to pay a real estate agent a fee in order to get Internet exposure similar to that provided by the MLS.

Post the property on the Internet

According to the 2005 NAR Profile of Home Buyers and Sellers, 77% of all buyers used the Internet to locate the home that they eventually bought.[19] The use of the Internet as an essential part of a buyer's search process continues to grow each year.

Another survey done by the California Association of Realtors (CAR) in 2006 showed that nearly 70% of all homebuyers used the Internet as an integral part of the homebuying process. CAR's survey stated as the NAR survey intimated, that Internet buyers tended to be "younger, wealthier, better educated and more likely to be married than traditional buyers." The CAR survey also noted that, "Internet buyers also reported greater satisfaction with the home-buying process compared with traditional buyers."[20] These facts just repeat what I said above. In today's world, it is critical that your property have a presence on the Internet. If, as a FSBO, you don't want to go to the expense of having an MLS listing, at least consider using one of the other FSBO websites to promote yourself.

Put a sign in your yard

The 2005 NAR survey says that 71% of homebuyers used a real estate sign and its pocket for flyers as a source for information about the property they bought. Fifteen percent first learned about the home they later bought from a yard sign.[21] This signifies how important it is to place a quality sign in your yard along with informational flyers.

Where do you buy a sign? Look in your phone book or on the Internet for local sign companies. Call them and ask them if they have a standard metal "For Sale" sign for homes. Chances are good that they do. Many of the Internet FSBO companies also allow you to order signs online.

Wherever you get the sign, you will need to put your phone number on the sign. In addition, you want to purchase one of the containers that attaches to your sign that allows you to put your home flyers or brochures into it. A waterproof container is best. Once in your yard, make sure that you keep it well stocked with clean brochures.

Hold an Open House

Most sellers who list their home with a real estate agent usually insist that the agent offer regular Open Houses to attract prospective buyers. As a FSBO, it is important for you to know that Open Houses rarely attract an actual buyer. Most real estate agents hold Open Houses because sellers expect them, and it is an excellent way for agents to cultivate buyers for other properties.

As a FSBO, you aren't looking to generate business for an agent—your major focus is finding serious, qualified buyers. So, do I advise against Open Houses? Not necessarily. You may want to do an Open House once or twice in the beginning of your marketing program for a couple of reasons.

Reason One: Face it; your neighbors will want to know what your asking price is. Plus, they have probably always wondered what your house looks like inside. Use your neighbors' curiosity to your advantage. Hold an Open House and even go around and put flyers on their doorknobs inviting them to come. Then, once they are there, ask them to refer anyone who they think may be interested in your house. Every now and then, a person will know a friend or a relative that has always wanted to live in your neighborhood.

This is exactly how my husband and I found our present home. A friend knew that we were looking for a home in his neighborhood. He happened to see a neighbor put a FSBO sign in the yard and that an Open House was to be held that Sunday. After viewing the house, our friend called and said, "You've got to see this house since it would fit you both perfectly." He was right.

Reason Two: When you hold an Open House, other real estate agents will sometimes come by. Naturally, they think that when they talk to you and befriend you that you might eventually list with them. What you want to do is to pick their brains. After all, it is always possible that you will find one that so impresses you that you want to work with them. Never hesitate to ask an agent about the strength of sales in the local market and what they think about your house.

Ask them about your price and your property's condition. Ask them if there is anything they'd recommend you do to improve the way you market your home or locate buyers. Evaluate what they say with what you have learned in this book and through your own investigations. If it seems like their opinion is good advice, take it under consideration.

It is actually in your best interest to have as many people, real estate agents included, see your house. The more people that are aware of your home and that it is on the market, the more chances the right buyer will come along.

Creating a professional marketing flyer/brochure

One mistake I have repeatedly seen made by FSBO sellers is that they don't take the time or make the effort to create a marketing flyer for their home. In this age of computers and digital cameras, it is easily accomplished and is a valuable marketing tool.

If you aren't sure how to do it, make it a family project. Chances are good that your children have been learning how to do reports and make flyers in school. Get them to help you on the computer if you aren't computer savvy yourself. A good way to decide what your flyer should contain is to drive around and pick up a dozen or so from the homes for sale in your neighborhood. See which flyers look good and provide the best information.

Other than that, I recommend that your flyer contain:

1. At least one photo of the outside and perhaps one or two of the inside or back yard. Choose those shots which are the most spectacular and best represent your home.

2. Include the price. Nothing is more annoying to a prospective buyers than not seeing the asking price of the home on a flyer. Real estate agents often don't advertise the asking price because they want buyers to call them in an effort to convert them to clients. That type of self-promotion doesn't help you a bit. You want only those buyers who know your price and will contact you because they can afford it. Otherwise, any other type of buyer is just wasting your time.

3. Put down the number of bedrooms, bathrooms, and the square footage. If you don't know the square footage, ask your title insurance representative for that information. You should already be developing a relationship with a title person who can provide this information. If you do list the square footage, make sure you identify the source of the information if you have not verified its accuracy.

4. List all the improvements that make your home special. This can be a feature in the back yard, the kitchen, the bathrooms, etc.

5. Also list neighborhood qualities that might not be known to prospective buyers, like special local schools, a local library, playgrounds, shopping, or even bus line connections within the neighborhood.

6. Include your phone number. If you want to put a person's name, just use a first name—preferably a male name. Then, when people call, you can always say, "I'm sorry he isn't in right now—can I help you?"

   If you don't like taking calls directly, then get an answering machine or a voice mailbox and ask callers to please leave a message. Don't be afraid someone won't leave a message—if they don't, they aren't serious anyway. If you do take messages, be sure and return calls promptly.

7. If you have set up a website or have listed your property under a FSBO or MLS site, print the website address on the flyer so Internet buyers can then go online for further information.

Once you have made your flyer on the computer, you can either print them out or have them printed by a local copy center. Don't skimp on the price. You want color copies on paper that is heavier than plain copy paper. Businesses like Kinko's do this type of work on a regular basis, so call for prices. Remember, your brochure is a reflection of your home and yourself. If you want to present a favorable image to prospective buyers, then make sure your flyer looks great, feels friendly, and is helpful!

Advertising

In the past, newspaper and print advertising was essential. That was before the Internet. Now, most people who want to search out properties look to the Internet first. However, depending upon where you live, you may want to consider the newspaper. If there is only one local newspaper that everyone in the area reads, then it might be worth the expense.

As far as advertising in real estate magazines, I think it rarely justifies the expense. So too, with television. Sellers frequently like to see their home on TV, but it seldom brings in buyers. Most of the time, top producing agents use it as a way to get more sellers to list with them. The practice may bring in more clientele for an agent, but it does little to locate buyers and sell your home.

The value of staging

First impressions are vital to success in sales. That's where home staging comes in. Staging is doing anything and everything that shows your home in the best possible light. The practice of staging has always been an important part of selling a home, yet only within the last year or two has it been called staging and given such a high priority.

Even though most people attempt it on their own, others swear that by hiring professionals they not only recaptured the cost, they made an extra profit. Entire books have been written on the topic, and HGTV has a series with great examples. All deserve your study. At the very least you will want to research the practice on the Internet and do your best to apply what you learn.

Here are some of the most obvious ideas to get you started.

1. Furnishings: It may not be practical to go out and buy new or nice furniture before selling a house, but it is to your advantage to have clean furniture in good condition while your home is for sale. If an item is well worn or soiled, get rid of it. Furniture that looks shabby will make your home look shabby too, so move it out.

You should also know that a home always looks best when it has furniture in all of the rooms. For example, every bedroom should have a bed and preferably a dresser. Sometimes, you may need to move before you sell your home, but be aware that a vacant, unfurnished home will be a detriment to the sale of your home. If possible, always leave your home furnished during the showing period.

However, be careful of having too much furniture. Too much furniture forces prospective buyers to notice the furniture rather than the home. If you have any room in your house that has more furniture than it should, get rid of the excess pieces. If you can't easily walk into and around the room—and use it for what it was designed for—then remove the excess furniture before showing.

2. Get rid of clutter: Clutter is everything that is piled into closets and covering the walls and shelves. Box it up and store it elsewhere. In the last home I sold, we rented a storage unit and moved all of our clutter there for the three months it took to sell and close escrow. We also took down just about all the knick-knacks in our home, as well as family photos, which ends up being clutter to others. Of course, a few well chosen decorator items are good, but most homes—mine included—are filled with far too much personal stuff. This detracts from the home and makes it harder for prospective buyers to envision themselves living in the house.

Some people make collecting an art. Still, I recommend that if you have an elaborate collection of anything, then box it up and have it stored away from your property. I once bought a condo from a family that collected clowns. Thank goodness, I was able to see beyond the clutter of clowns. They hung on all the walls, were stacked on all the shelves, and layered the sofa and chairs. It was not cute, it was actually creepy. Even if you love your collection beyond life itself, chances are your buyers will find it distracting at best and offensive at worst. Do yourself a favor and box them up in anticipation of your move.

3. Clean it up: It may seem obvious, but when you start looking at other houses for reference, you will notice how few actually keep their house clean and tidy during the selling process. Granted, it can be a chore for some families to maintain a clean house, but the constant effort will pay off in the long run. Keep bathrooms, kitchens, windows, and walls as clean as possible.

Cleanliness also has to do with smells. If your home has any particular odor to it, do whatever it takes to neutralize it. A Royal LePage survey in 2006 attempted to find out what people noticed when buying a home. The survey found that, "53 percent of buyers believed strong odours such as pet and cigarette smells had a stronger impact on their impression of a home over overall tidiness and cleanliness."[22] With this in mind, if you have a pet, make sure his presence in the house in undetectable by anyone viewing it. If you or a family member smokes, you may want to ban the activity to outside, then check for smells within the drapes, carpet, and furniture.

4. If you paint it, make it neutral: Most buyers prefer colors and decorating that are simple and neutral. As tempting as it might be to paint or decorate in a way that sets a distinct style for yourself, the odds are that a prospective buyer has another style altogether. Since people tend to focus first on what they don't like, don't risk the chance that your style might be what turns a buyer off from buying your home.

I happen to prefer bright colors, but I know that I am in the minority. If you do have bright colors already painted in your home, and don't want the expense of repainting entirely, at least make sure that the paint is in good condition. Touch up any marks or scratches, and let the new buyers know that you will leave touch-up paint for them when you move.

5. Stage your yard with landscaping: The beauty of your property from the outside is sometimes called its curb appeal, and it is extremely important. Start by making sure that your lawn and bushes are mowed and trimmed. Plant flowers; they add color and are inexpensive. The first impression a buyer has is set the moment they pull up to the curb and see your home, so don't lose the opportunity to make it look as good as possible.

In some cases, landscaping reaps better returns than most interior upgrades. It has been claimed that the addition of trees, shrubs, plants, walkways, lighting, and patios can increase the value of some properties up to 20%! Although you may not be able to increase your home value so dramatically, enhancing your home's curb appeal should help you maximize whatever value you do receive and minimize the time needed to attract your buyer.

Don't forget the back yard. Remove old and ratty lawn furniture. Buy pots and fill them with colorful flowers. If you have pets that are destructive, confine them to a small portion of the backyard or put them in a lend-lease program for the time your home is for sale. Before showing your property, hose off outdoor furniture and the patio, and keep them clean.

When my husband and I first began buying houses, we lived in Colorado in an area where most of the homes were built in the late 1800s. At the time, we could not afford to remodel or update the inside of a home, so we instead focused on making sure that the outside looked great. That activity alone often made the sale, along with a nice profit. Obviously, you never want to ignore important inside features, but never forget that the yard is equally important as its appearance sets the tone for viewing the house itself.

If you do not want the expense of hiring a professional stager, then something else you might do is invite a friend who's keen on decorating to walk through your house with you. Ask them to view the house as critically as possible and provide as many ideas as they can, so you can use their input to make your house more presentable and sellable. If they are straightforward in their advice, you might receive some very valuable suggestions that you may have never before considered. Just don't take any of their ideas about the house personally!

If you are selling a home priced at the low end of the market, staging probably doesn't make much difference. But, if you really want to get top dollar for your home, or come out on top in competition with other homes for sale at the same time, then make it look as great as possible.

FSBO information from the NAR survey

What type of person typically becomes a FSBO? According to the NAR survey, a typical FSBO is 48 years old (slightly older than non-FSBOs) and makes $84,400 a year, which is slightly under the agent-assisted seller's income of $86,600.[23] This is understandable. If you have gone through the sale process before with an agent, you may be more likely to sell your home yourself. Also, the more income you make, the less likely you are to have the time or inclination to "do it yourself."

However, the most important reason that FSBOs sold their home themselves, according to the NAR survey, was because they did not want to pay the commission (53%). The next major reason was that 22% of them sold their home to a relative, friend, or neighbor. Next, 8% did not want to deal with an agent, 9% had buyers who contacted them directly, 3% had an agent who couldn't sell it so they ended up selling it themselves, and 3% had a real estate license themselves.[24]

As stated elsewhere, the NAR survey reported a major selling price comparison. In their survey FSBOs had an average selling price of $198,200, while the agent-assisted price was $230,000. As I mentioned in an earlier chapter, I think this statistic is not representative due to California's high home values.

When analyzed, the NAR report doesn't break down price by area. Other survey results were divided into five U.S. regions. Surely the price data would be different in different parts of the county? I also believe that the median price for a home dramatically affects whether a person wants to sell their home themselves or list it with a real estate agent. A two-income, busy family has little time to sell their house themselves. And the more expensive the home, the more likely people are to turn it over to a professional so they can conserve their time to make money elsewhere. Plus, when prices rise dramatically in a booming real estate market, sellers are more willing to share unexpected profits. However, when properties stop rising in value and there is less equity to carve up, more FSBOs will want to hang on to any profit they can generate.

In addition, the NAR survey also reveals that 39% of FSBOs knew their buyer before they made the sale.[25] This suggests that many FSBOs in the past have sold to family members or friends. As is often the case, special price concessions are made to such buyers.

How did FSBOs in 2005 market their home? The majority used a yard sign (61%). Beyond that, friends, neighbors or relatives provided 46% of their source for locating a buyer. Next, 37% used newspaper advertising, 29% held an Open House, 17% used the Internet, 3% used direct mail, and 4% advertised in a FSBO magazine.[26]

These statistics impart a significant reason as to why more people did not sell their house themselves—less than 20% used the Internet. If most available buyers use the Internet to find out about properties, that means most wouldn't even know about the FSBO property. Even though friends, neighbors, and relatives were very important, they cannot come close to the exposure provided by the Internet.

What did FSBOs find most difficult? At the top of the list, at 17%, is understanding and completing the paperwork. Next, 16% said that preparing or fixing up their home was difficult. Fourteen percent said that setting the right price was hard, and then 13% said that selling within the expected timeframe was most difficult. Only 9% had trouble finding buyers, and 8% said that having enough time to devote to selling the home themselves was challenging. Three percent said they had difficulty helping the buyer find financing, and 20% had other difficulties.[27]

This information shows that paperwork and pricing are indeed two of the more difficult things you face as a FSBO. Now, because I have explained these in great detail, those should not even be on your list of foreseeable difficulties.

Of all the FSBOs who sold their home without an agent in 2005 as reported in the NAR survey, over 53% would do it again. Only 34% weren't sure. Fourteen percent said they would use a real estate agent instead.[28] Clearly, the majority of those who sold their home themselves are willing to do it again. That should give anyone else considering the prospect the encouragement to do it as well.

Other survey results

Another consumer survey done in 2006 by RealEstate.com provides and clarifies seller activities. The survey results are from 500 homesellers who sold a home during the last three years and offers the following data:[29]

1. According to this survey, 65.2% of those surveyed listed the home with a real estate agent and 27.6% sold their home themselves. These results vary widely from the NAR report. I believe the reason for that is because the NAR survey was a mail out survey from NAR itself rather than an independ-

ent survey company. In my opinion, an independent survey is less biased. The survey also reported that 7.2% used a real estate company that let them pick the services they wanted to use, as with discount brokers.

2. The survey stated only 52.8% would use a real estate agent the next time they wanted to sell their home. At the same time, 33.2% said they would sell it themselves. Fourteen percent said they would use a service that lets them pick and choose. Clearly, those who sold it themselves were happy and some who used a real estate agent wished they hadn't.

3. The top priority when getting the home's exterior ready for sale was to spruce up the lawn and/or landscaping, at 51.6%. Next, sellers felt that it was important to paint the exterior and/or trim (24%), as well as the front door. Following that, lighting and/or potted plants (14.2%) was considered. Finally, sellers suggested making sure that the house numbers were visible from the street.

4. The sellers surveyed said that they thought prospective buyers were most interested in the kitchen (37.8%) when looking inside the house. Next came the family room, at 31%. After that, the living room was important at 15%, and the master bedroom at 11.8%. Finally, the master bath was only important to 4.4% of those looking at houses to purchase.

5. Those surveyed believed that particular neighborhood conditions were important to buyers. These included local school systems at 48.2%, proximity to conveniences at 30.2%, proximity to highways and commuting at 15%, and access to public transportation at 6%.

6. When getting a home ready to show, 50.4% of sellers felt that cleaning everything as thoroughly as possible was the best action. Once clean, sellers believed they should make the home as well lit as possible (19%). After that, putting away personal items and removing clutter came next at 14.2%. A few thought that they should leave the house in an "as-is" lived-in look (9.6%). (I suspect they were just lazy!) Finally, 6.8% said that baking cookies or pie for a sweet smell was a good idea.

Final marketing details—showing your home

There is an art to showing your property correctly. Don't believe me? Then in the weeks leading up to putting a sign in your yard, attend every Open House you see advertised. Watch the owner or the agent and see what works and what feels awkward or pushy. Take notes and rate reactions to review later before you do your own Open House. If you pay attention, you'll see that there are a number of things that make a house show better—and there are just as many that detract. Here are a few of the do's and don't's.

Do:

1. Stage your home before showing it to anyone. See the previous section on home staging for more information.

2. Ask buyers to make appointments—then stay flexible. I recommend that you put on your "For Sale" sign, "by appointment only." Normally, this won't deter most actual buyers and should cut down on any who won't hesitate to knock on your door during dinnertime. Remember, you are in the driver's seat, and you do not have to show your house at inconvenient times if you are simply unable.

   However, with that said, you may want to do your best to make sure your house is as available as possible. If buyers only see 6-10 homes before they actually buy, your home may be the right one at the right time. You can never tell. My advice is to do your best, but never so much that it drives you crazy.

3. Pick one person in the family (or a good friend) who is the best at showing and have them take on this duty. The rest of the family should be as absent as possible (including pets) and stay out of the way. This is a good time to take a long drive around the block.

4. Ideally, one person should take on the showing duties, but always keep safety issues in mind. Make appointments as carefully as you would for any other reason. Have the entire family present when the buyers arrive, and if something seems out of the ordinary, make sure everyone stays. Ask the buyers before they arrive if they will be coming alone, as a couple, or with children. That should also give you an indication of what to expect.

5. Select a good time to show your property. Every home looks better at different times of the day. Usually, it is sometime during the daylight hours. If it is your choice when to show it, pick the time of day you think your home shows at its best.

6. Stay with your prospective buyers as they walk from room to room. This is your home and you want to know what they are looking at. Tell them to feel free to open doors or closets and ask questions—but for the most part, follow silently. Be discreet, but present.

7. Put away any valuables or private information that you don't want others to see. If you have jewelry or other valuables that are easily removed and are sitting around, I suggest that you put them away in a safe location for the entire time you are marketing your home. That way, the home is always ready for a showing and you won't have to keep an eye on your valuables.

8. Have a stack of flyers for your home on the table or on the kitchen counter. If the person viewing your home is a real estate agent, always ask for a card. If it is a buyer alone, ask if they have a business card too. Tell them the card will help you remember their name, and most of the time, people will give it to you. Another option is to have a sign-up sheet for everyone's name and address.

9. Realize in advance that most of the people looking at your home are just lookers. That doesn't mean they don't know someone that might be interested, only that they are there just to take a quick look and move on. Don't take it personally if they don't want to talk or get to know you. Remain friendly, but not attached to their reactions.

10. I also recommend that if your prospective buyers seem halfway interested, ask them what their goals are. It is best if you know upfront whether the people have the motivation to actually buy your home. If you ask, you may get an answer that leads you to further discussion about your home.

Don't:

1.   Don't chatter nonstop. Otherwise, it is impossible for anyone to focus on what they are seeing. Keep quiet for the most part. If prospective buyers have a question, they will ask. If there is something very important that they are unlikely to notice unless you draw their attention to it, then ask them if you can show them the "such and such."

2.   Do not follow the prospective buyers around stating the obvious, like, "this is the kitchen and this is the living room." Avoid saying anything that is obvious by looking.

3.   It is fine to ask people a few questions about themselves, but if they are quiet or introspective, follow their cue. If they start asking questions, then it is clear they want more information about the house. After that, you can begin getting to know them. Otherwise, they are probably just lookers.

4.   Never let a buyer wander through your house unescorted. This is your home and you want to keep an eye on things. Just stand to the side and let them look.

5.   Don't make appointments with anyone who won't give you their name and phone number. If they sound suspicious for any reason, tell them that you can't pick a time at the moment and will need to call them back. If they are less than sincere, they will likely never provide their phone number.

6.   Don't let them privately use the facilities within any bathroom where you keep medications or prescription drugs.

7.   Ignore any of their complaints or criticisms in regard to your house. Yes, some people will unconsciously say some of the most ignorant or rude things. Others may even be attempting to set the stage so they can ask for a discount in price later. Pay no attention to such comments.

8.   Take nothing personally! This includes the good things they say as well as the bad. Some people, who go on and on about loving your home, will never be seen or heard from

again. Others who act picky and judgmental might be doing it because they are really interested. Try not to get excited about anyone who looks at your home until they have been back at least once. Until then, they are all just lookers.

9. Don't leave junk lying around. Every real estate agent can tell you horror stories about some of the homes they have shown buyers. If you have read the section about staging your home, you should already have most of the clutter reduced in your home. But if the kids have been playing with toys before the prospective buyers show up, pick them up! If you routinely change your clothes and leave them where they fall, pick them up! If you usually don't do dishes until late in the evening, do them now! In the end, your mess may not affect the value of your home, but it will dramatically affect what the buyers see when they look at it. Junky houses have a discounted value. If you want to achieve the best price possible, clean it up!

What does this all mean?

It has been my goal in this chapter to show you what is normally done to market homes for sale. If you were to list with a real estate broker, few will do more than what is listed above. Obviously, as a FSBO, you can do just about everything as well. While not difficult, the tasks do require commitment and focus. Yet, as you have probably already calculated, the time and effort of selling your home as a FSBO pays off quite well!

CHAPTER FOURTEEN
Troubleshooting

In the process of selling or buying a home, dozens of events and activities take place that must be addressed if the transaction is to be completed. Many are just activities that will occur without consequence. However, some events have the potential to destroy the sale if not handled correctly. In this chapter, I will discuss some of the common challenges that accompany every home sale.

Marketing challenges

1. No one is even looking at the property or seems interested in buying my home.

If you have few or no prospects looking at your home, then chances are good that your marketing program to attract prospective buyers isn't aggressive enough to generate interest. Some homes have the advantage of being located on easily accessible streets. Others are hard to find, even with a map! If your home is in a gated community or far off the beaten track, you must go above and beyond normal marketing to attract a buyer.

The slower the market and the more difficult it is to locate your house, the more likely it is that you will want to pay to list your property on a local multiple listing service (MLS). The last house I sold was in a country club. The only people who knew it was for sale were a few neighbors who saw the "For Sale" sign. While that may have been enough in a great market, through our local MLS we offered to pay a 3% commission to any buyer's agent who brought us a ready, willing, and able buyer who would ultimately purchase our property. When you offer to pay a buyer's agent's fee in a slow market, you benefit from having your home widely exposed to the real estate community. However, remember that it is always possible to offer even less than what is considered the standard going rate in your area, say 2-2.5%, as the fee paid to a buyer's agent.

Also, go back and review Chapter 13 where I explained the basics of marketing a home. Be sure that you are doing everything suggested to the best of your abilities. If your property is for sale and no one is looking, then chances are good that you've missed some of the necessary steps.

Remember that a buyer's agent's fee is not the same amount as a listing fee! It is usually half, or even less, than what is traditionally a full listing fee. To familiarize yourself with the practice of "MLS for less," see the explanation in Chapter 13.

2. No one is making any offers to buy my home.

There is a saying in real estate that goes something like this, "Any home will sell, as long as the price is right." If no one is even looking at your home and you have done nearly everything suggested in the marketing section in this book, then chances are good that your property is priced too high to attract a buyer in the current market. People will not make the effort to even look if they think your asking price is ridiculously high.

Regardless of the condition of your property, as long as your price reflects the value of that condition, then there is a buyer who will eventually pay something close to your asking price. No matter where it is located, if your price takes that location into account, someone will find it.

Unfortunately, most sellers hope that their property has more value just because that means more money in their pockets. That hope is completely understandable, but not realistic. As mentioned in the chapter on pricing, the market value of your home is what a ready, willing, and able buyer will pay and what you will sell it for under normal circumstances. That value rises and falls with the market, not with your dreams and desires.

Sometimes, the greatest benefit a real estate agent can provide is to compel you to be realistic about your price. Of course, that doesn't always happen. Some agents will take a listing at any price, just to get the listing. But listing your property at a high price won't serve you because homes rarely sell when overpriced. Eventually, in order to generate interest, that listing agent will ask you to lower the price so a buyer can be found.

Clearly, I don't believe you need a real estate agent to set your asking price, but I do urge you to be extremely realistic by investigating and comparing the recent sales in your area. Even if you want to price your home 10-15% higher than what you believe it will sell for, make sure the minimum price you believe you should get is as realistic as possible. If priced much more than 10-15% above market, buyers won't even look at your property, much less make an offer to purchase it.

Additionally, find out the average time it now takes for a home in your area to sell. If your home has been sitting on the market for longer than six months with little or no positive action, then most likely your price is too high.

3. All of my offers are lower than the asking price.

That's to be expected. If you have received a number of offers at prices that are significantly lower than your asking price, then you are ignoring the message. If legitimate, nonspeculating homebuyers have taken the time to make an offer, and then disappeared when you wrote a counteroffer negotiating for a higher price, then chances are good that you have a desirable property, but are just asking for too much.

However, if you are quite confident that your price is reasonable, then ask the buyers (or their agents) how they came up with their offering price. This is a great question that is seldom asked. The usual answer from buyers and/or their agents will be that they checked the data on the sales of comparable homes and the comps told them what your home is worth.

If you have done your homework by gathering your own comparables and preparing a Comparative Market Analysis (CMA) to set the market value of your property, this would be an excellent time to pull out that folder and show them your CMA and explain how you arrived at your asking price. If you can show them homes in your neighborhood that have recently sold which have features similar to yours with sales prices justifying your asking price, then you may convince them to raise the price in their offer. (See Form 318)

4. I lowered the price, but I'm still not selling. Why is it taking so long?

There is no simple answer for how long it takes to sell your home. As long as your price is right and you've completed the basic marketing suggestions I have given you, then you simply have to wait out the time it takes for the right buyer to come forward.

I'm impatient too! The last home we sold took about twice as long as I expected. I did everything that I advise in this book, and my price was right and my marketing program was extensive. However, it still took time for the right buyer to come along.

My advice to you is to lengthen your time-frame expectations for finding your buyer. Don't take it personally that you don't get an offer, and don't get too anxious. Should a sale occur right away, you can always be pleasantly surprised. Remember, in a Seller's Market with many buyers, property will sell quickly after placing it on the market. In a Buyer's Market with lots of sellers, it just takes more time and effort.

5. The buyer's wife said something sarcastic and rude about the color of my bathroom walls (or the carpet, or the playpen in the back yard, or the bushes out front, etc.), yet they still want to make an offer. What should I do?

Unfortunately, not everyone is as tactful as they should be when looking at homes and voicing their opinions out loud. Not only that, they disregard the fact that your home has been a very special part of your life, and that you selected colors and decorating items that you liked for a wide variety of personal reasons they will never understand. Even though they may be out of line for expressing their thoughts in a rude manner, make every effort not to take things personally. In fact, when people are looking at your home, try to imagine yourself as a sales agent so you can disassociate yourself from any personal comments they may make.

In some cases, you might not even like the people who are buying your house. Realize that upfront. Think about it. If a buyer's conduct or personality is going to deter you from selling your home, and you are unable to change your attitude, maybe you aren't the best salesperson for your home.

If questions or comments disturb you too much, or dealing with people you dislike is offensive to you, then you might want to consider putting another family member in charge of the showings and negotiations. Certain people are born with better temperaments for handling these types of interactions. If you can't find a family member to take on this task, perhaps you should strongly consider hiring a real estate agent.

6. My asking price is reasonable and the house is in great condition, but still no offers. Is there something else I can do to attract attention?

Yes. Although it often seems that the price is the deciding factor in most home sales, there are often little incentives that can make a big difference to prospective buyers. One strategy is to offer some sort of bonus to the buyer. Examples of popular bonuses include:

- offering an item of furniture or a fixture that appeals to a particular buyer;
- advertising that you'll include home warranty insurance with the sale of your home;
- including some furniture or outdoor playground equipment that appeals to the buyer's children;
- offering a free vacation week in a time-share or second home you own; and
- offering a car you own.

Keep in mind that all of these items are freebies to the buyer, but a cost to you. However, if you have some reason to believe that they might make a difference and the cost is not too great, use them. You might also want to consider highlighting your advertising with the bonus as a lead-in. Something like, "Buy a house and get a free vacation!" might grab the buyer's attention among all those ads in the newspaper and produce a call.

You can also add incentives for real estate agents. You can advertise saying that you will provide a bonus of 1% or more to any real estate agent that shows and sells your property this weekend. Remember, a bonus doesn't have to be big—you mainly want to use it to get attention and be a call for action. Agents are also attracted to free vacations, so don't hesitate to offer that incentive to professionals as well. Just remember when including an incentive for a buyer or an agent to always set a deadline to generate immediate action.

7. What happens if my home is worth less than what I owe on it?

Real estate prices are cyclical. During the recent real estate boom of 2004 and 2005, house prices were soaring as creative lending allowed many buyers to purchase and finance homes with little or no money down. Unfortunately, many of those buyers who bought at the highest prices now owe more on loans than their house is presently worth. The good news is, as long as the loans are purchase-money loans on a primary residence, they are considered nonrecourse loans.

In other words, because you used the loan money to fund the purchase of your house, your bank or lender has "no recourse' to recover the loan amount from you personally if you default. If you elect to stop making payments on the loan, the only option the lender has is to foreclose and absorb any losses they may have due to the foreclosure sale. However, if you refinanced the loan for any reason, the refinancing is considered a recourse loan. If the loan is a recourse loan, and the lender chooses to judicially foreclose, you could be responsible for any deficiency in the value of the property to cover the loan amount at the time of the foreclosure sale.

So, what are your options if you owe more than the property is worth? My initial advice to you is to wait out the market until the cycle of pricing returns to higher values. Historically, even when the real estate market goes through a down phase, it will recover and your home value will return and even increase after a number of years. Meanwhile, as you wait for market values to rise, you have the benefit of living in your own home.

However, if you must sell your home as a matter of necessity, you do have a couple of choices. Contact your lender and tell them you cannot sell your property for the amount of money you now owe on it and request information about giving the lender a deed-in-lieu of foreclosure. What that means is that rather than foreclosing and taking ownership of your property, you want to just deed your house directly back to the bank and be done with it. (See Form 406)

Why would a lender do that? A lender knows that if his loan is a nonrecourse loan, he cannot require you to pay any deficiencies in the value of your home to fully cover the loan amount upon foreclosure. Rather than face all of the costs, fees, and time necessary to foreclose and resell the property in a Buyer's Market, it is usually in the lender's best interest to accept the deed-in-lieu. But just because they can do it, and sometimes do, doesn't always mean they will, until the downward cycle in the real estate market becomes undeniable. Some lenders believe that it is still to their benefit to go through the foreclosure process because the title is then completely wiped clean of any claims others may have on your ownership when they repossess the property at a foreclosure sale.

There is one other approach to consider when your loan amount is greater than what the property is worth. It is called a short sale. A short sale is where you find a buyer and enter into a contract to sell your property for the highest price possible at the time, contingent on the lender agreeing to accept a lower payoff amount than what is actually owed on the loan. Obviously, this still requires you to market and sell your house, and at the same time, negotiate with the lender. Plus, you lose any equity you may have and the time and effort it will take to sell the property. (See Form 274)

DATE: _____, 20_____, at _____, California.

Items left blank or unchecked are not applicable.

FACTS:

1. This is an addendum to the following agreement:
   - ☐ purchase agreement   ☐ Counteroffer
   - ☐ escrow instructions   ☐ _____

   1.1   dated _____, 20_____, at _____ California,

   1.2   entered into by _____, as the buyer, and

   1.3   _____, as the seller,

   1.4   regarding real estate referred to as: _____

   _____

AGREEMENT:

In addition to the terms of the above referenced agreement, the buyer and seller agree to the following:

2. Close of escrow is conditioned on the seller obtaining payoff demands at a discount from the lienholders of record in full satisfaction of all amounts owed them.

   2.1   The discounts are to be amounts which collectively allow the seller to fully perform on this agreement and escrow instructions without the need for escrow to call for funds from the seller to close escrow.

   2.2   Seller on opening escrow to promptly request payoff demands from the lienholders, directly or through escrow, and diligently assist each lienholder in their analysis of their discount and processing of their payoff demand by providing them with information and documentation on themselves and this transaction.

3. After _____, 20_____, this agreement may be terminated by either the buyer or the seller should the seller be unable to obtain written payoff demands or consent from the lienholders to accept seller's proceeds from this transaction which remain after disbursement of all costs incurred by seller in the full performance of this agreement and escrow instructions. [See **ft** Form 183]

4. Seller may accept backup offers contingent on the cancellation of this agreement.

   4.1   If backup offers are received, they will be submitted to the lienholders for payoff demands which may be accepted by the lienholders in lieu of a payoff demand on escrow under this agreement.

   4.2   Should lienholders submit a written payoff demand in a backup offer acceptable to the seller, the seller may terminate this agreement. [See **ft** Form 183]

I agree to the terms stated above.	I agree to the terms stated above.
Date: _____, 20_____	Date: _____, 20_____
Buyer: _____	Seller: _____
Buyer: _____	Seller: _____
Signature: _____	Signature: _____
Signature: _____	Signature: _____

Short sales work best with local institutional lenders or carryback sellers. If you can show these types of lenders that the market value of the home has been reduced, and that they'll get the property back in foreclosure if they don't cooperate with a short sale, then they may go along with your plan. Again, this requires negotiation with your lender, as well as the ability to market and sell your property for the highest amount possible.

Either way, you will not walk away worry free. Although you are free of the loan, this process will negatively affect your credit. Chance are, it will take a few years and an otherwise good credit and job history before another lender will finance a house for you, so the deed-in-lieu of foreclosure or the short sale should be considered only as last options, short of actual foreclosure.

Purchase agreement challenges

1. You entered into a purchase agreement and now you want to back out of the transaction before it closes.

Normally, the only time one of the people in a transaction can cancel their agreement is when there is a legal excuse or justification. So, what can you do if you do change your mind and decide not to sell your house after you have entered into a purchase agreement with a buyer? You may still have rights to cancel under contingency provisions in your agreement calling for your approval or consent before you are required to proceed. Also, if the buyer promised to accomplish something by a specific date that has not happened and was to benefit you as the seller, then you may be able to exercise a right to cancel the purchase agreement and escrow.

On the other hand, if all the contingencies have been eliminated, and then you want to back out of the sale, what can you do? It depends. If the buyer has already done everything necessary to close escrow, and you then back out by canceling the transaction, the worst-case scenario would see the buyer taking you to court and forcing you to close escrow, or recovering money from you for all his losses caused by his inability to now acquire your property. Whether the purchase agreement contains an attorney fee provision has a lot to do with the likelihood of litigation if you wrongfully cancel. The purchase agreements in the accompanying CD do not include provisions for attorney fee recovery in an effort to avoid litigation. In the long run, what happens and how much it costs will depend upon what kind of people your buyers are and what they are willing to do to get your house.

Possible remedies include:

1. You could explain the situation and ask the buyers to let you out of the transaction by mutual cancellation of the purchase agreement and escrow instructions. (See Form 181)

2. You could offer to pay all costs the buyers have incurred up to that point.

3. You could offer to pay your buyers a cancellation fee (an amount you would negotiate).

212

4. You could retain a lawyer for advice on any vague conditions or contingencies in your purchase agreement, escrow instructions, or buyer activities that you might be able to use as a legitimate basis for backing out of the transaction.

Remember, if all contingencies are removed and the buyer wants to force the issue since he is ready to close escrow, he can take you to court and force you to sell him your house on the terms in the purchase agreement. With that in mind, you may want to negotiate a number of concessions. If you end up in court, the contract will be enforced and you will probably still lose the house and much of the profit in attorney fees and costs. If you even think you might not want to sell in the future, don't put your property on the market for sale.

2. The buyer changed his mind and doesn't want to buy.

If a buyer backs out after all of his contingencies have been removed, you have three options:

1. You can take the buyer to court and force him to perform as agreed in your purchase agreement by buying the property or paying you for any drop in the property's value at the time he breached your agreement.

2. You can agree with the buyer to cancel the purchase agreement and escrow instructions, and then proceed to re-sell your property as quickly as possible without further concern with that buyer. (See Form 181)

3. You can choose not to sell your property and stay put.

But what happens to the buyer's good-faith deposit now held in escrow? Unfortunately, as mentioned before, there is a great deal of misunderstanding surrounding the good-faith deposit made by the buyer when he entered into the purchase agreement. Regrettably, some of the misunderstanding is promoted by the real estate brokerage community out of their desire to get a piece of the deposit if the transaction falls apart.

As mentioned in previous chapters, if the buyer defaults or breaches the contract after all contingencies in his favor have been removed, then the seller can only withhold an amount from the buyer's deposit equal to the actual money losses he incurred due to the buyer's breach. Normally, those losses are limited to:

- the operating and carrying costs for the time period between the moment the buyer breached and the moment the seller was able to resell;

- the nonrecoverable costs or fees paid by the seller under the terms of the purchase agreement; and

- the interest on the seller's net equity from the date scheduled for closing to the date a resale is closed (less actual or imputed rent if the property is occupied by a tenant or yourself).

Keep in mind, however, that should you actually lose money and the buyer refuses to voluntarily release that amount from the good-faith deposit, recovery can become a major battle. You will need to consider the disadvantages over having yourself and possibly your property tied up in a court proceeding to determine whether you are entitled to any part of the deposit if the buyer refuses to cooperate. Will it be worth it? Only you can make that decision.

3. What happens if my buyer dies before the close of escrow or if I do?

If one or more of the buyers die during the process of purchasing your property, your transaction will not close as planned, if ever. Chances are good that the buyer was applying for a new loan to purchase the property, and if he or she is not present, the loan will not be approved, much less funded. Obviously, escrow will not close and the purchase agreement will need to be canceled, unless the successor to the deceased buyer's interest decides to close the transaction.

On the other hand, if a seller dies, the purchase agreement still remains enforceable and escrow will close without a problem as long as the seller had previously delivered the grant deed into escrow. Once the seller enters into a purchase agreement, the only remaining activity required for the seller to perform is the exchange of his deed for money. Although chaos within the seller's family may occur and possibly delay the closing if the deeds are not already in escrow, the sale will usually finalize and the proceeds be dispersed to the survivors of the deceased seller.

4. The buyer wants to renegotiate the transaction after the purchase agreement is signed.

Occasionally, a buyer will come back to you and ask for things that you didn't previously agree to do or provide. Technically, there is nothing that can keep a buyer from asking, but you are not required to change the terms of your agreement once you have signed the contract unless the buyer pays something for that modification.

However, and this is a big however, if some of the contingencies in the transaction still need to be satisfied, then the buyer may be in a position to request changes that the seller should consider. As the seller, you will then have to decide once again what you are willing to do to keep the transaction alive.

For example, if you did not provide the buyer with the property's Transfer Disclosure Statement (TDS) prior to entering into the purchase agreement, he has three days to read and approve the document or cancel the transaction. If, within those three days, he comes back to you and says that he wants to pay less for your property or he will pull out because of unexpected disclosures, he can legally do so. Your choice will be whether you agree to the change or refuse to agree and wait to see if the buyer will cancel the purchase agreement.

As long as contingencies remain that give the buyer the option to cancel the purchase agreement, the buyer can come back to you with other requests. That is why it is so important for you to either avoid contingencies altogether or to proceed through contingencies as quickly as reasonably possible. Most of the time, buyers will not use their contingency provisions to squeeze you for a better deal, but there are those who make it a habit.

Your best move is to always deliver documents and disclosures before entering into a purchase agreement and to aid in loan processing activities in concert with the buyer as quickly as possible after going under contract. By following all the suggestions that I offer in this book, you should be able to eliminate most causes that allow a buyer to renegotiate after the purchase agreement has been signed. Remember, if you give a buyer the opportunity to renegotiate, you should expect that he will.

5. A water pipe broke and flooded the house while the property was in escrow. Who has to fix it, and what happens now?

Sometimes property is either damaged or destroyed before the close of escrow. Because this is always a possibility, the purchase agreement Form 157, on the accompanying CD deals with physical damage to the property in Section 12.8. If the property is materially damaged prior to closing, the condition-of-property provision gives the buyer the right to terminate the agreement.

In other words, if the house is flooded and the damage it causes adversely affects the value of the property, then the buyer has the option of canceling the transaction. If you talk to the buyer and together determine that the flooding can be fully repaired, then the buyer has the option of continuing with the transaction.

Basically, any damage to the property that affects its value puts the buyer in the position of deciding what comes next. Of course, if he proposes something, such as asking for a credit that is out of proportion to the cost of the repair, then you have the right to disagree and force the buyer to decide whether to proceed or cancel.

6. There is a cloud on the title that I didn't know about. Escrow says that it will likely take beyond the closing date to remove it. What happens now?

As mentioned in a previous chapter, a cloud on your title is something that makes the title to your property unmarketable under the terms of your purchase agreement. Before you can close escrow, you must clear up the cloud. The most common cloud is created when a previous loan was paid off, but the proper paperwork was never filed to release the loan amount. Until the proper papers are provided to remove the cloud, it will remain on your title and delay closing.

If for any reason your title is not marketable due to a cloud on the title, then the buyer has the option to cancel the purchase agreement. However, if the buyer can be assured that the cloud will be removed within a reasonable period of additional time and agrees to an extension of the closing date, then the transaction can proceed even though its closing will be delayed.

7. The buyer's previous home hasn't sold, but he still wants to buy my house. What can I do?

You always have the option of extending the time period for closing your purchase agreement to accommodate your buyers. This may even be an easy decision if you haven't received other purchase offers or if there aren't any other prospective buyers seriously looking to buy your property. An extension can be added to the time period for the elimination of any contingency, as long as you both agree.

Plus, if an agent is involved and purchase agreement Form 150 is used, he has the automatic right under Section 10.2 to extend the period for satisfying contingencies and closing escrow for up to one month.

8. The buyer made a low-ball offer, so I submitted a counteroffer. He never even responded. Is that normal?

Sometimes. If your buyer was just testing the water to see if you would accept a low-ball offer, he might not respond to you because he couldn't buy your house at a bargain-basement price. However, if you countered his offer at your full asking price, that will most likely turn off your prospective buyer. Many interpret a full price counteroffer to mean that you won't budge on your price whatsoever. If you won't and they don't think your property is worth your asking price, they won't bother countering you with another price lower than your asking price.

If you counter with an offer in the spirit of compromise since you are both interested in a common goal—the sale of the property—then the buyer will most likely respond. If they don't, you have every right to call them and ask them why. It is possible that his circumstances have changed since he first made you an offer. It is also possible that he found another property that he likes better. Even if that is true, it is important to know where your price and your property stand in the marketplace. So, if you really want to know why the buyer has not gotten back to you, call him. That is what a real estate agent would do. As a For Sale By Owner (FSBO), you need to take the initiative since you do not have an agent conducting negotiations on your behalf.

9. The buyer and I agreed on a price, but the appraisal by the lender came back for a lower amount. What do I do now?

No guarantee exists to assure you that the lender's appraisal will match or exceed the sales price you and your buyer have negotiated. As mentioned in the chapter on arriving at a price, I explained how even when the data on comparable properties are similar, different appraisers interpret the data in very different ways. In any event, the lender's loan amount is based on a percentage of the property's value, and a lower-than-sales-price appraised value means that the property's value does not support the full amount of loan the buyer has applied for to buy your home. So what happens now?

Basically, if the appraised value is lower than the price you and your buyer have agreed to, the buyer has the option of canceling the purchase agreement. The buyer has this right because the property's value does not allow him to satisfy his loan contingency provision in the purchase agreement. If a lower-than-sales-price appraisal happens to you as a seller, you have a couple of choices:

1. The most obvious choice is for you to lower your price to the appraised amount and continue with the sale. While this may save your sale, it will also reduce your net proceeds by the full amount of the price reduction.

2. If you are fairly certain your home is priced correctly, you can stick to your guns and insist on the price. At that point, the buyer will have to decide if they still want to pay your price, usually by increasing the amount of the down payment, or if not, to cancel the purchase agreement. If your buyer cancels, you have repurchased your house for the amount that represents the difference between what the appraiser says your property is worth and what you believe. If you can accept the fact that another buyer may not come along right away, then hold fast to your price and wait, especially if the sales market appears to be strengthening.

    If an appraisal comes in for less than expected, that means the loan amount will be less, hence a larger down payment. In that case, the buyer must come up with more cash. Another option would be for you to provide the difference between your asking price and the appraised price by financing that amount in a seller carryback note.

    If a buyer is determined to buy your home, he will probably pay whatever you are asking regardless of the appraisal. However, it is unusual for most buyers to want any particular house that badly, unless little money is involved in the difference and they either have the cash or can borrow it elsewhere.

Real estate agent problems

1. A real estate agent keeps calling and bugging me to list my house. Is there anything I can do?

When explaining how the real estate business works, I mentioned earlier that all real estate agents work for a broker. If an agent is pestering you to the point of rudeness, I suggest you contact the office where the agent works. Explain that you need to speak to the office manager or the managing broker of the office. Once connected, explain that a particular agent from his office has crossed the line and you want to complain.

Be specific. Say that you do not want this agent to contact you again or you will be forced to complain to the California Department of Real Estate (DRE) about his conduct. Brokers know that they are 100% responsible for overseeing the conduct and actions of their agents and will resolve the problem, even though they might explain that the agent is an independent contractor.

2. The buyer wants to use his real estate agent. Do I have to pay his agent a commission?

If a buyer uses the services of a real estate agent to submit an offer which asks you, the seller, to pay a brokerage fee, you have three choices:

1. You can say no and reject the offer as long as a broker is involved. Of course, you must then be prepared for the possibility that the agent will convince the buyer to look at other homes to purchase. Shifting the buyer to another property whose owner will "cooperate" with the agent by paying a fee does occasionally happen.

2. You can negotiate the amount the buyer's agent is to receive as his fee. Even if the agent initially asks for the customary 3% selling agent's fee, you can always offer to pay less. You can start with an offer of 1%, which the agent might agree to if he has only spent a small amount of time with the buyer. Just remember that if you are anxious to sell, it may be in your best interest to make a deal satisfactory to the agent. Do not alienate the agent unless you are willing to lose the buyer as a prospect for your home.

3. You can negotiate by adding the amount of the real estate fees to the asking price of the house in a counteroffer. If the buyer agrees, you may well have sold your home.

With these suggestions in mind, be sure to remember how you arrived at your asking price. Did you price the property 10% over what you believed was its market value? If you asked a slightly higher amount, knowing you would take a slightly lower offer, then consider that fact when negotiating the brokerage fee. If a buyer offers a full price offer and you know you have 10% to play with, giving an agent 2-3% may turn into a very good deal. Keep in mind that a buyer's agent is usually not in the negotiations as a hostile adversary. A buyer's agent actually provides the buyer with advice and assistance that will make your transaction go more smoothly.

3. The buyer's real estate agent is making demands after we signed the purchase agreement.

My parents sold their house several years ago. Before closing escrow, the buyer's agent just about blew the deal. The agent was a fast-talking, pushy individual who insisted that the abandoned TV antennae on the house be removed. My father, who didn't like the agent in the least, argued against doing it. However, the agent continued to insist and threatened to walk away with the buyer if it wasn't removed. My father removed the antennae to end the dispute. After the closing, my father spoke to the buyer and pointed out the absent antennae. The buyer casually remarked it was not he who was concerned about the antennae. In other words, the agent was the one who wanted the antennae removed, not the buyer.

My point with this example is that you should find out from the buyers themselves what is important. If they do work with an agent, explain that whenever there is a request for you to do something outside of what the purchase agreement states that you would like to speak to the buyers yourself. Nothing prohibits you from speaking with the buyers when an agent is attempting to assert control over the transaction. Insist on it, and ask the buyer directly.

4. The buyer's agent wants to use his broker's escrow company to close the transaction. Is that okay?

Usually, it is up to whoever is paying the costs of a service to select the company to use. If both parties split the charges, as is most often the case with escrows, then selecting the escrow officer is a negotiable item.

My only recommendation would be that you avoid using a broker-owned escrow company, unless it is licensed by the Department of Corporations (DOC) as an independent escrow company. A broker-owned escrow company operates under the broker's real estate license and is controlled only by the DRE with a recovery fund limited to $20,000 per licensee involved. Similarly, title company escrows are not required to provide specific insurance for any losses they might cause a buyer or seller to suffer when they handle the escrow. However, independent escrow companies licensed by the DOC are required to bond their employees and carry special insurance against losses.

Remember, the escrow company you choose will be holding your buyer's deposit, down payment, and eventually the new loan proceeds in the transaction—not to mention your net proceeds when the sale closes. You want to make sure that your funds are protected as much as possible.

5. The buyer's real estate agent says we can't use the forms on my CD if he is involved. Is that true?

No. The forms on the accompanying CD contain all the necessary contract and disclosure provisions to buy and sell residential property in the state of California. The agent might not be as familiar with them as you are and therefore would prefer to use a form he knows backwards and forwards. Likewise, you will want to use the enclosed forms because they are the ones you know. While it is your choice which form you use, if he repeatedly insists on using his form, then the agent is more concerned about his personal needs than about yours or your buyer's. If you do agree to use his form, make sure the agent fully explains every provision on his contract, why it is included, and what it does for you in contrast to provisions in the form you want to use. Make the agent work to educate you by clarifying what he is forcing you to use before you sign anything. Too often, agents expect blind obedience from sellers and buyers.

6. The buyer's agent says if I don't pay him a fee, he will talk the buyers out of buying my home. Can he do that?

Yes. The real estate agent is under no obligation to you. He does not have to find you or even present you with a buyer. The agent represents the buyer as a buyer's agent and is duty bound to care for and protect his buyer's best interests in buying a home. He has every right to ignore your needs as a seller. Is it proper conduct? Maybe not, especially if his sole motivation for talking the buyer out of buying your house is your failure to pay a fee. It may not be nice, but it still happens.

Of course, that doesn't mean that you can't call the buyers and encourage them to deal directly with you when the agent is upset about the fee arrangements. If the buyers are in love with your home, they might consider going around their agent and buying from you directly. Still, if they do go around their agent, you will want them to sign a provision that releases you from any obigation whatsoever to their agent.

Although you may be able to go around the agent to the buyers, I recommend you work to compromise. If the agent has been working with the buyers for any length of time, they probably have built up loyalty to him. It may be in your best interest to pay the real estate agent something, by either increasing the purchase price slightly to cover a small commission or resorting to the margin in your original asking price for a discount.

Remember, even though saving a commission may be a strong motivation for not listing your home with a broker, your primary goal is to sell your home. Keep focused on your goal of locating a buyer at all times, and weigh the benefits of having a ready buyer at your disposal in exchange for paying a small percentage as the agent's fee. Negotiation does not mean that you win and everybody else loses. It means that you, the buyers, and maybe even the agent all win too. Chances are good that you will get a price greater than the lowest one you would have accepted and the buyer will get their dream home.

7. I listed my property on the local MLS though the Internet and offered to pay a buyer's agent a 3% fee. However, an agent's buyer offered much less than my asking price. I need to sell, but don't want to pay that 3%. Do I have to?

No. When you list in any MLS environment, you merely make an offer to pay a broker a percentage fee to find a buyer for your property based upon your asking price. If a real estate agent brings you a buyer that submits a full price offer, you owe a commission because he produced a buyer at your price and thus accepted your offer to pay a fee. However, if the price the agent brings you is less than the listed price, you have the right to negotiate a new fee amount you are willing to pay since he did not comply with your original MLS offer.

For example, if you listed your home on the MLS for $500,000, offering to pay a buyer's agent a 3% fee, and an agent brings you an offer for $475,000, your original fee agreement is negated since the offer he submitted does not conform to your offer. You now have the right to negotiate any fee amount you wish. Just keep in mind that if you can't negotiate the fee so that both you and the agent are happy, the agent may begin to work against you.

Very few sellers know that the brokerage fee they offered in the MLS is negotiable if the price offered by a buyer comes in lower than the asking price. Of course, if the agent has clearly been working very hard to bring you a good offer and the price is close to what you expected, the agent has delivered a buyer at substantially your asking price so you should, but are not bound to, pay the advertised fee. Just remember, if you are asked to dramatically compromise your price, don't be afraid to ask the agent to share by reducing his fee.

8. The agent working with the buyer says that if I pay him a fee and he is involved in the transaction that my liability exposure is less. Is that true?

No. The only time an agent has the duty to protect you against liability is when he is employed by you under a listing. In that case, he then undertakes the duty to see to it that you do all the things required of you in a transaction. When you are represented by a listing agent and he does not advise you to provide your disclosures as you are required to do by law, then you can hold him responsible if the buyer later comes back against you for money losses. However, when you sell your home yourself, the agent submitting a purchase offer represents the buyer and you cannot rely on him for anything except to answer your inquiries truthfully and to the best of his knowledge.

A buyer's agent should help with the buyer's loan application and other activities necessary to complete the sale. There are also a number of other buyer activities that should benefit from the help of a buyer's agent. Ideally, a competent buyer's agent is a positive voice in a transaction, but his existence will not affect your liability exposure or risk of loss whatsoever.

9. I don't want to be a FSBO anymore. Is there anything I should know before I list with a broker?

Yes. First, if you dealt with any prospective buyers that were somewhat serious about your home during the time you marketed the property yourself, ask that those buyers be excluded on the listing with your new broker. By excluding all previous prospective buyers, you avoid having to pay a fee to your listing agent if those buyers return to buy your house. After all, you found them yourself, whether or not they have their own agent.

Next, be aware that you can negotiate the fee the listing agent will receive. If you have been marketing your home for some time, you now know that the listing agent will do little more than put your home on the MLS. You have already prepared all your property disclosures and obtained all the inspection reports that a buyer should be handed before making an offer, so you have reduced what a listing agent can now offer you. If MLS exposure to locate a buyer is the major benefit you now seek, then you may want to consider a discount broker who will merely list your property on the MLS and charge you a small flat fee for that service.

If you have already been on the MLS and still want to list with a broker, get them to put in writing all the things that they will do beyond what you are now doing to market the property and locate buyers. Ask them to list each and every action they intend to do to market your home. Analyze that list carefully before you agree to list your home with that agent.

A proficient agent is usually worth the fee they charge—especially if they are involved from the very beginning. However, if a home has been sitting on the market for a long time and not selling despite the fact that comparable homes are moving, then there are usually two things to consider:

- your price is too high; or
- the market is presently very slow and it's going to take more time than originally anticipated.

If both of these conditions exist, your home isn't going to sell right away, with or without an agent. Keep these things in mind if you consider entering into a listing.

10. I have listed my property with a real estate broker and now I want to cancel it and become a FSBO. What do I need to know?

If you signed an exclusive listing employing a real estate broker in your area, you have agreed to pay them their fee at the moment they bring you a ready, willing, and able buyer at the full listing price. However, if they are not acting diligently to market your property and locate a buyer, then they are not performing their services as an agent and you have every right to cancel the listing and go else-where. Yet, some agents will tell you that you cannot cancel the list-ing without paying their fee. Are they right? Yes, if they have worked continuously and competently, using all readily available methods to market your property and locate a buyer.

If you asked your broker to do specific things to market your home that were quite costly, and the broker did as required, then he has met his obligations to you and earned his fee. If you then cancel your listing agreement, you are liable for a fee as though he had sold your property.

Currently, most listing agreements you are asked to sign include a withdrawal-from-sale and termination-of-agency provision. These listing terms require that you pay a fee if you cancel the listing or withdraw your home from the market without legal justification. Have a clear understanding of these listing provisions before you em-ploy a broker so you know exactly what will happen and how much it will cost you if you back out.

However, should your agent agree in the listing agreement to perform specific marketing activities for your home and those things are not done, then he has breached his agreement and his agency du-ties, and you probably owe nothing. On that basis, you can cancel the listing because the agent has not exercised due diligence when per-forming his duties.

What is due diligence? Due diligence is the bundle of inspec-tions, actions, and care that can be reasonably expected in the market-ing of the property by an agent. If the agent hasn't fully performed, he cannot hold you to his listing agreement. If you want out, write a letter to the broker or office manager of the office requesting a release from the listing for failure of the agent to diligently represent your best interests. Make a follow-up call. Be sure to get the cancellation in writing on Form 121 in the accompanying CD before you begin marketing on your own or you could still owe a commission, even if you sell it yourself.

11. My listing expired and then I sold my home myself. The former agent says I now owe him a fee. Is that true?

Whether you owe a fee under an expired listing depends on who your buyer is and when you agreed to sell to that buyer. Fee provisions in all listing agreements contain safety clauses stating that the broker has earned a commission if you sell your property to prospective buyers the broker negotiated with prior to the listing expiring.

As you might imagine, some homeowners have been known to take advantage of the services of a real estate agent and then cancel the listing agreement, only to turn around and sell their home to someone that the agent had worked with in the past. Listing agreements contain provisions to protect agents from such malicious action.

An agent protects his previous time and effort under a safety clause included in the listing agreement by providing a list of names of those prospective buyers the agent introduced to your home and provided information to during the listing period. Should any of those buyers return to buy your house during the safety period after the listing expires, you will owe that agent a fee. Normally, the safety period has a time frame of anywhere from 3-12 months. If your listing expires and you sell your home yourself, make sure that your buyer was not listed on the agent's notice of prospective buyers. If listed as a prospective buyer and your negotiations to sell to that buyer occurred during the safety clause period, you will owe a fee.

12. A prospective buyer of my home was working with a real estate agent when he viewed my house and now wants to work directly with me. Do I have to pay anyone a fee?

Generally, no. Because you never employed an agent under a listing agreement or any other type of fee arrangement, you aren't liable as their client. Therefore, you can work freely with any buyers interested in your home without owing a fee. However, a slight chance may exist that the buyer had signed a buyer's listing agreement employing an agent or created some other obligation to an agent. In this case, the buyer would be liable for any fee. To be safe, you may want to require the buyer to indemnify and hold you harmless should any broker they have worked with make a claim on you for a fee.

13. Do I have to enter into a listing agreement to pay a broker a fee?

No. You do not need to employ a broker in order to pay him a fee. If you aren't getting any action on your home and want to try something, put an ad in the paper with your address and phone number and write in something like, "Will cooperate with brokers." This means that you will pay a fee if an agent brings you an offer from one of the buyers he is presently working with.

Again, the amount of the fee you will pay is strictly negotiable. Chances are good that the agent will call and ask about the fee arrangement you will agree to before he brings his buyers to see your house. Have a ready answer. You might tell them that if you receive a full price offer you will pay 3%. If you get less than full price, you will pay somewhat less. That usually works.

Should the agent submit an offer from his buyer, he will probably request 3%, even if the offer is less than full price. You know what to do. Simply negotiate the amount along with the other terms of the offer. If the agent keeps insisting on 3%, then ask him or his buyer to pay for other items that you might otherwise pay, like the premiums on a home warranty or title insurance policy. Agents and buyers are not barred from paying those expenses, and it might make the deal work.

Other questions that might pop up

1. I have a good friend who says he will help me sell my house if I pay him a fee. He isn't a licensed agent, but I think he'd do a good job. Is there a problem with that?

Yes. In California, it is quite clear that only people licensed by the California DRE, or as an attorney, can accept a fee for helping you sell your house, unless they are licensed as an attorney. This licensing requirement is meant to protect the public from dishonest, corrupt, and incompetent individuals, but it sometimes limits your options.

On the other hand, friends might be a tremendous help in locating buyers. What you can do is offer them a finder's fee if they introduce you to someone who buys your house. However, once they put the buyer in contact with you, they are not allowed to show your property, provide data, or negotiate terms. They can only put you in touch, and for that you can pay them a fee. (Of course, friends can always help you, you just can't pay them a fee for it.)

How much can you offer as a finder's fee? There is no limit on the amount or how you pay it. If you decide to go the finder's fee route, Form 115 on the accompanying CD is for this purpose. The finder's fee can be paid on the close of escrow by fee instructions given to escrow, or you can just pay it yourself after closing.

Another thing you might want to consider as a marketing plan is to offer a bonus (finder's fee) to any neighbor that brings you the person who buys your home. A good time to introduce that would be when you hold a Neighborhood Open House and invite all the neighbors. A bonus that might get attention would be anything that sounds really fun or unique without costing too much. Again, if you have a time-share that you seldom use, you could offer a week's vacation along with $1,000 spending money. Or what about tickets for the whole family to go to Disneyland? If you can offer something that will get the neighborhood talking, you've done your job. Even if none of your neighbors ends up referring a buyer, you will still have the entire neighborhood talking up your sale.

2. What about "For Sale" signs? My Homeowners' Association (HOA) says that I can't place one outside my unit. Is that right?

In most cases, yes. Unless you have written permission from your HOA, you are restricted from displaying your real estate sign within the common area. In a condominium, you usually only own the airspace inside your unit. You can always place a sign on the inside of your window. However, if you live in a Common Interest Development (CID), the association cannot bar you from placing a "For Sale" sign on your property and advertising it for sale with directions, names, and contact information.

Then again, government agencies can restrict the size, color, and shape of signs that are used. Cities always restrict your placing signs in public right-of-way areas or along highways. Sellers and agents are also prohibited from using a neighbor's property for signs or directional indicators without permission.

3. Do I have to use an attorney?

In some states in the United States, you must hire an attorney to review your closing documents and/or provide their opinion. Not so in California where much of the process is standardized, allowing sellers and their agents to fill in forms of their liking and proceed to closing using a non-attorney escrow service. Neither is the sales process controlled nor the type of form mandated. It's an open market. The same is true with documents used by the escrow holder.

The only time you might want to get an attorney involved is when something unusual or unique about your property or your transaction is brought to your attention. Should the use of an attorney be necessary, I recommend that you seek out a lawyer who specializes in real estate. Few attorneys do. Those that don't often end up being more disruptive than helpful for lack of experience.

If necessary, an experienced real estate attorney will clarify and resolve issues if that is your goal and will be well worth their hourly charge. To locate a real estate attorney, ask several real estate brokers who they would recommend. A common name will usually pop up as the attorney to use.

4. Is there anything I need to know about discrimination and/or fair housing requirements before I begin marketing my property?

My best advice is to treat all individuals equally and fairly by not discriminating against anyone simply because they are from a particular class of people. As long as you treat all prospective buyers without regard to their race, color, religion, sex, marital or familial or domestic status, ancestry, national origin, sexual orientation, physical handicaps, or other distinguishing features, you will be fine.

You will find yourself in trouble if you apply a different standard and treat others differently simply because they belong to a legally protected class of people. The only time discrimination to eliminate people as buyers is permitted is when evenly applied, and is not selective to eliminate a protected class of persons who might be buying. For example, a buyer who cannot qualify for a loan, or has no savings for a down payment, makes a poor prospect to buy your home and may be discriminated against. In other words, insolvent individuals are not a protected class of people.

Obviously, if you refuse to show your property or accept an offer, or purposely avoid contact with anyone with the intent to avoid them based on his or her status as a member of a protected class, you could be accused of discrimination. If that happens, you could find yourself before a government agency.

These are just a small sample of some of the things that can pop up during your transaction. Some sales go so smoothly that nothing extra is necessary. Others have one thing after another to deal with on a regular basis. Interestingly enough, whether or not you have challenges is seldom tied to whether you sell your property yourself. I have seen some sales go horribly wrong precisely because they did use a real estate agent, so don't let your fears of dealing with a buyer yourself keep you from doing the job. Just know that you will be able to handle anything that comes along.

CHAPTER FIFTEEN
Final considerations when selling your property

If you've gotten this far in the book and still want to sell your home yourself, good for you! I have explained as thoroughly as possible what you will face and have attempted to make it as uncomplicated as possible. Throughout this book I've insisted that most people can sell their home themselves and save a lot of money. However, what I think doesn't really matter. In the end, you need to decide if the savings will justify the time and commitment required of you.

In this last chapter, I will clarify a few more pieces of the puzzle and offer you some final advice. As you can see from the many items and tips included in this book, numerous routine details are involved with every transaction. Obviously, it is impossible to cover every single instance, but I think that as long as you understand most of what I've explained, you will know what you need to do to market and sell your home yourself as quickly and effectively as possible.

Income taxes

As mentioned elsewhere in the book, capital gains taxes on the sale of a principal residence are currently very favorable for homeowners. In the past, you needed to purchase another home to avoid paying tax on your profit. That has changed. If you have owned and lived in the home you are now selling for two out of the last five years (consecutive or not), you qualify for up to a $250,000 tax-free exclusion on the profit from the sale of your home. If you are married—and file a joint tax return—you both can take the $250,000 allowance for a total of $500,000. Let me repeat that, you can now make up to $500,000 per couple tax-free every two years! At a capital gains rate of 15%, that's up to $75,000 in taxes you can avoid paying. This is an amazing savings for most people.

Your profit on a sale is the amount your principal residence has increased in value beyond the amount you paid for it. About the only other limitation, besides the two-year owner-occupancy requirement, is the fact that the property has to be your primary home (no second homes allowed) and you can only claim the allowance once every two years. If you rented it out and depreciated the property for tax purposes, you still get the full amount of the profit tax exclusion on all the profit after your depreciation if you owned and lived in it two out of the five years prior to the sale.

But what happens if you have lived in your home for less than two years before you sold it, and have a substantial profit? The Internal Revenue Service (IRS) has created exemptions that may allow you to avoid paying taxes on some of your profit. These exemptions include:

- an act of God, war, or terrorism that results in a casualty to the resident;
- death;
- getting fired from work and going on unemployment;
- a significant change in employment or self-employment that makes housing costs impossible to pay;
- divorce or legal separation;
- multiple births resulting from the same pregnancy; and
- involuntary conversion of the residence, in other words, condemnation.

If you or your family qualify for any of these hardships and need to sell your property prior to the two-year, own-and-occupy rule, you may qualify for a pro rata share of the $250,000 exclusion and pay no taxes on that amount of your profit. Other exemptions may be allowed, but you would be required to address the IRS directly and they would be decided on a case-by-case basis.

It is important to determine how your sale will affect your tax liability in advance. If you are close to the two-year residency requirement and anticipate a profit from the sale, you might want to make sure to delay closing any sale until after the two year owner-occupant mark has passed.

What about federal and state tax withholding, and why should you care?

If you are a citizen or resident of the United States and you are selling your home, you probably will not be affected by the federal or state tax withholding requirements. The federal tax withholding law, called the Foreign Investment Real Property Tax Act (FIRPTA), and the state withholding law, called the California Foreign Investment Real Property Tax Act (CAL-FIRPTA), collect profit taxes from nonresident aliens through escrow in order to insure that those sellers pay taxes on any profit they made on property they sold.

If you are a nonresident foreigner, the IRS is to be paid 10% of your sales price at the close of escrow. The good news is that if the property is sold for less than $300,000 and the buyer will occupy it as his principle residence, then escrow will not even report your sale to the IRS. Even better news is that escrow will handle all the paperwork, including the forms necessary to prove that you are exempt.(See Form 301)

CAL-FIRPTA is similar in that escrow will provide all the forms that need to be filled out prior to closing. If the home is a personal residence, or less than $100,000 in value, then a seller is exempt from this withholding tax. If the property is an investment, it gets more complicated. While your escrow officer cannot help you fill out the forms, there are instructions available which will help you compute any withholding you would be required to fulfill. If you think you might fall into that category, you may want to research CAL-FIRPTA in advance or talk to a tax advisor prior to the sale of your property so you will know what tax liability you may be facing before the actual closing.

Homeowners' insurance

Even though homeowners' insurance or property-hazard insurance is normally an obligation that belongs to buyers, you may want to be aware that the buyer's failure to promptly apply for coverage commonly delays a closing. For some reason, in light of all the details the buyer must take care of to close escrow, insurance is frequently overlooked until the last minute. If it isn't in place, or a binder hasn't been issued when the new loan is ready to fund, then everything grinds to a halt and everyone must wait for the insurance agent to act.

It is in your best interest to assist the buyer with property insurance contacts. By sharing with them what company you have used in the past and reminding them to follow through, you will get them past this common roadblock before the date scheduled for closing.

Normally, the buyer contacts an insurance company, then fills out all the necessary applications and paperwork required for the insurance company to issue a policy, which is then passed on to escrow.

The buyer either pays the premium in advance or arranges for it to be paid though escrow. Either way, the application for a policy should be completed prior to a week or two before the final loan documents are drawn.

Also know that every claim you have ever made will affect the buyer's hazard insurance policy. Insurance companies now rate all future risks for a particular property based on claims made by prior owners of the property. That data affects the property for all time.

If you do end up listing with a real estate broker

If you ultimately decide after reading this book that you want to go ahead and list your property for sale by employing a real estate agent, I have a couple of last minute suggestions.

Suggestion 1.

Remember, the brokerage fee charged to sell a property is negotiable. Of course, you may have to negotiate with the broker rather than his agent, who has contacted you. Just don't let dealing with the agent's broker deter you from asking. Understand that although some agents and their brokers will not negotiate their fee, many will do so.

Suggestion 2.

If you intend to buy a house when you sell the one you are in, ask your agent if he will reduce his fee since you will be dealing with him on both your sale and the replacement home. For example, if the customary brokerage fee for a home sale in your area is 5%, ask your agent if he would instead list your home for 4%. At the same time, guarantee him you will buy your next home using him as your agent. Although he will earn a smaller than traditional fee on the sale of your property, he will receive a full buyer's agent fee when you buy a replacement property. In this case, a prudent agent will want you to sign a buyer's listing agreement employing him to help you locate and purchase a home in the future. The main benefit to you is a discount on the brokerage fee when selling your home.

Suggestion 3.

Remember that the more expensive the property, the more the total dollar amount of the brokerage fee. For that reason, you should be able to pay a reduced fee based on a smaller percentage of the sales price or a flat fee on the sale of a high-priced home, and pay a slightly higher percentage on a less expensive one.

For example, the standard real estate fee for a vacant lot used to be 10%. That was because a vacant lot was usually so inexpensive, the only way you could get an agent to work on one was to offer a higher than average fee amount. Not any more. Because lots are much more expensive now, brokerage fees for lots are comparable to many homes.

Unfortunately, a number of die-hard agents refuse to recognize that they are asking for the same percentage fee on multi-million dollar homes as they do on mom-and-pop fixers. However, these properties aren't the same animal! When it comes down to it, most agents know that it takes a similar amount of time to sell an inexpensive fixer-upper as it does to sell a mansion. With that in mind, if you have an expensive property, don't be afraid to ask for a reduction in the percentage fee amount right from the beginning. Often a flat fee, not a "fat fee", can be negotiated.

Suggestion 4.

Take the time to find an agent that you respect, then stick by him. Proficient agents with a history of exemplary service to sellers deserve your loyalty. I hope I have explained throughout this book that although a good agent is hard to find, when you find one, you should respect that agent and their expertise! Plus, if you want your agent to work hard and be there for you, then compensate him fairly.

Suggestion 5.

If you do come across an agent that clearly knows less about real estate than you do after reading this book, tell them you're not interested in dealing with them. Don't waste your time educating and correcting a novice. While they may be wonderful people, chances are the fee they would like to charge will be the same as if you were working with an experienced agent. You actually assist the real estate industry when you support agents who are competent and refuse to work with those who are not.

Suggestion 6.

Don't expect the same quality of real estate agent across the board, especially if you list with a discount broker. One complaint heard frequently is that a seller listed with a discount broker and then received no benefit from that broker other than placing the home in the local multiple listing service (MLS). Obviously, that is why he is called a "discount" broker! I personally believe that offering limited service at a discount is a great option, but never with the expectation that the broker will do more than provide the minimum level of service advertised.

Suggestion 7.

Recognize upfront that some buyer's agents will give less consideration, if any, to your property if you list your property at a lower fee or with a discount broker. In this current transitional stage of the real estate sales industry, many agents refuse to adapt and change. A number of agents have enjoyed receiving excessive fees due to the rising price of real estate and changing market conditions. Rather than adjust, some agents shun anyone, other brokers included, who are attempting to sell real estate in a new way at even lower fees for their services.

If you list agreeing to pay a smaller than what is considered a standard fee in your area, some agents will refuse to show your home to their buyers. Although seldom in the buyer's best interest, and quite unethical as it is a failure of the agent to care for his client, it still happens. You need to know about and expect to see such behavior, and not suffer from the illusion that all real estate agents do what is best for their clients and the public. You and all other sellers need to weed out such agents by refusing to work with them!

With that said, most agents work very hard and very ethically to serve their clients. Realize that for the sale of your property, you are better off searching for a skilled and experienced agent rather than attempting to deal with a less desirable one you would have to constantly police.

Suggestion 8.

If you do list your house, and the broker brings you an offer that is less than full price and not on the terms solicited in the listing, then you don't owe the full amount agreed to in your listing agreement. After all, if the broker expects you to accept a price for less than what you listed it for, it is not improper to ask the broker for a reduction in what you owe him since he has not performed as agreed. However, the adjusted amount of that fee has to be negotiated *before* you sign the fee arrangement which is part of the buyer's purchase agreement.

Often, sellers are so excited to get an offer that they fail to understand that they are also setting the dollar amount of the brokerage fee on that sale at the same time they accept the offer. And remember, if you make any changes to the purchase offer, brokerage fee provisions included, then a counteroffer has been made and must be accepted by the buyers to form a contract. But if the price isn't right and the terms aren't enough to make the sale work for you, see if the broker can help by reducing his fee.

Suggestion 9.

If you do decide to list, you may want to write a special provision into the listing agreement regarding the real estate fee to address what amount is due the broker if the broker brings you an offer for less than your full asking price. Include in your listing agreement language stating:

- "If Seller receives a full price offer, then the brokerage fee is _____. If Seller receives $10,000 less than full price, then the brokerage fee is _____ (perhaps .5% less). If Seller receives $20,000 less than full price, then the brokerage fee is _____ (perhaps 1%, and so forth)."

This provision would let your broker know up front that, unless they bring an offer at the full listed price, you will not pay them the full brokerage fee. It should also induce the agent to price your property very close to market.

Suggestion 10.

After reading this book, you now have a pretty good idea what a real estate agent should do to market your property and locate a buyer. Make sure they actually do it. Before you list your home, make a list of the actions you expect your agent to carry out, and then hold them to it. If they don't perform as outlined, then fire them and get another agent who is more attentive. Actually, if your expectations are expressed in writing on the listing contract, it is much easier to cancel the listing if they do not conduct themselves as agreed.

Remember, you can fulfill these activities yourself if you want to, so don't accept anything less from your agent.

Suggestion 11.

If you do list your property, list it for the shortest period of time possible, and hopefully not longer than for three months. Within the first month of any listing, you will see the agent working as hard as possible. They know that they need to expose your property to prospective buyers, and since they don't want a long, lingering listing with a cranky seller, they know they must act fast. As long as they are providing the service you expect, assure them that if need be, you will extend the listing period if the property does not sell. You need to use the elements of time and deadlines to your advantage to manage the conduct of your agent.

Of course, some agents will say that their broker will not allow them to take less than a six-month listing. If that happens, and you really want to use that agent because they have been highly recommended, be sure and complete a very thorough list of items they will be performing as recommended in the section above. Consider requiring the broker to increase services after three months if the property does not sell.

Suggestion 12.

If you do find an agent you can work with and who goes the extra mile for you, refer them to others! Think about how difficult it was for you to find someone you could trust and was willing to be of service; now support them so they stay in the business. A gifted real estate agent who cares for and protects his client is hard to find. An average or incompetent agent is far too easy to locate. Help those who strive to provide quality and effective service by refusing to work with less competent agents.

Leasehold properties

> **Note:** Now you can even "review" a real estate agent online! Go to www.homethinking.com and let others know if you found a good one—or one not so good!

A small quantity of homes in California are on ground or land leases. I live in the Palm Springs area where a number of properties exist on Indian leased land. While it is always possible to sell your home yourself, even when the property is on leased land, you will need to have additional advice to make the transaction go smoothly since your buyer will be buying your leasehold interest in the real estate by an assignment, not a fee-simple deed.

There are basically two complications created by land leases. First, you must get past any buyer hesitations. The major buyer concerns are the time period remaining on the lease and the fact that, while the buyer will possess the land and improvements for that time period, he will not own them. Also, a lease has a monthly or annual rent that is paid in addition to the loan payment and taxes. Obviously, if you are selling a home that sits on a leasehold, not a fee simple parcel, you need to be able to explain the financial and legal realities of leasehold ownership. However, if you aren't completely convinced that owning a home on a leasehold is a good way to go, then you may have a difficult time convincing a prospective buyer.

Naturally, your best bet will be to find a buyer who not only understands leaseholds, but appreciates them as well. Even though not as many buyers understand or are willing to entertain buying a home on a ground lease as compared to fee simple land, they do exist. If you do not feel confident about selling the concept, your best alternative may be to find an agent who handles the sale of leasehold homes with continued success.

Your second hurtle is to make sure you adequately disclose the details of the ground lease to the buyer. Disclosure includes such things as the remaining term of the lease, the monthly rent, any and all rental adjustments or increases, and any alienation clauses, together with a copy of the lease or sublease.

Your escrow officer will prepare all the necessary paperwork to assign the lease (instead of a grant deed) and obtain the landowner's consent before you can close escrow. Make sure your escrow officer is experienced with leasehold sales as their lack of skill can delay or permanently hinder your sale. Remember, the landowner must consent to the assignment before the lease can be transferred so make sure that all details are handled by an escrow officer who has successfully closed dozens of them.

Last but not least, you will want to assist your buyer in locating a lender who has a history of making loans on leasehold properties. Unless the lender understands the leasehold interest, either an inadequate appraisal or a denied loan approval could postpone and even terminate your transaction.

Leasehold sales are common in many resort areas and appear where a single owner controls large parcels of real estate, such as the Native Americans or the early settlers of Orange County. If your property is located on one, make sure you surround yourself with competent advisors before you attempt to sell your interest in the property yourself.

Lease with an option

Another term loosely thrown around in most For Sale By Owner (FSBO) books is a lease with an option to buy, or a lease-option transaction. Some writers imply that if you can't sell your house, your best bet might be to enter into a lease-option agreement with a prospective buyer. Unfortunately, lease-option sales transactions are not common and are more complicated and risky than traditional sales. Actually, they shouldn't be called a lease option at all, as it is a misnomer.

If you are unable to sell your home by finding a buyer with cash or a new loan, you do have the option of renting it to a tenant who might eventually like to purchase your home. If you sign a lease with your tenant agreeing to sell the home to him, and if any of the monies you receive under the lease apply to the price he will pay for the property should he exercise the purchase right you gave him, you have legally agreed to sell your home under an installment sale, a type of credit sales transaction. The only way that a lease option is truly a lease and an option is when there is no set price for the property, other than its market value at the time the option is exercised, or when no option money or rent is credited to the price, which would build up an equity in the property.[1]

Structured unconventionally as a lease and a purchase option, a lease-option sales transaction with monies applied to the purchase price is actually seller carryback financing. If the price is set, the seller is receiving regular payments from the buyer that in part apply to the price, and the buyer has both the right to occupy and later own the property by paying the balance due on the price, then the transaction is really a sale—with unnecessarily complicated documentation and terms.

There are a couple of distinctions you should note. First, if you grant an option to purchase with a set price, and by its terms some portion (or all) of the monies received by the seller on the option and under a lease is applied to the price, then the buyer has *equitable* ownership to your property. If the buyer then defaults on this type of arrangement, it isn't like evicting a tenant to get rid of him. On his default, you must eliminate the equity he has built up in your property by foreclosure, usually in a lawsuit, unless the lease-option terms include authority for a trustee's foreclosure sale. After you foreclose and clear your title of the buyer's lease-option rights, only then can you evict the buyer and recover possession to your property. A carryback note and trust deed sale is always a better "option."

A lease-option is not for inexperienced sellers. Furthermore, the IRS treats these leases with an option to buy and an equity build up as an installment sale and require you to pay taxes as though you sold the home. Of course, the $250,000 per owner profit tax exclusion would apply.

If you do decide to go ahead and attempt a lease option, Form 163 is included for that purpose on the accompanying CD. Just know that a lease option is more complicated than a regular carryback sale, and both are more involved than a cash-to-new-loan sale.

Arbitration—what happens when the deal goes south?

Most real estate contracts, although not the purchase agreement included with this book, suggest that if you have a problem with your buyer or the transaction you can avoid the court room by going to arbitration. Arbitration cases have been promoted as being swifter and less costly than traditional court cases.

Unfortunately, arbitration does not live up to the hype. Compared to the filing fees for litigation, the filing fees for arbitration are excessively high. Beyond that, arbitration proceedings can be drawn out for years when the dispute becomes complicated. Even worse, if the arbitrator decides the case erroneously, it is not subject to judicial review and cannot be corrected. Unlike a judge in a court of law, an arbitrator is not bound by the law when arbitrating a dispute. The arbitrator's decision is final and binding on all parties as it cannot be corrected on an appeal or by the arbitrator himself as with a court decision.[2]

The only time you or the arbitrator can overturn an arbitrator's decision is if you can prove he exceeded his powers, he acted with fraud or corruption, or the award was procured by misconduct or fraud. Once you know how your rights are limited through arbitration, you will probably never agree to it given the alternative of a trial court with judicial oversight.

Don't let anyone say you can't do it!

In the spring of 2006, a Realtor Association in Orlando, Florida created an interesting ad campaign geared towards FSBOs called, "Don't it yourself!"[3] Although no longer available online, this campaign was a cute and funny way for the real estate community to attempt to discourage homeowners from ever trying to sell their property themselves.

Although I admire their creativity, the ad promotion showed how nervous the real estate community is about the success homeowners are having as FSBOs. They equate selling your home to conducting surgery on yourself or performing a root canal. It's not! To compare the minimal entry requirements and experience of many real estate agents to the education and experience it takes to become a doctor or lawyer is clearly the proclamation of a worried group of people.

It has been my intention throughout this book to share the difficulties and the challenges involved in selling your own home, but I certainly don't believe that it can be compared to performing brain surgery, much less on yourself. As I said in the beginning, too many homeowners jump into the task of selling their home without preparation and without sufficient resources. However, now that you have read this book and have followed along with the forms, I believe you have what it takes.

California and its residents are known for being adventurous and willing to take on new experiences. Because of that, it is the perfect place for the FSBO revolution to take hold and show the real estate community that it needs to change with the times. Real estate brokerage has been conducted much the same for the last 50-plus years. But the demands of the buying and selling public are changing.

The public deserves to have skilled real estate agents working for them, not against them by use of outdated marketing and sales procedures, and antiquated fee structures, as is often the case. Perhaps the only way that will happen is if more FSBOs demonstrate that they can, and will, do it themselves if agents and their actions don't adjust with the times.

So, in the end, selling your home yourself might not be easy since the real estate market itself influences your results. Nonetheless, I know without a doubt that you now know enough to successfully sell your home yourself and save a large sum of money as a result.

Notes

Chapter 1

1. Remodeling Magazine Research Team, "Remodeling Cost vs. Value Report 2006," *Remodeling Magazine*, November 2006, http://www.remodeling.hw.net/content/CvsV/CostvsValue-project.asp?articleID=381305&sectionID=173 (accessed December 13, 2006).

2. Clay Risen, "Realtors v. The Internet," *The New Republic*, May 2, 2005, http://www.tnr.com/doc.mhtml?i=20050502&s=risen0502205 (accessed November 13, 2006).

3. U.S. Government Accountability Office, *Real Estate Brokerage: Factors That May Affect Price Competition*, report to the Committee on Financial Services, House of Representatives, GAO-05-947, http://www.gao.gov/atext/d05947.txt.

4. Robert W. Hahn, Robert E. Litan and Jesse Gurman, "Bringing More Competition to Real Estate Brokerage," *AEI-Brookings Joint Center for Regulatory Studies*, working paper 05-11, http://www.aei.brookings.org/admin/authorpdfs/page.php?id=1159 (accessed November 28, 2005).

Chapter 3

1. GAO, *Real Estate Brokerage*, (see Chap. 1, note 3).

2. Comparative Production Statistics, State of California, RE149, Department of Real Estate, June 2006.

3. California Association of Realtors, "Typical home buyer now an Internet buyer, according to the '2006 Internet Versus Traditional Buyer Survey'", http://www.car.org/index.php?id=MzYyMzg= (accessed May 22, 2006).

4. Paul C. Bishop, Ph.D., Shonda D. Hightower and Harika Bickicioglu, *The 2005 National Association of Realtors Profile of Home Buyers and Sellers*, The Research Division of the National Association of Realtors, Item #186-45-0506, page 68.

Chapter 5

1. Bishop et al., *2005 NAR Profile*, page 68, (see Chap 3., note 4).

2. Reuters, "Fewer Seen Able to Afford a Home," *Los Angeles Times*, February 10, 2006.

Chapter 7

1. *first tuesday* Real Estate Practice, Fourth Edition, (2006), Chapter 25.

Chapter 8

1. *first tuesday*, Real Estate Practice, Fourth Edition, (2006), Chapter 28, (see Chap. 7, note 1).

2. Ibid., Chapter 31.

3. California Civil Code §1102.6b.

Chapter 9

1. Wikipedia, "Title insurance," http://en.wikipedia.org/wiki/Title_insurance (accessed April 11, 2006).

2. Beth Bresnahan, "One-Third of Residential Real Estate Transactions Have Title Issues, Survey Says," April 17, 2006, http://www.rismedia.com/index.php/article/articleprint/14213/-1/1 (accessed April 17, 2006).

3. California Department of Real Estate, "Title to Real Property," *Reference Book: Information Relating to Real Estate Practice, Licensing and Examinations*, (2000).

Chapter 12

1. *first tuesday*, Real Estate Finance, Fifth Edition, (2005), Chapter 6.

Chapter 13

1. Bishop et al., *2005 NAR Profile*, page 3, (see Chap 3., note 4).

2. Ibid., page 10.

3. Ibid., page 18.

4. Ibid., page 22.

5. Ibid., page 18.

6. Ibid., page 19.

7. Ibid., page 20.

8. Ibid., page 24.

9. Ibid., page 28.

10. Ibid., page 29.

11. Ibid., page 19.

12. Ibid., page 29.

Notes from Chapter 13 continued

13. Ibid.

14. Ibid., page 36.

15. Ibid., page 37.

16. Ibid., page 59.

17. Ibid.

18. Ibid., page 65.

19. Ibid., page 29.

20. CAR, "Typical home buyer," (see Chap. 3., note 3).

21. Bishop et al., *2005 NAR Profile*, page 29, (see Chap. 3, note 4).

22. Royal LePage, "Image is Everything: Creating a Positive First Impression is Key to Selling Your Home," http://www.agentinhamilton.com/Home_Staging/page_1795958.html.

23. Bishop et al., "Typical home buyer," page 68, (see Chap. 3, note 4).

24. Ibid., page 69.

25. Ibid.

26. Ibid., page 70.

27. Ibid.

28. Ibid., page 71.

29. Realestate.com, *Realestate.com Consumer Survey*, http://www.realestate.com/customer-service/surveys/ConsumerResults.htm.

Chapter 15

1. *first tuesday*, *Real Estate Matters, 2nd Edition*, (2005), page 107.

2. Ibid., page 86.

3. Orlando Regional Realtor Association, http://www.dont-it-your-self.com.